The Playful Politics of Memes

Memes work as rhetorical weapons and discursive arguments in political conflicts. Across digital platforms, they confirm, contest, and challenge political power and hierarchies. They simultaneously create social distortion, hostility, and a sense of community. Memes thus not only reflect norms but also work as a tool for negotiating them. At the same time, memes meld symbolic and cultural elements with technological functionalities, allowing for replicability and remixing.

This book studies how memes disrupt and reimagine politics in humorous ways. Memes create a playful activity that follows a shared set of rules and gives a (shared) voice, which may not only generate togetherness and political identities but also increase polarization. As their template travels, memes continue to appropriate new political contexts and to (re)negotiate frontiers in the political. The chapters in this book allow us to chart the playful politics of memes and how they establish or push frontiers in various political, cultural, and platform-specific contexts. Taken together, memes can challenge and regenerate populism, carve out spaces for new identity formations, and create togetherness in situations of crises. They can also, however, lead to the normalization of racist discourses.

This book will be of interest to researchers and advanced students of Media and Communication Studies, Information Studies, Politics, Sociology, and Cultural Studies. It was originally published as a special issue of the journal *Information, Communication & Society*.

Mette Mortensen is Professor and Deputy Head of Department for Research at the Department of Communication at the University of Copenhagen, Denmark. Her work focuses on media and conflict, including the mobilization of images through social media and visual evidence.

Christina Neumayer is Associate Professor at the Center for Tracking and Society at the Department of Communication at the University of Copenhagen, Denmark. Her research focuses on the role of media technologies, digital data and methods for political contention, protest, activism, racism, civic engagement, social movements and more broadly political communication.

The Playful Politics of Memes

Edited by
Mette Mortensen and Christina Neumayer

LONDON AND NEW YORK

First published 2023
by Routledge
4 Park Square, Milton Park, Abingdon, Oxon, OX14 4RN

and by Routledge
605 Third Avenue, New York, NY 10158

Routledge is an imprint of the Taylor & Francis Group, an informa business

Chapters 1, 2, 4–6 and 8 © 2023 Taylor & Francis

Chapter 3 © 2021 Samuel Merrill and Simon Lindgren. Originally published as Open Access.

Chapter 7 © 2021 Tommaso Trillò and Limor Shifman. Originally published as Open Access.

Chapter 9 © 2021 Tina Askanius and Nadine Keller. Originally published as Open Access.

With the exception of Chapters 3, 7 and 9, no part of this book may be reprinted or reproduced or utilised in any form or by any electronic, mechanical, or other means, now known or hereafter invented, including photocopying and recording, or in any information storage or retrieval system, without permission in writing from the publishers. For details on the rights for Chapters 3, 7 and 9, please see the chapters' Open Access footnotes.

Trademark notice: Product or corporate names may be trademarks or registered trademarks, and are used only for identification and explanation without intent to infringe.

British Library Cataloguing-in-Publication Data
A catalogue record for this book is available from the British Library

ISBN13: 978-1-032-44950-0 (hbk)
ISBN13: 978-1-032-44952-4 (pbk)
ISBN13: 978-1-003-37471-8 (ebk)

DOI: 10.4324/9781003374718

Typeset in Minion Pro
by codeMantra

Publisher's Note
The publisher accepts responsibility for any inconsistencies that may have arisen during the conversion of this book from journal articles to book chapters, namely the inclusion of journal terminology.

Disclaimer
Every effort has been made to contact copyright holders for their permission to reprint material in this book. The publishers would be grateful to hear from any copyright holder who is not here acknowledged and will undertake to rectify any errors or omissions in future editions of this book.

Contents

	Citation information	vi
	Notes on contributors	viii
1	The playful politics of memes *Mette Mortensen and Christina Neumayer*	1
2	Messy on the inside: internet memes as mapping tools of everyday life *Sulafa Zidani*	12
3	Memes, brands and the politics of post-terror togetherness: following the Manchester bee after the 2017 Manchester Arena bombing *Samuel Merrill and Simon Lindgren*	37
4	Memetising the pandemic: memes, COVID-19 mundanity and political cultures *Maria Francesca Murru and Stefania Vicari*	56
5	'Don't panic people! Trump will tweet the virus away': memes contesting and confirming populist political leaders during the COVID-19 crisis *Nete Nørgaard Kristensen and Mette Mortensen*	76
6	'#OkBoomer, time to meet the Zoomers': studying the memefication of intergenerational politics on TikTok *Jing Zeng and Crystal Abidin*	93
7	Memetic commemorations: remixing far-right values in digital spheres *Tommaso Trillò and Limor Shifman*	116
8	Sharing the hate? Memes and transnationality in the far right's digital visual culture *Jordan McSwiney, Michael Vaughan, Annett Heft and Matthias Hoffmann*	136
9	Murder fantasies in memes: fascist aesthetics of death threats and the banalization of white supremacist violence *Tina Askanius and Nadine Keller*	156
	Index	175

Citation Information

The chapters in this book were originally published in the journal *Information, Communication & Society*, volume 24, issue 16 (2021). When citing this material, please use the original page numbering for each article, as follows:

Chapter 1
The playful politics of memes
Mette Mortensen and Christina Neumayer
Information, Communication & Society, volume 24, issue 16 (2021) pp. 2367–2377

Chapter 2
Messy on the inside: internet memes as mapping tools of everyday life
Sulafa Zidani
Information, Communication &Society, volume 24, issue 16 (2021) pp. 2378–2402

Chapter 3
Memes, brands and the politics of post-terror togetherness: following the Manchester bee after the 2017 Manchester Arena bombing
Samuel Merrill and Simon Lindgren
Information, Communication &Society, volume 24, issue 16 (2021) pp. 2403–2421

Chapter 4
Memetising the pandemic: memes, COVID-19 mundanity and political cultures
Maria Francesca Murru and Stefania Vicari
Information, Communication &Society, volume 24, issue 16 (2021) pp. 2422–2441

Chapter 5
'Don't panic people! Trump will tweet the virus away': memes contesting and confirming populist political leaders during the COVID-19 crisis
Nete Nørgaard Kristensen and Mette Mortensen
Information, Communication &Society, volume 24, issue 16 (2021) pp. 2442–2458

Chapter 6
'#OkBoomer, time to meet the Zoomers': studying the memefication of intergenerational politics on TikTok
Jing Zeng and Crystal Abidin
Information, Communication &Society, volume 24, issue 16 (2021) pp. 2459–2481

Chapter 7
Memetic commemorations: remixing far-right values in digital spheres
Tommaso Trillò and Limor Shifman
Information, Communication &Society, volume 24, issue 16 (2021) pp. 2482–2501

Chapter 8
Sharing the hate? Memes and transnationality in the far right's digital visual culture
Jordan McSwiney, Michael Vaughan, Annett Heft and Matthias Hoffmann
Information, Communication &Society, volume 24, issue 16 (2021) pp. 2502–2521

Chapter 9
Murder fantasies in memes: fascist aesthetics of death threats and the banalization of white supremacist violence
Tina Askanius and Nadine Keller
Information, Communication &Society, volume 24, issue 16 (2021) pp. 2522–2539

For any permission-related enquiries please visit:
http://www.tandfonline.com/page/help/permissions

Notes on Contributors

Crystal Abidin is socio-cultural anthropologist of influencer cultures and social media pop cultures, especially in the Asia Pacific region. She is Professor of Internet Studies, Founder of the TikTok Cultures Research Network, and ARC DECRA Fellow at Curtin University, Perth, Australia.

Tina Askanius is Associate Professor in Media and Communication Studies at Malmö University, Sweden, and Affiliated Researcher at the Institute for Futures Studies in Stockholm, Sweden. Her research concerns the interplay between online media, social movement mobilization, and political radicalization.

Annett Heft is Head of the research group Digitalisation and the Transnational Public Sphere at the Weizenbaum Institute for the Networked Society, Berlin, Germany, and Senior Researcher at the Institute for Media and Communication Studies at Freie Universität Berlin, Germany. Her main fields of research are the comparative study of political communication in Europe with a focus on digital public spheres, right-wing communication infrastructures, transnational communication, and cross-border journalism as well as on quantitative research methods and computational social science.

Matthias Hoffmann is Postdoctoral Researcher at the Department of Communication at the University of Copenhagen, Denmark.

Nadine Keller is Research Assistant at the School of Arts and Communication and affiliated with the research platform Rethinking Democracy at Malmø University, Sweden. She holds an MA in Media and Communication Studies.

Nete Nørgaard Kristensen is Professor of Media Studies at the Department of Communication at the University of Copenhagen, Denmark, where she serves as Head of Section of Media Studies. She specializes in media and popular culture, cultural journalism and cultural criticism across platforms, and political communication.

Simon Lindgren is Professor of Sociology and Director of the Centre for Digital Social Research at Umeå University (DIGSUM), Sweden. His research is focused on the relationship between digital technologies and society with a particular emphasis on politics and power relations.

Samuel Merrill is Associate Professor of Sociology at Umeå University's Department of Sociology and Centre for Digital Social Research (DIGSUM), Sweden. He specializes in digital and cultural sociology, and his research interests include the intersections between collective memory, digital media, social movements, and cultural heritage.

NOTES ON CONTRIBUTORS

Jordan McSwiney is a Postdoctoral Fellow at the Centre for Deliberative Democracy and Global Governance at the University of Canberra. His research focuses on the far right, with a particular interest in the organisation of far-right parties and movements, and their use of social media.

Mette Mortensen is Professor and Deputy Head of Department for Research at the Department of Communication at the University of Copenhagen, Denmark. Her work focuses on media and conflict, including the mobilization of images through social media and visual evidence.

Maria Francesca Murru is Associate Professor of Sociology of Culture and Communication at the University of Bergamo, Italy. Her research interests include digital public spheres, mediated citizenship, and local journalism.

Christina Neumayer is Associate Professor at the Center for Tracking and Society at the Department of Communication at the University of Copenhagen, Denmark. Her research focuses on the role of media technologies, digital data and methods for political contention, protest, activism, racism, civic engagement, social movements and more broadly political communication.

Limor Shifman is Professor at the Department of Communication and Journalism at the Hebrew University of Jerusalem, Israel. She is currently the PI of the ERC-funded project "DigitalValues: The Construction of Values in Digital Spheres".

Tommaso Trillò is Postdoctoral Researcher at the Department of Communication and Journalism of the Hebrew University of Jerusalem, Israel. Tommaso holds a PhD in Political Sciences from the University of Łodz, Poland, where he worked as part of the Marie Skłodowska-Curie ITN GRACE.

Michael Vaughan is Research Officer at the International Inequalities Institute at the London School of Economics and Political Science, where he researches digital political communication and participation.

Stefania Vicari is Senior Lecturer in Digital Sociology at the University of Sheffield, UK. Her research interests include the general areas of digital participatory cultures, digital health and digital methods.

Jing Zeng is an assistant professor at the Department of media and culture studies at Utrecht University, the Netherlands. Her research interests include digital culture, online activism, and digital methods.

Sulafa Zidani is Assistant Professor in Comparative Media Studies at the Massachusetts Institute of Technology, Cambridge, USA, where she studies global creative practices in digital civic engagement.

The playful politics of memes

Mette Mortensen and Christina Neumayer

ABSTRACT
This special issue emphasizes memes as an avenue for researching vernacular expressions of the political. Memes disrupt and reimagine politics in humorous ways. Spreading across platforms, they confirm, contest and challenge political power and hierarchies. In this introduction, we contend that *playfulness* connects the humorous and the political in memes. While memes may be created to disrupt, challenge, and reimagine politics in a humorous way, we argue for a critical examination of how they playfully demarcate and move frontiers between 'us' and 'them' in the political. Memes constitute a playful activity that follows a shared set of rules and gives a (shared) voice, which may create togetherness and political identities but also increase polarization. As their template travels, memes continue to appropriate new political contexts and to (re)negotiate frontiers in the political.

Introduction

Memes work as rhetorical weapons and discursive arguments in political conflicts. They confirm, contest, or challenge political power and hierarchies. In so doing, they simultaneously create social distortion, hostility, and a sense of community (e.g., Segev et al., 2015). Memes thus not only reflect norms but also work as a 'social tool for negotiating them' (Gal et al., 2016, p. 1700; see also Mortensen & Kristensen, 2020). At the same time, memes meld symbolic and cultural elements with technological functionalities, allowing for replicability and remixing (Shifman, 2013).

Memes are easily generated, disseminated, and consumed – but also easily forgotten. In the techno-commercial infrastructure of social media based on personalization and filtering processes, memes tend to revolve around current spectacular and controversial topics (Bayerl & Stoynov, 2016; Neumayer & Struthers, 2019). Their ephemerality, recognizability, and humorous form can both politicize and depoliticize conflict and divert attention to and from the issues at stake. While there is agreement that memes constitute an everyday shared practice and engagement in politics, research has not yet fully captured the diversity of ways in which memes are political.

From being a phenomenon of 4chan and similar fringe sites, memes have over the past years become an inevitable and intrinsic part of visual communication in relation to political debate and conflict. They circulate back and forth from niche to mainstream cultures. As they travel across various platforms, political contexts, and corners of the internet, the politics of memes come to the forefront in various ways: Actors from the far-right propagate their ideology through memes (e.g., Greene, 2019). Images from political protests are memefied, such as the Pepper Spray Cop from student protests at UC Davis (Bayerl & Stoynov, 2016; Huntington, 2016) or the Riot Hipster from the G20 protests in Hamburg (Neumayer & Struthers, 2019). Memes have addressed injustice and inequality by deconstructing stereotypes of people living in poverty (Dobson & Knezevic, 2017), and protested the lack of political responsibility for refugees, for example by placing the figure of the deceased refugee child Alan Kurdi on the roundtable of a UN summit (Mortensen, 2017; Olesen, 2018). Other memes continue the tradition of satirizing political figureheads. For instance, the general election in Brazil in 2014 was coined 'The Election of Memes' due to the mass dissemination of memes mocking the candidates (Chagas et al., 2019), and former US president Donald Trump, himself referred to as a 'meme president', has been portrayed in memes as Pepe the Frog and Lord Farquaad from *Shrek* (e.g., Denisova, 2019; Peters & Allan, 2021).

Efforts to understand the political role performed by memes have led to the creation of concepts such as 'memetic protest' (Olesen, 2018), 'the memefication of politics' (Dean, 2019), 'the memefication of political discourse' (Bulatovic, 2019), and 'weaponizing memes' (Peters & Allan, 2021). These concepts foreground the political. In this introduction, we argue for the necessity of considering the *playfulness* that connects the humorous and the political in memes. We begin by addressing the link between humour and politics in memes before conceptually locating the politics of memes at the intersection of play (Sicart, 2014), the political (Laclau & Mouffe, 1985; Mouffe, 2005), and memes as a humorous form (e.g., Shifman, 2013; Milner, 2018; Miltner, 2018). Within this conceptual framework, we introduce the articles in this special issue and finally discuss how the playful politics of memes may enhance our understanding of shifting frontiers constructing 'us' and 'them' in the political.

Politics and humour in memes

Memes should be seen as a continuation of the long tradition of political humour. Satire, parody, comedy, and other genres have sustained democratic public culture by exposing the hypocrisy of those in power and testing the limits of free speech (e.g., Chen et al., 2017; Hariman, 2008). What sets memes apart from previous forms of political humour is their fluidity of context and content. Memes differ from earlier types of political humour in that they are created by unspecified groups of media users as part of participatory digital culture. They mostly emerge outside of institutional contexts and are disseminated without a known creator (Ross & Rivers, 2017; Shifman, 2013; Wiggins & Bowers, 2015). The constant, collective process of creation and creative expression, which was discussed early on as an element of internet culture (Jenkins, 2006), means that their content is also in flux. Due to this fluidity, the intersection between politics and humour is often more difficult to grasp in memes than in genres such as political cartoons, which are typically anchored by a clear institutional affiliation and an identifiable author. The specific political message in memes is often up for interpretation. At the same time, humour is a driver of both inclusion and exclusion – strengthening a feeling of belonging and group identity among those appreciating the joke and creating a gap to those who do not.

Research concerning the politics of memes tends to emphasise either the humorous or the political. For example, Denisova (2019, p. 3) contends that the meme 'has no inherent political or cultural connotation except for the promise of entertainment.' By contrast, Shifman (2013, p. 120) argues in her early work on memes in internet culture that humour is more or less pronounced in political memes, but basically they make 'a point – participating in a normative debate about how the world should look and the best way to get there.' Similarly, Wiggins (2019, p. 11) highlights the political in his definition of internet memes 'as a remixed, iterated message that can be rapidly diffused by members of participatory digital culture for the purpose of satire, parody, critique, or other discursive activity' and downplays humour as 'merely the surface-level entry point for social salience.' In this special issue, we foreground neither the political nor the humorous, arguing instead that memes perform humour and politics through play.

Playful humour and politics

We conceptualize the politics of memes as playful appropriations of contexts that occur at the intersection of the political and the humorous. In Miguel Sicart's (2014, pp. 71–72) understanding, play is distinguished by 'its appropriative nature and the creativity that ensues.' Playfulness may facilitate a critical approach to a political context through creative appropriation. As such, play can be used creatively to express political ideas at the nexus of form, appropriation, and context (Sicart, 2014, p. 76). Such creative political expressions are often facilitated by subversive appropriation of mainstream cultural forms, for example through political memes that are heavily shared and appropriated, de-contextualized, and re-contextualized (Mortensen, 2017). Memes are political in their critical engagement with and appropriation of a context – usually, but not always, in a humorous way – and their production of double-edged meanings. They are a play activity in themselves but also express political meaning, which accords with Sicart's (2014, p. 80) definition of playfulness. Being inherently playful, memes allow for creative expression of politics in situations of oppression and crises, collective identification, and togetherness. Memes thus constitute a playful activity that follows a shared set of rules and gives a (shared) voice.

To address the playful in memes as part of politics in contemporary internet culture, we employ Laclau and Mouffe's (1985) radical democracy perspective (see also Dahlberg, 2007; Neumayer & Svensson, 2016; Svensson et al., 2015). Radical democracy provides a conceptual framework for understanding political expression surrounding processes of identification, highlighting difference and dissent in the playful politics of memes. This enables us to widen the sphere of political engagement beyond institutions of democracy. According to radical democracy, the political can never include all political positions since majority decision-making always favours one position over another (Mouffe, 2005). As Mouffe (2005) further contends, ideals of deliberation and communicative rationality (see Habermas, 1990 [1962]) may also conceal differences, conflicts, and power relations beneath a veneer of agreement and consensus.

We conceptualize the politics of memes as a playful expression of different subject positions in the political. This allows us to map out a coalition of excluded opinions, perspectives, and expressions, which may be overlooked or communicated in different ways within the liberal parliamentary political arena. While memes playfully appropriate political contexts to negotiate identities, express difference and communicate political positions in a digital media environment, it should be taken into account that every identity is relational and consequently exists by affirmation of difference to another identity, which is the essence of how antagonisms arise (Mouffe, 1993, p. 2). Radical democracy thus emphasizes the construction of frontiers to an outside other and the formation of unity across diversity against a common enemy (Mouffe in Carpentier & Cammaerts, 2006) which may provide new impulses in a democracy. The 'radical' in radical democracy refers to such expressions of difference and includes conflict and dissent as important elements in a democracy. As constructions of a 'we' and a 'them' (see Mouffe, 1993), memes offer a creative and playful way for groups to express their identity and to raise their voice.

As a playful expression of politics, memes travel particularly well due to 'their textual flexibility,' which allows 'them to be taken up and imbued with new meaning by different groups' (Miltner, 2018, p. 415). The humorous element of memes makes them well suited to political commentary, statement, or critique (Milner, 2018; Miltner, 2018; Shifman, 2013). Although all memes possess politics to some degree, we can observe changes as they travel – often from the political being foregrounded to an almost exclusive focus on humour and creative expression or *vice versa* (Jensen et al., 2020; Bayerl & Stoynov, 2016). At the same time, identity politics are at the core of internet memes defined as 'units of popular culture that are circulated, imitated, and transformed by individual Internet users, creating a shared cultural experience in the process' (Shifman, 2013, p. 367). From a rhetorical perspective, memes are driven by three factors: political expression on social media, cultural evolution, and games and play (Seiffert-Brockmann et al., 2018).

The origins and motivations for creating memes are not always political. Memes also emerge as an impulse for appropriating visual content that happens to be political or in which the political offers a space for creative expression (Jensen et al., 2020; Seiffert-Brockmann et al., 2018). This occurred, for instance, when Brussels was in security lockdown after a terror threat in 2015, and memes of LOLcats were disseminated on Twitter to create a feeling of togetherness and solidarity (Jensen et al., 2020). However, memes are also sometimes generated with a direct political intent that deploys humour to promote a certain message. This occurred, for instance, when the international hacktivist collective Anonymous declared 'meme war' on ISIS and circulated memes ridiculing this terror network's propaganda imagery by inserting rubber duck heads onto ISIS combatants, replacing machine guns with toilet brushes, etc. (McCrow-Young & Mortensen, 2021).

Memes may thus foster the formation of shared collective identities or cohesive groups through individuals taking part in the playful activity of producing and sharing them online (Katz & Shifman, 2017). Users who engage in this must, however, first have acquired the shared knowledge of how memes are meant to be appropriated and reappropriated. In other words, the relational rules applied to play (Sicart, 2014) manifest themselves in shared 'subcultural knowledge' and 'unstable equilibriums' that require constant negotiation concerning the correct use of memes and their deployment as 'discursive weapons' directed at the political other (Nissenbaum & Shifman, 2017, p. 483).

Knowledge of these rules is part of how 'othering' takes place in memes. Tuters and Hagen (2020) find in their analysis of the triple-parentheses meme on 4chan's /pol/ board that the 'us' and 'them' formulated through this meme may not be recognizable to outsiders who are unfamiliar with 4chan's /pol/ and the particular meaning of the triple parentheses. This propensity for in-group lingo constitutes another means by which memes establish frontiers against a political 'other'.

Identifying an outside other is important in this construction of a temporarily coherent 'us'. That is, collectives gather around specific and more or less fleeting political demands. Since radical democracy offers a normative perspective, it also provides a yardstick for evaluating how positions are expressed (Neumayer & Svensson, 2016). Focus on difference and conflict goes to the core of the political. For Laclau and Mouffe (1985), this constitutes a 'democratic pluralism' that brings differences to the fore. However, this entails respecting the other as an adversary and not an enemy to be eliminated. By outlining the notion of agonism, in contrast to antagonism, Mouffe (2005) suggests a conception of the other as an adversary to be acknowledged, which is important for displaying the heterogeneity of conflictual forces constituting the political. Even though expressions and representations of war (e.g., in literary fiction and games) may include ludic elements of play (Huizinga, 1949), this relationship cannot be seen as agonism, given that elimination of the enemy is projected as the ideal outcome. From a normative perspective, this constitutes the tipping point of the playful appropriation and reappropriation that are essential to the politics of memes.

Connecting the political and the humorous as they occur in internet culture with a conceptual understanding of the processes occurring through play, we can map the politics of memes in recurrent elements: the construction of 'us' and 'them' on a continuum from adversary to enemy; the sociocultural, technical, and rhetorical rules underlying playful engagement with memes; the normative yardstick reaching a tipping point when appropriations are taken too far through constructing the 'them' as an enemy that should be eliminated; and the shifting frontiers within which playful appropriations of political contexts take place through memes.

Mapping the politics of memes: articles in this special issue

In the articles included in this issue, we can observe blurred boundaries in the playful ways in which memes humorously appropriate political contexts. They move not only between online and offline as 'more or less digital' forms (Merrill & Lindgren, this issue) but also between the subversive, the subcultural, and the mainstream (McSwiney et al., this issue) and between challenging and reaffirming the political context they appropriate (Kristensen & Mortensen, this issue). All the contributions play into well-established political contexts and conflicts such as generational gaps (Zeng & Abidin, this issue); commemoration cultures after terror attacks (Merrill & Lindgren, this issue); visual culture surrounding political figureheads (Kristensen & Mortensen, this issue); everyday life in prolonged conflict in Palestinian cities (Zidani, this issue); vernacular politics during the COVID-19 lockdown (Murru & Vicari, this issue); and visual culture of the far-right (Askanius & Keller, this issue; McSwiney et al., this issue; Trillò & Shifman, this issue). In the following, we introduce the seven articles, focusing on how the humorous memes in question playfully appropriate political contexts and form frontiers between 'us' and 'them'.

In her article, Sulafa Zidani uses memes to map the physical and symbolic borderlines between Israeli and Palestinian youth and their everyday lives in prolonged conflict. The memes on Instagram created by young Palestinians in Israel offer insight into the navigation of life in mixed cities. By proposing a conceptual framework of memes as 'mapping tools of everyday life,' the study shows how memes, as a digital culture vernacular, navigate contested cultural spaces and help carve out spaces for Palestinian youths across cultural diversity.

Samuel Merrill and Simon Lindgren study how the Manchester bee became a symbol of post-terror togetherness following the 2017 bombing at the Ariana Grande concert in Manchester. By analysing Instagram images as 'more or less digital' across and beyond social media platforms, they explore the memetic revival and brand adoption of the civic symbol of 'the worker bee'. They find that although the memefication of the bee produced a form of post-terror togetherness, political tensions were later obfuscated through the integration of the bee into the official city branding strategy.

Maria Francesca Murru and Stefania Vicari explore 'mundane memetic practices' of quarantined Italians during the COVID-19 lockdown. In a study of memes shared on Twitter, they identify a mundane political culture building upon playful rituals through which political identities are established. The memes express sentiments such as anti-elitism and anti-scientism, humorously producing an 'us-versus-them' polarization that feeds into wider populist discourses and allows potentially conflicting political identities to surface.

Nete Nørgaard Kristensen and Mette Mortensen show how memes criticize populist leaders while reinforcing the communicative logics of the populists themselves, thereby both contesting and propagating populism. Using search engines as an entry point, they analyse memes of British Prime Minister Boris Johnson and then US President Donald Trump during the COVID-19 crisis. They conclude that the memes conflate affirmative and critical power, as they criticize the populist leaders but also confirm their communicative patterns and worldviews.

Jing Zeng and Crystal Abidin demonstrate in their study that memes form a collective us of 'Gen Z' (or the 'Zoomers') in opposition to 'Boomers' by wittily negotiating generational boundaries in TikTok video memes. They investigate how young people utilize TikTok videos to advocate for their political culture. The memefication of intergenerational politics takes place through short videos produced by the TikTokers, who express a collective generational identity of Gen Z, with Boomers as the collectively imagined other.

Tommaso Trillò and Limor Shifman study 'alternative calendar commemorations' on Twitter and Instagram as a photo-based meme genre memorializing figures and events central to the Italian far-right imaginary. They argue that memes contribute to a mainstreaming of the far-right which is protected from criticism due to the respectability associated with commemorations. Their findings point to a clash between far-right values such as collectivism, patriotism, and tradition on the one hand and values coupled with memes such as individualism, self-direction, and authenticity on the other.

Jordan McSwiney, Michael Vaughan, Annett Heft, and Matthias Hoffmann question common key assumptions concerning the transnationality of far-right memes and their role in visual culture. In an analysis of far-right memes by alternative media and non-party organizations in Australia, Germany, Italy, and the US, across Facebook, Twitter, and Telegram, they find that, quantitatively, memes play a limited role in visual culture. Far-right memes do not easily circulate transnationally, but they nonetheless express transnationality as 'fascist continuity, western civilization identity, and pop cultural appropriation.'

Tina Askanius and Nadine Keller argue that far-right meme culture transcends symbolic boundaries between mischievous subcultures and violent extremism. They trace the 'memefication of white supremacism' in an analysis of memes published on the neo-Nazi group Nordic Resistance Movement's online hub Nordfront.se. They conclude that the memes contribute to mainstreaming far-right ideas through their interplay between jokes, playfulness, and ambiguity on the one hand and serious, violent threats of white supremacy and murder fantasies embedded into historical events on the other.

Playful appropriations: moving and demarcating frontiers

The articles in this special issue allow us to chart the politics of humorous memes and how this genre establishes or pushes frontiers in various political, cultural, and platform-specific contexts. Taken together, the template underlying memes can be seen to challenge and regenerate populism (Kristensen & Mortensen, this issue), carve out spaces for new identity formations (Zeng & Abidin, this issue; Zidani, this issue), and create togetherness in situations of crises (Merrill & Lindgren, this issue; Murru & Vicari, this issue). They can also, however, lead to the normalization of racist discourses (Askanius & Keller, this issue; McSwiney et al., this issue; Trillò & Shifman, this issue).

In some instances, memes allow us to look beyond spectacular political events and produce insight into the politics of everyday vernacular culture (Murru & Vicari, this issue; Zidani, this issue). As Zidani (this issue) argues, they enable us to map the politics of inclusion and exclusion and the spaces in between, thereby creating the potential for critical reflection. While a particular meme may stay within subversive subcultures, such as the far-right (McSwiney et al., this issue), it can playfully appropriate a new political context and generate new frontiers between 'us' and 'them'. The constant playful appropriation of contexts and the demarcating of new frontiers allow memes to effortlessly travel between subcultures and the mainstream, between the platform-specific and wider media ecologies.

It can be difficult to pinpoint when precisely a meme works toward politics of inclusion or exclusion, as frontiers are constantly moving, creating new constellations of 'us' and 'them'. Although their potential to travel is dependent on the political context (see McSwiney et al., this issue), memes are produced and diffused by members of participatory internet culture. They cite popular culture, are created with intertextual awareness of other memes, and are distributed online by numerous participants. As memes are rapidly diffused across political contexts and digital platforms, the messages they convey and the memetic visuals themselves become remixed, iterated, and often decontextualized (see also Ibrahim, 2016; Boudana et al., 2017). In some instances, this opens a space for political identity formation (Zeng & Abidin, this issue), while in others it dilutes any political significance (Merrill & Lindgren, this issue) or may contribute to polarization and hostility (Askanius & Keller, this issue; Trillò & Shifman, this issue).

As memes flow between the subcultural and the mainstream, they may normalize or move fringe political perspectives along with them. Askanius and Keller (this issue) remind us of a striking example of how memes can contribute to mainstreaming extremist views. During the siege on the US Capitol on January 6, 2021, a mob of supporters sought to overturn the electoral defeat of outgoing president Donald Trump. In their staging of this attack, the insurgents drew heavily upon the iconography of white supremacy, known from memes as well as alt-right visual culture more generally. This includes Pepe the Frog and the green-and-white flag of Kekistan, which references the German Empire's Reichskriegsflagge. These symbols not only travelled from subcultures to the mainstream but also moved as 'more or less digital' (Merrill & Lindgren, this issue) from analogue media to online and were ultimately reproduced in physical protest. As Askanius and Keller (this issue) contend, the violence and turbulence of the attack, during which five people were killed and over a hundred injured, contrasts strikingly with the humour in memes with murder phantasies. Memes can be mobilized to move white supremacist violence into the mainstream and push the boundaries of what is deemed acceptable. In the political, these memes do not create frontiers against the 'other' as recognized adversary (as e.g., in Zeng & Abidin's contribution in this issue) but instead create the 'other' as an enemy that needs to be eliminated. The memes thus reach the normative tipping point of acceptability in playful appropriations of political contexts.

While not necessarily reaching this tipping point, other memes may contribute to mainstreaming political critique or entrenching existing power relations. Kristensen and Mortensen (this issue) identify how memes of populist political leaders seemingly contest their irresponsible handling of the COVID-19 crisis while nevertheless reproducing populist values and communicative styles. This emphasizes how political parody and satire inevitably reference and/or reproduce the target of their criticism, thereby risking amplification of extremist ideologies or indeed populism (Kraidy, 2018; McCrow-Young & Mortensen, 2021). As the contributions in this issue show, however, this ambiguity may be difficult to grasp in memes due to their constant authorless remixing, reproduction, and dissemination in various contexts (Kristensen & Mortensen, this issue; Merrill & Lindgren, this issue; Murru & Vicari, this issue). From a normative perspective, memes can contribute to political discussion in a productive way, but we must differentiate 'between memes that enhance democratic public debate and those which degrade it' (Boudana et al., 2017, p. 1228).

As they travel as artifacts of and in social media, memes are governed by social media logics. They are simultaneously used to destabilize politics and to create new identity formations (Murru & Vicari, this issue; Zeng & Abidin, this issue; Zidani, this issue). Several articles in this special issue demonstrate how memes operate in a grey zone between the market and bottom-up political participation. Memes creating post-terror togetherness (Merrill & Lindgren, this issue) are appropriated by the city council for branding strategies, and the generational politics of the Zoomers have generated spin-off merchandise in the form of keychains, t-shirts, and stickers inspired by meme videos mocking 'Boomers' (Zeng & Abidin, this issue). Such commodification emphasizes the ambivalence of meme's playful politics. That is, memes entangle the political and the humorous through play but this also commodifies the political. By the same token though, the commodified, humorous politics of memes are part of the playful everyday engagement with politics.

The contributions in this special issue show the various ways in which memes reinforce, create, transgress, and challenge political boundaries. They politicize and depoliticize. They personify but also de-personify. They stay within the subversive and create frontiers to political elites and the mainstream, but in their playful appropriation of political contexts, they may challenge and push these very same frontiers. Memes provide means of creating togetherness and political identities while also increasing polarization by constantly drawing and redrawing the boundaries between 'us' and 'them' – in some instances reaching the tipping point of what is acceptable. As their template travels effortlessly, memes continue to playfully appropriate new political contexts and to (re)negotiate frontiers in the political.

Disclosure statement

No potential conflict of interest was reported by the author(s).

Funding

This work was supported by Velux Fonden [Grant number 13143].

References

Bayerl, P. S., & Stoynov, L. (2016). Revenge by photoshop: Memefying police acts in the public dialogue about injustice. *New Media & Society*, *18*(6), 1006–1026. https://doi.org/10.1177/1461444814554747

Boudana, S., Frosh, P., & Cohen, A. A. (2017). Reviving Icons to death: When historic photographs become digital memes. *Media, Culture & Society*, *39*(8), 1210–1230. https://doi.org/10.1177/0163443717690818

Bulatovic, M. (2019). The imitation game: The memefication of political discourse. *European View*, *18*(2), 250–253. https://doi.org/10.1177/1781685819887691

Carpentier, N., & Cammaerts, B. (2006). Hegemony, democracy, agonism and journalism: An interview with chantal mouffe. *Journalism Studies*, *7*(6), 964–975. https://doi.org/10.1080/14616700600980728

Chagas, V., Freire, F., Rios, D., & Magalhães, D. (2019). Political memes and the politics of memes: A methodological proposal for content analysis of online political memes. *First Monday*, *24*(2), https://doi.org/10.5210/fm.v24i2.7264

Chen, K. W., Phiddian, R., & Stewart, R. (2017). "Towards a discipline of political cartoon studies: Mapping the field". In J. M. Davis (Ed.), *Satire and politics: The interplay of heritage and practice* (pp. 125–162). Palgrave Macmillan.

Dahlberg, L. (2007). Rethinking the fragmentation of the cyberpublic: From consensus to contestation. *New Media & Society*, 9(5), 827–847. https://doi.org/10.1177/1461444807081228

Dean, J. (2019). Sorted for memes and gifs: Visual media and everyday digital politics. *Political Studies Review*, 17(3), 255–266. https://doi.org/10.1177/1478929918807483

Denisova, A. (2019). *Internet memes and society: Social, cultural, and political contexts*. Routledge.

Dobson, K., & Knezevic, I. (2017). 'Liking and sharing' the stigmatization of poverty and social welfare: Representations of poverty and welfare through internet memes on social media. *tripleC: Communication, Capitalism & Critique*, 15(2), 777–795. https://doi.org/10.31269/triplec.v15i2.815

Gal, N., Shifman, L., & Kampf, Z. (2016). 'It gets better': Internet memes and the construction of collective identity. *New Media & Society*, 18(8), 1698–1714. https://doi.org/10.1177/1461444814568784

Greene, V. S. (2019). "Deplorable" satire: Alt-right memes, white genocide tweets, and redpilling normies. *Studies in American Humor*, 5(1), 31–69. https://doi.org/10.5325/studamerhumor.5.1.0031

Habermas, J. (1962, reprint 1990). *Strukturwandel der Öffentlichkeit. Untersuchungen zu einer Kategorie der bürgerlichen Gesellschaft* [The Structural Transformation of the Public Sphere]. Frankfurt am Main: Suhrkamp.

Hariman, R. (2008). Political parody and public culture. *The Quarterly Journal of Speech*, 94(3), 247–272. https://doi.org/10.1080/00335630802210369

Huizinga, J. (1949, reprint 2014). *Homo ludens: A study of play-element in culture*. Routledge.

Huntington, H. E. (2016). Pepper Spray Cop and the American dream: Using synecdoche and metaphor to unlock internet Memes' visual political rhetoric. *Communication Studies*, 67(1), 77–93. https://doi.org/10.1080/10510974.2015.1087414

Ibrahim, Y. (2016). Tank man, media memory and yellow duck patrol. *Digital Journalism*, 4(5), 582–596. https://doi.org/10.1080/21670811.2015.1063076

Jenkins, H. (2006). *Fans, bloggers, and gamers: Exploring participatory culture*. NYU Press.

Jensen, M. S, Neumayer, C., & Rossi, L. (2020). 'Brussels will land on Its feet like a cat': Motivations for memefying #Brusselslockdown. *Information, Communication & Society*, 23(1), 59–75. https://doi.org/10.1080/1369118X.2018.1486866

Katz, Y. & Shifman, L. (2017). Making sense? The structure and meanings of digital memetic nonsense. *Information, Communication & Society*, 20(6), 825–842. https://doi.org/10.1080/1369118X.2017.1291702

Kraidy, M. M. (2018). Fun against fear in the Caliphate: Islamic Stateï¿½s spectacle and counter-spectacle. *Critical Studies in Media Communication*, 35(1), 40–56.

Laclau, E. & Mouffe, C. (1985). *Hegemony and socialist struggle*. 2nd ed. New York: Verso.

McCrow-Young, A., & Mortensen, M. (2021). Countering spectacles of fear: Anonymous' meme 'war' against ISIS. *European Journal of Cultural Studies*, 24(4), 832–849. https://doi.org/10.1177/13675494211005060

Milner, R. M. (2018). *The world made meme: Public conversations and participatory media*. MIT Press.

Miltner, K. M. (2018). Internet memes. In J. Burgess, A. Marwick, & T. Poell (Eds.), *The SAGE handbook of social media* (pp. 412–428). Sage.

Mortensen, M. (2017). Constructing, confirming, and contesting icons: The Alan Kurdi imagery appropriated by #humanitywashedashore, Ai Weiwei, and Charlie Hebdo. *Media, Culture & Society*, 39(8), 1142–1161. https://doi.org/10.1177/0163443717725572

Mortensen, M., & Kristensen, N. N. (2020). De-celebrification: Beyond the scandalous. *Celebrity Studies*, 11(1), 89–100. https://doi.org/10.1080/19392397.2020.1704385

Mouffe, C. (1993). *Reprint 2005). The return of the political*. Verso.

Mouffe, C. (2005). *On the political*. Routledge.

Neumayer, C., & Struthers, D. M. (2019). Social media as activist archives. In M. Mortensen, C. Neumayer, & T. Poell (Eds.), *Social media materialities and protest: Critical reflections* (pp. 86–98). Routledge.

Neumayer, C., & Svensson, J. (2016). Activism and radical politics in the digital age: Towards a typology. *Convergence: The International Journal of Research Into New Media Technologies, 22*(2), 131–146. https://doi.org/10.1177/1354856514553395

Nissenbaum, A., & Shifman, L. (2017). Internet memes as contested cultural capital: The case of 4chan's/b/board. *New Media & Society, 19*(4), 483–501. https://doi.org/10.1177/1461444815609313

Olesen, T. (2018). Memetic protest and the dramatic diffusion of Alan kurdi. *Media, Culture & Society, 40*(5), 656–672. https://doi.org/10.1177/0163443717729212

Peters, C., & Allan, S. (2021). Weaponizing memes: The journalistic mediation of visual politicization. *Digital Journalism*, online before print. https://doi.org/10.1080/21670811.2021.1903958

Ross, A. S., & Rivers, D. J. (2017). Digital cultures of political participation: Internet memes and the discursive delegitimization of the 2016 U.S presidential candidates. *Discourse, Context & Media, 16*, 1–11. https://doi.org/10.1016/j.dcm.2017.01.001

Segev, E., Nissenbaum, A., Stolero, N., & Shifman, L. (2015). Families and networks of internet memes: The relationship between cohesiveness, uniqueness, and quiddity concreteness. *Journal of Computer-Mediated Communication, 20*(4), 417–433. https://doi.org/10.1111/jcc4.12120

Seiffert-Brockmann, J., Diehl, T., & Dobusch, L. (2018). Memes as games: The evolution of a digital discourse online. *New Media & Society, 20*(8), 2862–2879. https://doi.org/10.1177/1461444817735334

Shifman, L. (2013). *Memes in digital culture*. The MIT Press.

Sicart, M. (2014). *Play matters*. The MIT Press.

Svensson, J., Neumayer, C., Banfield-Mumb, A., & Schossböck, J. (2015). Identity negotiation in activist participation. *Communication, Culture & Critique, 8*(1), 144–162. https://doi.org/10.1111/cccr.12073

Tuters, M., & Hagen, S. (2020). (((they))) rule: Memetic antagonism and nebulous othering on 4chan. *New Media & Society, 22*(12), 2218–2237. https://doi.org/10.1177/1461444819888746

Wiggins, B. E. (2019). *The discursive power of memes in digital culture: Ideology, semiotics, and intertextuality*. Routledge.

Wiggins, B. E., & Bowers, G. B. (2015). Memes as genre: A structurational analysis of the memescape. *New Media & Society, 17*(11), 1886–1906. https://doi.org/10.1177/1461444814535194

Messy on the inside: internet memes as mapping tools of everyday life

Sulafa Zidani

ABSTRACT
This paper presents the first systematic analysis of memes created by Palestinians in Israel. An analysis of 150 memes reveals how memes are used to reflect on and intervene in Palestinian youths' navigation of life in mixed cities under prolonged war and colonialism. I analyze these memes at three different levels: global popular culture and politics, in relation to the Israeli State, and Palestinian in-group dynamics. The analysis reveals a divide between Palestinians and Israelis despite living in mixed cities, putting the myth of coexistence in such cities into question. Memes appear to function both in navigating the contested cultural and spatial politics and carving out space in the cultural landscape for youths' aspirations. I propose a framework that conceptualizes Internet memes as mapping tools of everyday life. I argue that memes map out the social, cultural, and political landscape in which meme makers live and operate, and further reveals the intricate ties between new media technology and the political, cultural, and spatial arenas.

Introduction

In August 2020, Israel, and the United Arab Emirates (UAE) reached an agreement to normalize their diplomatic relationship, a step labeled by some politicians (mainly in the United States) and journalists as a 'historic peace deal' (BBC, 2020; Estrin, 2021), despite there never being an official war between Israel and the UAE. This deal normalizes trade deals that existed prior to the new agreement (Friedman, 2010). Palestinian meme makers responded to the deal through memes. They compared Haifa's Ministry of Interior's Sail Tower to Dubai's iconic tower, Burj Al Arab. They revived a mockery of the Haifa tower (colloquially called the 'rocket building' عمارة الصاروخ) which had launched at the time of its construction in 2002 (Figures 1–5).

Meme makers also self-deprecatingly made fun of the fact that they do not have enough money to travel to Dubai themselves, and so instead, they buy a ticket to Haifa's light rail train to go see the 'rocket building.' They imagined the disappointment a citizen of Dubai must feel when faced with this armature version of Burj Al Arab, and pictured Emirati people at the beach in Haifa. The memes even planned a night out that starts in Downtown Haifa and ends in Dubai.

Figure 1. Meme Text: 'When you want to travel to Dubai but you only have money for a ticket to the [Haifa] light rail'; Caption: 'It's the company that matters anyway #HaifaOnTheMap'

Figure 2. Meme Text: 'When an Emirati comes to Haifa and sees the rocket building'; Caption: 'When you order Dubai from Ali Express #HaifaOnTheMap'

Figure 3. Meme Text: A map pin indicating (in Hebrew) the location is Haifa's Student Beach; Caption Text 'Live broadcast from Haifa Meme channel on one of Haifa's beaches!! #GetTheCooler #HaifaOnTheMap'

This article investigates the relationship between Internet memes, politics, and everyday life. Using Internet memes made by Palestinians in mixed cities in Israel as a case study, I propose a framework that looks at memes as mapping tools that outline social, political, and cultural boundaries. I open with this group of memes because they represent an example of a broader trend of memes made by Palestinians in Israel which situate them and illustrate the cultural dynamics which they navigate: between local and global, with the Israeli state, within broader Arab culture in the region, and their own culture, their neighborhoods, cities, and the diaspora.

What stands out about this Middle East 'peace deal' is that Palestinians, who are key figures impacted by the continued war and occupation by Israel, were not included or consulted in the process. In fact, the US administration bypassed Palestinians in brokering the deal between Israel, UAE, and Bahrain (Al Jazeera, 2021). This is not unique to the UAE-Israel peace deal. Rather, this deal sits atop of a stack of other so-called 'historic' and/or 'peace' agreements involving Israel that exclude Palestinians. From early examples like the Balfour Declaration in 1917 all the way to today's peace agreements with the UAE, Sudan, and Morocco. For the Palestinian people, these deals have not brought along peace, rather they have brought about a further normalization and solidification

Figure 4. Meme Text: 'When the outing starts in Downtown and ends in Dubai'; Caption: 'Oh, habibi! What a night!'

of the occupation and support for colonial capitalism in the region through business exchanges and tourism agreements. The peace deal with the UAE, for example, brought about 50,000 Israeli tourists to Dubai by December 2020 (McGinley, 2020), and Israel targeting UAE tourists (Kane, 2020), all during the COVID-19 pandemic.

Palestinian meme makers use globally-trending meme templates to create complex responses that critique current events and systemic issues. In the meme above, for example, @jean.paul.za3tar uses the 'starter pack' meme template to criticize normalization in its different forms. The meme points out the hypocrisy of political agreements and efforts that take place under the pretense of peace, focusing on superficial optics while oppression continues in practice. This starter pack includes, for example, Canary Mission, a self-proclaimed anti-hate site that has been condemned for spreading misinformation and slander targeting activists for Palestinian rights in the US (Jewish Voice for Peace, 2016). The starter pack also includes tourism between Tel Aviv and Dubai (top right corner), the pride parade in Tel Aviv (bottom right corner), appropriation of food (bottom left corner), or tattoos of the word 'peace' in Hebrew and Arabic (top left corner). In doing so, the meme outlines what normalization looks like in terms of specific trends in the cultural landscape.

This article examines memes on three Instagram pages made by Palestinians in mixed cities in Israel (Haifa and Nazareth) as a way to interrogate the role that memes play in

Figure 5. Meme Text: 'Normalization starter pack'; Caption: '@jean.paul.za3tar's Guide to Normalization: The Path to Peace (Tel Aviv-Yafo: Center for Contemporary Art Press, 2021).

navigating daily life under prolonged conflict and war. Taken together, these memes map out the contested space that Palestinians in mixed cities navigate under precarious conditions whereby they are, at best, invisible and abandoned by the State, and seen as enemies at worst, and often used simply as a tool to win elections. I begin first by contextualizing the memes within the field of meme research and give an overview of research on new media technology in the Palestinian context. Then I outline my method for investigating the memes and display my findings. This is followed by a discussion section where I propose a framework for viewing memes as mapping tools that chart out the cultural landscape and illustrate how Palestinian youth navigate life in this context. I end with concluding remarks reflecting on the implications of this framework.

Before I begin the analysis, I want to comment on the term 'Palestinians in Israel.' Despite having a similar relationship to the historical land of Palestine, the lived experience of Palestinian people and the ways they might identify are diverse. I use the term 'Palestinians in Israel' in this study to clarify its focus on memes made to comment on the life of Palestinians living within the Israeli State. 'Palestinians in Israel' acknowledges the diverse lived experiences of Palestinians and specifies the limits of the group of Palestinian people that is covered in this article, which does not cover Palestinian meme makers in the West Bank, Gaza, in refugee camps in other countries, or in the diaspora. I step away from terms like 'Palestinian citizens of Israel' or 'Arab Israelis' which contribute to a minoritization discourse that is problematic for two reasons: First, it further promotes the segmentation of Palestinian communities that has been instilled through colonial practices. Second, it erases the history of Palestinians as indigenous people to the land. The word 'citizens' does not represent the situation of Palestinians in Israel, who have been treated as un-citizens, enemies of the state. Although this citizenship status comes with certain mobility, like the ability to travel the conditions in which Palestinians live often tell a story of discrimination, population control, and surveillance (Kopty, 2018; Sa'di, 2014), and show that citizenship in itself is an unstable arena of conflict and negotiation (Azoulay, 2008). In fact, Palestinians have been markedly erased from discourse around citizenship (Azoulay, 2008). Through its examination of meme culture, this paper will further show the complex cultural position that Palestinians in Israel are connected to. Through my use of the term 'Palestinians in Israel,' I aim to push back against terms that contribute to segmentation and maintain the connection between Palestinian people in different places and situations while still acknowledging the divergence in human rights and lived experiences. Furthermore, this choice suits the methodology of this article which does not view memes solely within a framework of nation-state politics or institutional politics, but rather points to the complex relational configuration of culture as it is mapped out through the discourse of memes.

Internet memes and politics

An Internet meme is defined as a group of digital items with common characteristics that are created with awareness of each other, then circulated, imitated, and/or transformed by Internet users (Shifman, 2014). Memes have been theorized as cultural building blocks that bridge between personal and political meanings (Shifman, 2014), between the past and present (Hristova, 2013), and between politics and humor, or seriousness and silliness (Mina, 2019; Shifman, 2014; Tay, 2014). According to Shifman, memes can function as forms of political advocacy, grassroots action, and as modes of expression and public discussion (Shifman, 2014). Memes can also do political work that includes exposing the inauthenticity or flaws and manipulations of politicians (Shifman, 2014), and inviting people to connect in solidarity movements and civic efforts (Mina, 2019).

Memes have been used across the world both to reinforce and disrupt power relations in the political and cultural landscape. Indigenous activists in Australia, for example, use memes to bring together a movement against the erasure of indigenous people and raise awareness about the ways in which Australian colonialism has been enacted over time (Frazer & Carlson, 2017). In China, Internet users deploy creative content including wordplay, memes, and parodic content to express political dissent or criticism as well as participate in community ritual (Fang, 2020; Yang & Jiang, 2015; Zidani, 2018).

Within the Arabic context specifically, scholars have shown how memes can be used as 'tactical social action' the subaltern uses in their struggle for justice (Ben Moussa et al., 2020), as 'laments' that express political dissent while saving face (Al Zidjaly, 2017), and as 'reorienting humor' that mixes cultures to interfere in the direction of global cultural flows (Zidani, 2020).

These theorizations of the political and cultural impacts of Internet memes inform my analysis of digital culture as an extension of 'offline' culture, rather than seeing the Internet as a separate space. In fact, power relations from the so-called 'offline' are reproduced online (Kopty, 2018). I frame memes as digital culture artifacts that are created and circulated in a way that is deeply connected to the social ties and the cultural and political experience in the everyday lives of their creators. It is especially the case in the context of Palestinians, who have been living under prolonged colonial rule, war, and continued civic unrest, that the separation between online and offline becomes even more muffled (Thompson et al., 2021). In this paper I argue that memes can be conceptualized as mapping tools that chart out the connection between cultural, political, and spatial boundaries, and participate in a playful negotiation of these boundaries. This framework is particularly useful for investigating memes in circumstances of prolonged conflict or war where space, culture, and politics are under constant change and negotiation. Palestinian meme makers navigate the dynamics of living under settler colonialism, global capitalism, and marginalization at the local and global levels, as well as their own cultural concerns – Palestinian diversity, gender equality, and youth issues that have to do with generational differences and popular culture.

Palestine and digital culture research

Scholars on digital culture in Palestine (Kamil, 2020; Nazzal, 2020; Tawil-Souri, 2016) problematize the assumption that new media technologies will bring with them a democratizing promise that will create peace across borders. While 'ICTs are assumed to function as bridges paving the way towards a 'global village' of peace and understanding' (Tawil-Souri, 2016, p. 108), the result for Palestinians is often a manifestation of contradictory borders (Tawil-Souri, 2016). Although new media technologies are built on the assumption of connection through disembodiment from space, space is actually central to their form and content. Palestinians have used new media technologies to recast ideas of access to land and space through, for example, an online tour of Al Aqsa or digitized oral history (Kamil, 2020). This use is particularly important for Palestinians and other indigenous communities across the world where settler colonial power enforces a disconnection from the land through an erasure of indigenous culture's historical connection to the land, limiting access of indigenous people to certain places, and segmenting the indigenous population. New media technologies are indeed part of a larger matrix of power in which Palestine's borders are continually constrained, Israel's are expansive, and the European Union's are fuzzy (Tawil-Souri, 2016). Tawil-Souri explains that:

> From the perspective of Palestine, a core contradiction arises as a back-drop against which to understand ICT infrastructures: the containment of Palestinians in narrowing and disconnected spaces occurs at the same time that hi-tech globalisation is posited as the route to openness and through which to overcome fragmentation and containment. In other words, new spatialities and bordering mechanisms are created, while others are eradicated. (p. 111)

By outlining the ways in which borders are simultaneously expanded and controlled in the advent of new media technology, Tawil-Souri demonstrates that 'the technological is (spatial-) political' and 'the (spatial-) political is also technological' (Tawil-Souri, 2016, p. 124). This technological-spatial-political relationship is manifested online through vague platform policies and discriminatory artificial intelligence on YouTube and Facebook, for example, and a promotion of Israeli content while silencing and censoring Palestinians (Nazzal, 2020). Palestinian youth also use Tiktok to connect with each other and promote their culture, but they have been met with backlash through comment sections and even erasure of their Tiktok accounts (Greig, 2021). Thus, the experience of Palestinians on social media platforms tends to be a mixed one, where they are able to form community and celebrate culture, but at the same time, they receive much backlash by the State, online trolls, if not platforms themselves.

When it comes to the online digital culture of Palestinian youth, it can be viewed in part within the context of the Arab World more generally. Previous studies have shown how Arab youth use creative expressions online to engage in public discourse around popular culture and politics. This includes practices that connect globalized culture with local Palestinian fandom such as the example with Korean popular music and soap operas (known as Hallyu culture; Otmazgin & Lyan, 2014). Arabic-speaking Internet users in the Middle East at large also participate in the creation and circulation of meme culture, remix and mashup culture, and parody videos, using humor and creativity to comment on politics, intervene in the direction of global cultural flows, and reimagine alternatives to their current situation (Elsayed, 2016; Elsayed & Zidani, 2020; Zidani, 2020). These engagements with different cultures are expressive of Palestinian youth's positionality within the world. They act as consumers and producers of both their own local culture, the regional or linguistic Arab culture, and global popular culture. This positionality results in language and culture mixing that is evident in the meme examples offered throughout this paper. Using memes as a mapping tool shows, for example, that US popular culture and politics are central in the cultural map of Palestinian memes.

Methods

Site of analysis

I examine memes made by Palestinians in Israel by focusing on the social media platform Instagram. Instagram was chosen as the main social media platform for this study because of its focus on visual culture and the wide dissemination of memes on that platform. Instagram has been conceptualized as a conduit for communication in the landscape of visual media cultures, and a key for understanding and mapping visual social media cultures both on the platform and off it (Leaver et al., 2020). As @mem3a_fe_alda5el put it in their Instagram profile description 'One page on Instagram is better than ten on Facebook' (referencing an Arabic proverb that a bird in the hand is better than ten in a tree). I focus mainly on three pages on Instagram: two meme pages from mixed cities in the north of Israel (Haifa Memes and Nazareth Memes or @haifa.memes and @nazarethmemes12 respectively), and a page dedicated to life 'on the inside' (referring to life inside Israel's borders established in 1948, the page is entitled ميمعة في الداخل 'Mess on the Inside' or @mem3a_fe_alda5el). All three pages have thousands of followers. At the time of writing this article, Haifa Memes was leading with 11.4 thousand followers, while Nazareth Memes and Mess on the Inside both had 7–9 thousand followers.

These Instagram pages are well suited for examining the relationship between memes and war and oppression that is prolonged, unlike a temporary or passing crisis event. The urban spaces of Haifa and Nazareth, just like the rest of the region, are continually changing and being contested. Both Haifa and Nazareth are rich with Palestinian history and cultural life. Although these cities are technically 'mixed' housing both Israeli Jewish and

Palestinian people, the neighborhood remain largely segregated. In the recent few years in Haifa, notably, middle-class youth are refashioning urban spaces into enclaves that center Palestinians and their culture and where Israeli Jewish citizens are considered guests (rather than the opposite; Withers, 2021).

Sampling

I chose the latest relevant 50 memes from each of the Instagram accounts for analysis. Relevance was defined as posts that (1) can be considered a meme, meaning that screenshots of news articles posted on the Instagram pages without being transformed into a meme were dropped out of the corpus. (2) In addition, I filtered out posts that focused solely on topics irrelevant to this paper. For example, posts that commented on the COVID-19 pandemic, like those that suggest how to wear a mask properly or memes that compare 2020–2021 were dropped out from the corpus. However, posts that discussed COVD-19 in the context of people's relationship to the State or the city were included. Altogether, I collected 50 memes from each of the three Instagram accounts, making up a totally of 150 memes for analysis.

Analysis

I conducted a systematic qualitative analysis based on grounded theory using criteria that rose from the data combined with prior knowledge (Strauss & Corbin, 1998). Thus, the criteria for analysis were chosen both based on common themes in the memes themselves and born out of prior research on culture and spatial politics. Here I use Doreen Massey's (2005) understanding of space as socially negotiated. In addition, Davi Johnson's (2007) theorization of memes (in their broader meaning, not necessarily as Internet memes) as a geographical concept which can be used as 'a methodological tool that is particularly suited to the analysis of popular culture discourses that transform social practices in spite of their apparent superficiality and triviality' (Johnson, 2007, p. 28). I also use prior knowledge on digital culture in Palestine specifically or in the rest of the world, some of which was reviewed in the literature review of this article.

The criteria for analysis noted places (towns, neighborhood, countries, etc.) and subcultures named in the memes, politicians and other key figures, languages included, and key words that help identify recurring themes.

The analysis included the visual part of the image (the meme) as well as the caption (the commentary posted on the platform alongside the image). The rationale behind including the caption is that the text was often not edited into the image, instead, the text portion which is typically part of the meme was placed in the caption. Thus, including the caption in the analysis followed meme makers' way of using the platform, and ensured that the commentary (or, oftentimes, the butt of the joke) are not filtered out the analysis.

Findings

Memes made by Palestinians in Israel can be organized on a few different levels that are detailed below. First, the global level reflecting how they navigate and intervene in global political dynamics. Seeing that the timing of this analysis coincided with the global COVID19 pandemic and events like the U.S.-brokered agreement, it is not surprising that many memes commenting on global politics brought up these events. Although these are specific current events, the way they are treated in the memes reveals something broader about global cultural, political, and spatial dynamics.

The second level is the state level, where I examine the memes' framing of issues involving the Israeli State and 'local' institutional politics, including Palestinian members of the Knesset as well as spatial and infrastructural issues that are raised in the memes.

The third level is that of in-group Palestinian diversity. This level looks into the ways in which diversity was reflected through the memes, both in terms of how the memes as a group portray a diverse group of people, and how there were intentional steps to emphasize that diversity and invite people from different places to join in on the meme conversation.

These three levels of analysis reflect the positionality of the youth making them. While I separate them aiming to organize the findings of this study, they are by no means separable. It is often the case that one meme can touch upon multiple levels simultaneously. In addition, it is worth emphasizing the convergence of these levels on each one of the meme accounts surveyed for this study.

Navigating global dynamics

The memes investigated in this paper reflect the dominance of the US on the global cultural stage. Many memes reference US politics and popular culture. This finding is not surprising since, first, US institutional politics directly impact local politics in Palestine, Israel, and the broader region, for example through the brokered 'peace deal' mentioned in the opening of this article, as well as US military aid to Israel. Many memes use the images of US politicians as funny mashup content and for the purpose of participating in a meme trend, such as the Bernie meme in Figure 6, which is a version of the *Bernie Sanders Wearing Mittens Sitting in a Chair Meme* that went viral after the original image was taken during the Inauguration of Joe Biden as US President. Other memes also express a lack of confidence in US politicians, both in their impact on their own country and in the possibility of them halting the empowerment of oppression locally. Former US president Donald Trump was a common figure in memes that mocked politicians, such as the meme in Figure 7, which fabricates a tweet by Donald Trump expressing a love towards 'the homeland' that is the exact opposite to what he practiced during his time in office. Or Figure 8, which shows a meme that highlights Trump's 'stop the count' slogan aimed at suppressing mail-in votes during the 2020 election.

The normalization of Israel's relationship with Bahrain and the UAE was another global political issue that came up in these memes. As shown in Figures 1–5, memes created parodical scenes mocking this relationship and emphasizing their lack of access to enjoy the perks it might provide some people. The text in the memes and captions repeated stated that they cannot afford a trip to Dubai and made fun of Haifa's rocket building compared to Burj Al Arab. Together, the groups of memes that brought up the normalization of Israel's relationship with the UAE reflect that tourism is one of the main ways that this relationship is practiced, highlighting that the economic benefits of this deal supersede actual peaceful relations between people.

Figure 6. A meme of Bernie Sanders wearing mittens sitting in a chair. This version has been edited to show him wearing a Palestinian kuffieh. The caption can be translated to 'It's super cold'

Secondly, the relevance (and dominance) of US popular culture in meme culture makes it so that participating in meme culture necessitates a level of fluency in US popular culture. This necessity for fluency in US culture is exemplified in the use of trending memes that include US politicians like the Bernie meme and Donald Trump's Twitter usage, as well as trending memes that draw on movies and television shows like The Office, Batman, or Dexter's Laboratory.

Figure 7. What looks like a tweet from Donald Trump (but is not a real tweet) saying 'You can take all the status and profits, just let me have the homeland'; Caption: 'I am a citizen.'

Figure 8. Meme text: 'When you watch a waiter calculating your bill Downtown'; Donald Trump's tweet: 'Stop the count!'; Caption: 'Bro, it's like they're just guessing the bill #HaifaOnTheMap'

With US culture dominating, it is also notable that many memes mixed languages and culture. This type of humor has previously been labeled as *reorienting humor*, a type of creative humorous digital content that is based on culture mixing, remixes, and mashups which Arab youth use to reorient the direction of global cultural flows in a way that centers their own culture (Zidani, 2020). Notably, although US cultural fluency is a prerequisite for participating in meme culture, mixing English was not encouraged. In fact, there was a hierarchy of languages that intersected with classed and gendered connotations to language choice that put colloquial Palestinian Arabic (including the different dialects) as the preferred choice. Colloquial Arabic was portrayed as the language of the middle-class youth, the meme culture community, while Modern Standard Arabic (also known as Fus'ha الفصحى) was portrayed are hipster and overly intellectual, mixing English was portrayed in the memes as classist (or trying to associate with a higher class) and un-masculine, and mixing Hebrew was mocked as an attempt at overcompensating or sometimes associated with fragile masculinity, or trying too hard. In terms of places, mixing English was more associated with Haifa while mixing Hebrew was more associated with Nazareth or with 'Dodim' culture which will be further explored below. For examples, Figure 9 shows a variation on the Swole Doge vs. Cheems meme portraying the different behavior of a Nazarene person in their hometown versus in Haifa. When visiting Haifa, a Nazarene person appears as Cheems, a smaller and less toned version of themselves who mixed English in their sentences. On the other hand, at home, a Nazarene person in Nazareth appears as Swole Doge, a larger and more muscular version of themselves who mixes Hebrew in their sentences and speaks in audible slang that is unique to Nazareth. This

24   THE PLAYFUL POLITICS OF MEMES

Figure 9. Cheems, the smaller dog, is labeled as a Nazarene person in Haifa saying 'the vibe in Downtown is so fire' (the words 'vibe' and 'downtown' are in English), Swole Doge, the larger muscular dog, is labeled as a Nazarene person in Nazareth saying in Nazarene slang 'I'm telling you I beat him up real good I swear.' The caption also imitates a Nazarene dialect 'We go to the city every weekend man #HaifaOnTheMap' ('city' and 'weekend' are in Hebrew).

example illustrates how language and dialect are part of the way in which Palestinian youth navigate the space around them and move between different spaces.

Ultimately, Palestinian meme makers' use of global political and cultural content in memes is both a reflection of their positionality – the way they navigate their lived reality – while it is also a way for them to intervene in that reality, place themselves in it, and reassign meanings to the cultures and politics they consume and create. It is a way to understand or make sense of the space, and to move between cultures and between spaces. Memes, then, reveal a map of cultural dynamics but also show what intervention or commentary are being made regarding that cultural map.

Navigating dynamics with the Israeli State

The lack of confidence in politicians extended to Israeli state politicians as well, including Palestinian members of the Knesset. When it came to Israeli political figures like Prime Minister Benjamin Netanyahu, memes pointed out a type of hypocrisy whereby politicians reach out to Palestinians for votes, but without taking any actions to improve the situation of Palestinians in Israel or the cities, towns, neighborhoods, or villages in which they reside. The memes expressed a deficiency in resources and infrastructure that impact the Palestinian community. One meme addressed this problem in Haifa specifically (Figure 10), citing the different treatment and resources that Palestinian neighborhoods like Abbas and Wadi el Nisnas get from the municipality in comparison to neighborhoods with a predominantly Jewish-Israeli population like Carmel.

THE PLAYFUL POLITICS OF MEMES 25

Figure 10. Meme text (top to bottom): 'Carmel,' 'Haifa Municipality,' 'Abbas,' 'Wadi el Nisnas'; Caption text: 'Please, the most important thing is Carmel and the high society #HaifaOnTheMap' (high society is in English).

Notably, at the time of writing this article (March 2021), the state of Israel is headed towards its fourth election in two years. Current Prime Minister Benjamin Netanyahu has won the past three elections by a narrow margin and nearly failed to create a government coalition between different parties. Much of this process is reflected in Palestinian meme pages. A series of memes containing on these pages speak directly to Netanyahu's efforts. 'We're all with you, Abu Yair,' one says sarcastically. The memes talk about how Netanyahu intends to 'milk' Arab towns and play games with people in attempt to lure some Palestinians into voting for him (see Figures 11 and 12).

Memes also expressed lack of confidence in Palestinian members of the Israeli Knesset. Many of them were portrayed in a mocking or parodic way. This was especially the case for The Joint List (المشتركة القائمة), an alliance formed in 2015 between four Palestinian-majority Knesset parties. Memes were used to criticize some Knesset members and point out their inauthenticity or hypocrisy, in line with Shifman's findings (Shifman, 2014). The example below shows Mansour Abbas, a common figure in the corpus, who separated the Muslim party from the Joint List and is portrayed as someone who is willing to go to extreme lengths in order to gain political power, even betraying his

Figure 11. Meme text (from top to bottom) 'The Arab society,' 'issalamu-alaykoom' (mocking Netanyahu's pronounciation of the Arabic greeting Assalmu Alaykum), 'racism, unemployment, illegal settlements, the deal of the century'; Caption text: 'Guess who is using us to play chess?'

own people's interests. In the meme below, Abbas is criticized for cozying up to Netanyahu and doing whatever he asks him (see Figure 13).

Other Palestinian Knesset members were mocked in memes less so for their politics and more for their mannerisms. The memes draw on certain traits of politicians, like Haneen Zoabi's enunciation, Ahmad Tibi's voice, or Ayman Odeh's choice of phrases and behavior. The meme below (Figure 14) shows how Ayman Odeh is mocked for displaying behaviors that might not match with the formality that is expected of a politician, and rather reminds meme makers of youth or students, thus making him more 'memable.'

The memes also raised issues concerning cultural erasure, commenting on the colonial practice in which Zionists appropriate on foods like hummus and falafel. Memes like the one below (Figure 15) reflect long-standing tensions rising from claims of hummus and falafel as Israeli foods (El-Jayyousi, 2019; Salaita, 2017).

Navigating Palestinian cultural diversity

The memes also expressed the diversity of Palestinian culture and subcultures, as well as common experiences of Palestinian youth. A recurrent theme, for example, consisted of

Figure 12. Meme text: 'Netanyahu's show for the Arab society: I am going to play ball with you'; Caption text: 'We the kind of people who .... You cannot play with us or use us to play.'

memes that were mainly concerned with the student experience. The tone in student memes was similar to the honest self-deprecating humor around student life described by Ask and Abidin (2018) whose work shows how students use memes to commiserate and build community around sharing daily struggles. Many Palestinian students leave their hometowns for universities in cities like Haifa, Tel Aviv, or Jerusalem, and return for the weekend to their hometown (commonly referred to as el-balad البلد). Student memes often point out the differences between their university town and el-balad, and share their common experience like traveling and searching for an apartment in a crowded city and living on a low budget. The memes also show how youth make sense of the different cultures that exist in each university, like Technion's casual dress versus Haifa University's more formal fashion approach (see Figures 16 and 17).

Cultural diversity was sometimes expressed in an inclusive way. For example, there were memes that emphasized and celebrated differences in Arabic accents or dialect. Memes also included captions calling on people from different places, acknowledging not only the diversity of the followers and fan base of these meme pages, but also the mobility of people within Palestine and their ties to different regions within Palestinian land. In this way, memes on the @arablocalmess Instagram page that give a sort of shout-out to people from Kofor Kanna, Iksal, Tamra, and other towns inviting them to participate, are not only giving a nod to their fans from these towns, but also illustrating an inclusive Palestinian group identity.

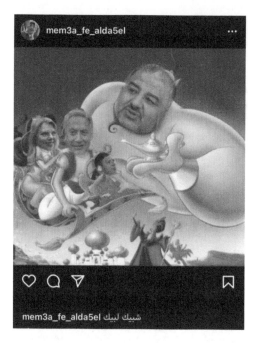

Figure 13. A shot from the Disney movie Aladdin which shows Benjamin Netanyahu with his wife Sarah and son Yair on the magic carpet, while Palestinian Knesset member Mansour Abbas is portrayed as the genie with a caption which can be translated to 'your wish is my command.'

However, cultural diversity was not always expressed in an inclusive way. Many memes mocked certain subcultures or expressed existing rivalries between cultural groups. First, some of the memes in this corpus generally portrayed a meme culture that is unwelcoming of women and LGBTQ people and non-heteronormativity in general. Some memes mocked women (commenting on make-up habits, poses for photos, and other stereotyping comments), and associated being gay with a lack of masculinity in a way that could potentially reinforce toxic masculine attitudes. Dodim culture was also a primary target for mockery. This is a culture of guys mostly from Nazareth and its suburbs or surrounding towns, who are associated with wearing sports brands like Adidas or slouchy jeans. Dodim also usually wear a chain necklace and a cap. In their linguistic practices, dodim tend to mix Hebrew words in their dialect. The label 'dodim' comes from the way they address each other as dod (דוד Hebrew for 'uncle'), – im is the plural masculine suffix in Hebrew. Dodim culture promotes an understanding of masculinity that builds on a combination of brand capital and cultural capital that comes from Hebrew language and Israeli music mixed within their own Palestinian Arabic repertoire. As demonstrated by the two memes below (Figures 18 and 19), meme makers mock this version of masculinity portraying it as forced or inauthentic, a masculinity that gives (and asks for) attention based on superficial and material things.

Several cultural rivalries came up in memes that compared one group to another, like Haifa versus Nazareth, Haifa University students versus Technion students, or Haifa's Carmel neighborhood versus its Downtown. These comparisons further highlight what has already been shown in the findings: that these memes are both reflective of and

Figure 14. Ayman Odeh in a tent during a days-long march protesting the Israeli government's treatment of Palestinians. Caption text: 'That moment when you remember at 1AM that you have a test tomorrow.'

also function for navigating the different dimensions of the Palestinian experience in the cultural and political landscape.

Memes as mapping tools, then, chart out the social stratification and indicate where the boundaries are drawn between different social groups and sub-groups within the group of Palestinian youth. They tell us how people from these different subgroups might experience space when they move in it, and who gets to go where in mixed cities. In addition, they show us who holds power to decide regarding mobility and resources.

Discussion: memes as mapping tools

Mixing popular culture and current events, memes connect lived experience of culture to the discourse around it and intervention in it. I suggest memes as mapping tools that introduce their consumers to the lay of the land – culturally, politically, and spatially, and allow their producers to comment on and intervene in those spatial political dynamics. Memes draw out not only the different spaces of neighborhood, cities, and the world, but also map out the social stratification related to these spatial politics, answering questions like: who can and cannot navigate these spaces easily? Who holds

Figure 15. An image from the January 6, 2021 storming of the United States Capitol which was circulated as a meme online. This version portrays Israelis as stealing falafel away proudly.

power in these spaces? Who decides where resources go? Or, to present some more concrete examples based on memes used in this article: Who owns Downtown Haifa on Thursday nights? Would dodim be welcome there? Which neighborhoods in Haifa are thriving, and which ones are drowning? How does a person from Nazareth appear in Nazareth versus in Haifa? Where do Palestinian stand on the chess board or in the soccer field of Israeli politics? Memes made by Palestinian youth in Israel map out the cultural and political terrain, showing where they stand on the map, their positionality in a complex web of cultural and political dynamics, and how they move within the cultural, political, and spatial landscape. The precarious 'citizen' status mentioned in the beginning of this paper is also reflected in the complex experience mapped out through the memes they make, which demand deep knowledge of the space, the languages, the cultures and subcultures, ways to behave to navigate the space smoothly, where to go for better resources or to find spaces with people with similar values. The meme content from these mixed cities is in line with narratives that break what has been labeled as 'the myth of coexistence' (Buttu, 2021) – the myth that Palestinians and Israeli Jews in mixed cities are a model for coexistence. The memes investigated here draw a picture whereby Palestinians and Israeli Jews do not spend time together in the same spaces and do not receive the same rights or infrastructural resources. This study showed a glaring segregation from Jewish Israeli society (apart from institutional politics).

The memes in this corpus mix popular culture from different parts of the world. Notably, in some memes, mixing cultures and languages is a way to celebrate or point out problems within Palestinian culture itself. Popular culture coming predominantly from the

Figure 16. Bernie Sanders meme originating from his presidential campaign for the 2020 US elections saying 'I am once again asking for your financial support.' Caption text: 'University students when they go back to el-balad.'

US and politics from other countries are thus deployed as a means for navigating the local cultural landscape.

The conceptualization of memes as a mapping tool complicates the liberatory potential of new media. New media has been and still is leveraged to combat the segmentation of Israeli settler colonialism (Kamil, 2020). Using memes as mapping tools allows us to assess where that cultural segmentation stands at a certain moment in time and from a specific cultural perspective. The memes focusing on mixed cities illustrate a segmentation between Palestinians in Israel and those who are in the West Bank, Gaza, and diaspora. It is important to pay attention to what is not mentioned in memes. Memes are a mapping tool from a particular perspective, and the perspective investigated in this study shows that, although there is an anti-colonial push in these memes, one that resists the erasure that has been enforced upon Palestinians and the disconnection from their land, these memes also show a potential normalization of the the divide and conquer approach that separates Palestinian in Gaza and the West Bank from Palestinians in Israel. The minimal presence of any mention of the West Bank, Gaza, or Palestinian refugees and the diaspora was a loud silence. The map that might be drawn with these memes indeed brings forth the voice or views of Palestinians 'on the inside.' However, this is not a complete map of the Palestinian people. This absence might be a sampling bias since this study focused on three Instagram accounts and specifically on mixed cities. But it may also be a product of the long-term segmentation of Palestinians limiting connection, which may have resulted in blockages in the landscape of meme culture as well. There

Figure 17. Meme text: (Right) How Haifa University girls go to school, (Left) how Technion girls go to school; Caption text: 'What about Ono Academic College?! #HaifaOnTheMap'

were memes in the corpus that commented on the accent of residents of the Golan Heights. The fact that they can access Haifa, for example, has led to a familiarity that lets the culture of Golan Heights people (or Jawlanis) come up in the imagination, and thus in the memes and cultural maps, of Palestinians in Israel. This reaffirms Tawil-Souri's argument that 'the technological is (spatial-) political' and 'the (spatial-) political is also technological' (Tawil-Souri, 2016, p. 124).

What these memes accomplish is carving out room for Palestinian youth within these cultural spaces that are difficult to navigate or where they experience risks or limitations. Memes become part of what Withers framed as a process of refashioning urban spaces into enclaves that center Palestinians and their culture (Withers, 2021). They use this digital culture vernacular as part of a larger culture shift to make room for and maintain connections across Palestinian culture. For example, by inviting participants with different accents and from different towns, meme makers push for a recognition of Palestinian lived experience and hold space for their cultural diversity. The memes map out Palestinian youths' aspirations for their culture, politics, and their desired values. They draw hard boundaries when it comes to politicians – Israeli or Palestinian – promoting settler colonialism and working against their interests. They point to a clear direction of what

Figure 18. Meme text: 'All dodim after the first rain'; Caption text: 'The complete one comes with a hat. #HaifaOnTheMap'

they think justice would look like: having fun with cultural diversity, equitable distribution of rights and resources, and a stop to colonial erasure and cultural appropriation.

Concluding remarks

This article is the first study of the meme culture of Palestinians in Israel. It offers a framework for viewing memes as mapping tools. This framework allows for a clearer view of the relationship between the cultural, spatial, and political, which is especially revealing under conditions where all these realms are contested because of long lasting colonial rule. The memes reveal, on one hand, a normalization of certain aspects of colonialism, like the segregation and segmentation of Palestinians and limitation of resources for Palestinian areas within Israel, and political and economic agreements with other countries that disregard the interests of Palestinians. They also show a criticism of this normalization and a push for recognizing what they viewed as games, hypocrisy, or control by politicians whether those are Palestinian, Israeli, American, or others.

This framework, then, reveals the cultural ties as well as the disconnections, and draws out the desired values and aspirations that are illustrated through meme culture. It shows how meme culture is simultaneously creating new possibilities for inclusion while it can also reinforce existing systems of power. Memes are not viewed here as a liberatory tool. They point to where their makers stand literally and metaphorically, in a cultural and political space that is contested. Through the creation and circulation of memes, meme makers also map out a space for themselves to avoid their erasure and promote

Figure 19. Meme text: (top) A dod riding a Mercedes wearing a Rolex happy with himself, (bottom) His parents who are paying and buying him everything; Caption text: 'I'm telling you, depend on your mommy and daddy.'

their aspirations. While this does not bring an end to or remediate oppression, it can create a gradual cultural push towards the justice values they want. Thus, we need to also pay attention to questions like: What is not mapped out in meme culture? What is being erased? How are things connected, segmented, linked, or divided? And what is called into question versus what is normalized?

Disclosure statement

No potential conflict of interest was reported by the author(s).

ORCID

Sulafa Zidani http://orcid.org/0000-0003-1337-0134

References

Al Jazeera. (2021, January 29). Trump went around Palestinians to get UAE, Bahrain, Israel accord. *Al Jazeera*. https://www.aljazeera.com/news/2021/1/29/trump-went-around-palestinians-to-get-uae-bahrain-israel-accord

Al Zidjaly, N. (2017). Memes as reasonably hostile laments: A discourse analysis of political dissent in Oman. *Discourse & Society*, 28(6), 573–594. https://doi.org/10.1177/0957926517721083

Ask, K., & Abidin, C. (2018). My life is a mess: Self-deprecating relatability and collective identities in the memification of student issues. *Information, Communication & Society*, 21(6), 834–850. https://doi.org/10.1080/1369118X.2018.1437204

Azoulay, A. (2008). *The civil contract of photography*. Zone Books.

BBC. (2020, August 13). Israel and UAE strike historic deal to normalise relations. *BBC News*. https://www.bbc.com/news/world-middle-east-53770859

Ben Moussa, M., Benmessaoud, S., & Douai, A. (2020). Internet memes as "tactical" social action: A multimodal critical discourse analysis approach. *International Journal of Communication*, 14(2020), 5920–5940. https://ijoc.org/index.php/ijoc/article/view/14534

Buttu, D. (2021, May 25). The Myth of Coexistence in Israel. *The New York Times*. https://www.nytimes.com/2021/05/25/opinion/israel-palestinian-citizens-racism-discrimination.html

El-Jayyousi, F. (2019, October 18). From Tahini to Sabra to sweet potato: The appropriation of hummus in Israel and the United States. *Medium*. https://farahwritesstuff.medium.com/from-tahini-to-sabra-to-sweet-potato-the-appropriation-of-hummus-in-israel-and-the-united-states-339f263b174b

Elsayed, Y. (2016). Laughing through change: Subversive humor in online videos of Arab youth. *International Journal of Communication*, 10(2016), 5102–5122. https://ijoc.org/index.php/ijoc/article/view/4795/1816

Elsayed, Y., & Zidani, S. (2020). Reimagining the Arab spring: From imagination to creativity. In H. Jenkins, G. Peter-Lazaro, & S. Shresthova (Eds.), *Popular culture and the civic imagination: Case studies of creative social change* (pp. 162–172). New York University Press.

Estrin, D. (2021, January 24). As Israelis flock to UAE, they see a new precedent: Peace deals without giving ground. *NPR*. https://www.npr.org/2021/01/24/956765027/as-israelis-flock-to-uae-they-see-a-new-precedent-peace-deals-without-giving-gro

Fang, K. (2020). Turning a communist party leader into an internet meme: The political and apolitical aspects of China's toad worship culture. *Information, Communication & Society*, 23(1), 38–58. https://doi.org/10.1080/1369118X.2018.1485722

Frazer, R., & Carlson, B. (2017). Indigenous memes and the invention of a people. *Social Media + Society*, 3(4). https://doi.org/10.1177/2056305117738993

Friedman, R. (2010, March 3). Israelis doing business in Dubai will wait out storm. *The Jerusalem Post*. https://www.jpost.com/Middle-East/Israelis-doing-business-in-Dubai-will-wait-out-storm

Greig, J. (2021, February 25). Young Palestinians are leaning into TikTok – even if their content gets deleted. *Vice*. https://www.vice.com/en/article/dy894y/young-palestinians-are-leaning-into-tiktok-even-if-their-content-gets-deleted

Hristova, S. (2013). Occupy wall street meets occupy Iraq: On remembering and forgetting in a digital age. *Radical History Review*, 117(117), 83–97. https://doi.org/10.1215/01636545-2210473

Jewish Voice for Peace. (2016, May 13). Canary Mission [web log]. *Jewish Voice for Peace*. https://jewishvoiceforpeace.org/canary-mission/

Johnson, D. (2007). Mapping the meme: A geographical approach to materialist rhetorical criticism. *Communication and Critical/Cultural Studies*, 4(1), 27–50. https://doi.org/10.1080/14791420601138286

Kamil, M. (2020). Postspatial, postcolonial: Accessing palestine in the digital. *Social Text*, 38(3), 55–82.

Kane, H. (2020, September 30). Israel targets 100,000 UAE tourists, eyes further potential. *Haaretz*. https://www.haaretz.com/israel-news/business/.premium-israel-targets-100-000-uae-tourists-eyes-further-potential-1.9195780

Kopty, A. (2018). Power dynamics in online communities: The Palestinian case. In C. Richter, A. Antonakis, & C. Harders (Eds.), *Digital media and the politics of transformation in the Arab world and Asia. Studies in international, transnational and global communications* (pp. 61–84). Springer VS.

Leaver, T., Highfield, T., & Abidin, C. (2020). *Instagram: Visual social media cultures.* John Wiley & Sons.

Massey, D. (2005). *For space.* Sage.

McGinley, S. (2020, December 17). UAE has attracted 50,000 Israeli tourists since Abraham accord. *Arab News.* https://www.arabnews.com/node/1778351/business-economy

Mina, A. X. (2019). *Memes to movements: How the world's most viral media is changing social protest and power.* Beacon Press.

Nazzal, A. (2020, November 27). YouTube's violation of Palestinian digital rights: What needs to be done. *Al Shabaka.* https://al-shabaka.org/briefs/youtubes-violation-of-palestinian-digital-rights-what-needs-to-be-done/

Otmazgin, N., & Lyan, I. (2014). Hallyu across the desert: K-pop fandom in Israel and Palestine. *Cross-Currents: East Asian History and Culture Review, 3*(1), 32–55. https://doi.org/10.1353/ach.2014.0008

Sa'di, A. H. (2014). *Through surveillance: The genesis of Israeli policies of population management, surveillance and political control towards the Palestinian minority.* Manchester University Press.

Salaita, S. (2017, Sep 4). 'Israeli' hummus is theft, not appropriation. *The New Arab.* https://english.alaraby.co.uk/english/comment/2017/9/4/israeli-hummus-is-theft-not-appropriation

Shifman, L. (2014). *Memes in digital culture.* MIT Press.

Strauss, A., & Corbin, J. (1998). *Basics of qualitative research techniques.* Sage publications.

Tawil-Souri, H. (2016). Between digital flows and territorial borders: ICTs in the Palestine-Israel-EU Matrix. In R. A. Del Sarto (Ed.), *Fragmented borders, interdependence and external relations: The Israel-Palestine-European Union Triangle* (pp. 107–128). Springer.

Tay, G. (2014). Binders full of LOLitics: Political humour, internet memes, and play in the 2012 US presidential election (and beyond). *European Journal of Humour Research, 2*(4), 46–73. https://doi.org/10.7592/EJHR2014.2.4.tay

Thompson, A., Stringfellow, L., Maclean, M., & Nazzal, A. (2021). Ethical considerations and challenges for using digital ethnography to research vulnerable populations. *Journal of Business Research, 124,* 676–683. https://doi.org/10.1016/j.jbusres.2020.02.025

Withers, P. (2021). Ramallah ravers and Haifa hipsters: Gender, class, and nation in Palestinian popular culture. *British Journal of Middle Eastern Studies, 48*(1), 1–19. https://doi.org/10.1080/13530194.2021.1885852

Yang, G., & Jiang, M. (2015). The networked practice of online political satire in China: Between ritual and resistance. *International Communication Gazette, 77*(3), 215–231. https://doi.org/10.1177/1748048514568757

Zidani, S. (2018). Represented dreams: Subversive expressions in Chinese social media as alternative symbolic infrastructures. *Social Media+ Society, 4*(4). https://doi.org/10.1177/2056305118809512

Zidani, S. (2020). Not Arabi or ajnabi: Arab youth and reorienting humor. *International Journal of Communication, 14*(2020). https://ijoc.org/index.php/ijoc/article/view/14133

ə OPEN ACCESS

Memes, brands and the politics of post-terror togetherness: following the Manchester bee after the 2017 Manchester Arena bombing

Samuel Merrill and Simon Lindgren

ABSTRACT
The 22 May 2017 bombing of the Manchester Arena, which killed 22 and injured over 800 more, triggered a massive public response leading to, among other things, improvised memorials, spontaneous vigils, dedicated hashtags, and viral videos. Within this response, the memetic reinvigoration and, subsequently, brand adoption of one of Manchester's oldest civic symbols – the worker bee – was clearly discernible. In this article, we explore how the spread of the bee after the bombing contributed to a politics of post-terror togetherness. Conceptualising memes as 'more or less digital', we 'follow' the bee across bodies, streets and social media platforms via the analysis of approximately 53,000 Instagram images. We show how the initial memeification of the bee carried with it grassroots expressions of togetherness while the subsequent use of the bee in official city branding strategies created and obfuscated various political tensions.

Introduction

At 10:31 pm on 22 May 2017, a bomb exploded in the Manchester Arena after an Ariana Grande concert. Quickly declared a terrorist attack by the Greater Manchester Police, the blast killed 23 people including the suicide bomber and injured over 800 more. The next day ISIS claimed the bombing had been carried out by a soldier of its caliphate who was eventually identified as a 22-year-old local man of Libyan descent.[1] On the same day, the UK government upgraded its terror threat level to its highest level allowing the deployment of troops to support armed police in guarding key government buildings and other potential terrorist targets around the country, the Mayor of Greater Manchester, Andy Burnham, presided over a vigil attended by thousands in the city's centre, and Grande temporarily suspended her concert tour and returned to the USA.

Unfolding against the backdrop of these cascading official reactions, the bombing also triggered a considerable grassroots public response characterised, in large part, by notions of solidarity, resilience, and cosmopolitan unity. This was evidenced by,

This is an Open Access article distributed under the terms of the Creative Commons Attribution-NonCommercial-NoDerivatives License (http://creativecommons.org/licenses/by-nc-nd/4.0/), which permits non-commercial re-use, distribution, and reproduction in any medium, provided the original work is properly cited, and is not altered, transformed, or built upon in any way.

among other things, improvised memorials and spontaneous vigils in Manchester and further afield, and the social media spread of dedicated hashtags and viral videos. Featuring prominently and being shared across these was one of Manchester's civic symbols: the worker bee. While before the bombing, the bee's official use had waned, by the time of its first anniversary this had changed with the bee featuring heavily in the branding of the commemorative events organised by the city's council.

In this article, we approach the bee as a meme, and subsequently a brand, with the aim of better understanding its reinvigoration and how this contributed to a post-terror politics of togetherness. We ask the following research questions:

(1) When and to where did the bee spread memetically after the bombing and how did it facilitate togetherness?
(2) How and for whom did the bee become a brand and with what political consequences?

These questions indicate that we are concerned with 'the political' rather than 'politics' (Edkins, 1999). In short, the post-terror politics that we are interested in relates to, but also exceeds, the politics of responses to terror attacks offered by politicians, political parties and governments that usually stress security concerns,[2] by also pertaining to the politics of emotion and place branding (Closs Stephens & Vaughan-Williams, 2009; Hutchison, 2013). In this respect, we suggest that the case of the Manchester bee is instructive because it reveals how the 'soft visceral side of politics' (Hutchison, 2013, p. 127) can be refracted through branding practices that often have overlooked political consequences and have rarely been explored in post-terror contexts (cf. Cassinger et al., 2018).

We start by summarising some of the literature concerning the interfaces between memes, politics and brands. We then discuss the relationship between social media and the politics of post-terror togetherness in order to provide a theoretical framework for our later analyses. Here we conceptualise memes, and specifically the bee, as being 'more or less digital'. After this, we introduce our materials and methods. These involve the analysis of around 53,000 Instagram images using a machine learning method for image classification and the closer qualitative exploration of selected images and their captions, as enacted in two subsequent sections. In the first of these, image similarity plots are used to understand the timing and diversity of the different trajectories of the bee's memeification. These plots are visually interpreted to help understand how the bee became political by encouraging a hybrid togetherness that crossed more and less digital terrains. In the second analysis section, the images and their captions are 'close-read' to provide a richer understanding of some of the political tensions that were created or obfuscated by the bee's brand adoption. We conclude by summarising the article's main empirical, conceptual and methodological contributions.

Literature review: memes, brands and politics

'Internet memes' are digital variants of the transferable units of culture referred to as 'memes' although these two terms are now often used interchangeably (Dawkins, 1976). While memes take many representational and gestural forms, internet memes are usually digital or digitised videos, animations (including GIFs) and still images including photographs, artworks and image-macros. As Shifman (2013) outlines, they are: (1) individually produced and circulated but can scale-up to shape the views and actions of social groups; (2) reproduced through mimicry and remix in line with different intentions and actions; and (3) diffused through competition and selection depending on their context.

Much research has addressed internet memes within wider circuits of digital culture, and their impact as creative and humorous expressions (Knobel & Lankshear, 2007). Scholars have also considered their political impact. Shifman (2014) has detailed how they have enrolled in political advocacy and/or persuasion; grassroots action; and the public expression of political opinions. Bayerl and Stoynov (2016) have demonstrated the influence of politically orientated internet memes on public debate. Others have highlighted the role that internet memes can play within official election campaigns (Chagas et al., 2019) and how they can help normalise fringe political opinions (Merrill, 2020a).

Denisova (2019) has noted that memes can also aid political branding. However, the literature that addresses the overlap between memes and branding mostly concerns commercial contexts (Murray et al., 2014). Here, brands are usually conceived of as taking advantage of memes through 'memejacking' (Hsu, 2018). While the defining characteristic of internet memes is their digital transmission and that of brands is the creation of distinguishable identities to serve commercial or other competitive ends, these characteristics can be shared by both phenomena. For example, internet memes can serve commercial ends and diffuse through competition (Shifman, 2014) and branding is often a participatory process that involves co-production and the uptake and transmission of brands at the grassroots level (Zenker & Erfgren, 2014).

Memes and brands have also both been approached as mutable objects (see Lunenfeld, 2014; Murray et al., 2014). With brands, this mutability has been highlighted by studies of branding within digital activism. In political protests, branding has, for example, been perceived as helping to establish dynamic action frames within which social actors can develop different activities, meanings and interpretations (Poell et al., 2016). The place-based branding of national and municipal governments is another way by which brands become political (Marsh & Fawcett, 2011). Here, the sorts of participatory place branding that involve residents are further facilitated by social media platforms in new ways, including through personal branding (Brems et al., 2017; Thelander & Cassinger, 2017; Zenker & Erfgren, 2014).

Overall, when memes and politics have been studied together, this has mostly relied on a narrow understanding of the latter as relating to political movements and parties, politicians, governments, parliaments and state apparatuses – 'politics'. Meanwhile, when memes and branding have been studied together, emphasis has tended to land on commercial matters rather than on 'the political'. Studying the Manchester bee at the intersection of, and as it crosses, these three empirical terrains (memes, brands and politics) helps diversify this earlier research. Furthermore, considering the memeification and brand adoption or 'brandification' of the bee as interrelated processes points towards 'the political' rather than 'politics'. This is because even if branding is influenced by official political actors, this is counterbalanced by those memetic processes that lend greater agency to grassroots actors. Therein lies the opportunity to interrogate 'the political' as those processes through which phenomena gain political status or political consequences in a broader sense – those processes that in other words index 'mutations of the social or symbolic order' (Edkins, 1999, p. 3). Given the empirical context in which the Manchester bee was memetically reinvigorated – in response to a terror attack – the case also presents the chance to conceive 'the political' also in terms of the politics of emotion via feelings of post-terror togetherness. Finally, studying a metropolitan, locally specific, symbol like the bee adds to those perspectives that have stressed the ritualistic and emotive use of more universal and/or national digital templates following terror attacks including 'pray for' hashtags and heart emojis (Eriksson Krutrök & Lindgren, 2018; McCrow-Young, 2021; Pitimson, 2016).

Theoretical framework: social media and the politics of post-terror togetherness

Terror attacks impact societies deeply, leading among other things to expressions of unity, solidarity, and resilience, as well as political debates about notions of community (Closs Stephens, 2007). These attacks now enter people's lives not only via broadcast and printed media but also via social media. The latter allows people to rapidly respond to terrorism by, among other things, digitally sharing expressions of togetherness (Eroukhmanoff, 2019). The use of social media in this way can also occur later, including around anniversaries, when terror attacks are often commemoratively reactivated (Merrill et al., 2020). In an era when a variety of new ways of being together are being facilitated by digital media and technology (Bakardjieva, 2003), social media have thus become implicated in the transformation of individual grief into 'collective trauma' and the (re)construction of social groups and identities after events like terror attacks (Alexander, 2012). Their enrolment in such processes is political because it contributes to determining to whom post-terror togetherness extends and to whom it does not.

At the same time, social media platforms often facilitate forms of being and acting together that are dynamic and multifaceted, episodic and fragmentary. The feelings of togetherness that they make possible do not necessarily rely on physical copresence and often take shape through different 'trajectories of publicness' – including those of a spatial, temporal and material character – contributing to broader networks of connection (Couldry, 2020; Kavada & Poell, 2020; van Haperen et al., 2020). Such trajectories can also be affective insofar as emotional connectivity allows 'fundamentally different actors, identities, and perspectives to temporarily come together' (Poell & Van Dijck, 2016, p. 232). This has implications for the everyday politics of emotions – creating new possibilities for the negotiation of hegemonic structures of feelings (Beattie et al., 2019). It also indicates how social media parallels the city in providing space for affective moments of togetherness – such as during the aftermaths and anniversaries of terror attacks – when a different politics of belonging is practiced and experienced in a pluralistic manner (Closs Stephens et al., 2021).

Following on from this, we avoid conceiving the post-terror togetherness that social media supports as relying *only* on digital practices, infrastructures and connections. Rather we approach this togetherness as being 'hybrid', blurring the so-called online and offline with the potential to involve copresence or not (Lindgren, 2014; Merrill, 2019). Hybrid togetherness has characterised the public responses to numerous terror attacks. For example, the public response to the January 2015 shootings at the Charlie Hebdo offices in Paris saw people come together under the banner of the 'Je Suis Charlie' slogan and logo not only on social media but also in the urban spaces of the French capital and other cities (Eroukhmanoff, 2019). However, 'Je Suis Charlie' was also fraught with political tensions and its inference of a universalist frame of belonging was critiqued for erasing social difference and hegemonically amplifying certain groups' perspectives over those of others (Payne, 2018; Lentin, 2019). Thus, even those hybrid public responses to terror that initially appear to emphasise cosmopolitan forms of togetherness and unity by stressing the inclusion of 'otherness' within collective forms of self-identification (Beck, 2003) can still prove exclusionary, and thus political, in different ways.

In this article, we further convey the hybridity of post-terror togetherness using the phrase: 'more or less digital' (Merrill et al., 2020; see also Merrill & Lindgren, 2020). This phrase acknowledges that in societal contexts characterised by widespread digital technology and social media use, distinctions between the so-called 'real' and 'virtual' or 'offline' and 'online' are losing analytical utility. Various phenomena including spaces, activities, behaviours and objects are not only *more or less* digital, but also more *and* less digital in the extent to which they are digitally or non-digitally constituted. Acknowledging this encourages the consideration of not only the digital mediatisation of previously non-digital phenomena but also the non-digital materialisation of digital logics (Merrill et al., 2020). It also allows for greater analytical scrutiny to be applied to the material underpinnings of digital content that is often perceived as immaterial, whether these be spatial, corporeal, artefactual, technological or infrastructural (Kinsley, 2014; Merrill, 2018). As online traces of offline embodied actions, performances and practices, social media content can thus be approached as both digitally and non-digitally constituted (Merrill, 2018; 2019). Social media content and platforms are therefore rarely *just* digital.

Accordingly, we conceptualise internet memes as more or less digital vehicles of hybrid togetherness. This actually encourages a subtle return to earlier conceptions of memes (see Dawkins, 1976) with the 'internet' prefix increasingly rendered obsolete as society in some parts of the world approaches a post-digital state (Lindgren, 2017). Furthermore, given the convergence of old and new media forms, and the prevalence of remediation and remix practices (see Bolter & Grusin, 1999; Jenkins, 2006; Knobel & Lankshear, 2007), internet memes are now rarely restricted to the internet and memes, regardless of whether theyoriginated online or not, are now often manifested in both more and less digital ways. Therefore, in the remainder of this article we simply use the term 'meme'. The memetic spread of the bee after the Manchester bombing helps illustrate these ideas.

Material and method: 'following' the Manchester bee

The 'worker bee' has been a symbol of Manchester since the industrial revolution, featuring on the city's coat of arms since 1842. Later in the nineteenth century, it became linked with the city's cooperative movement and started to feature in the city's architecture, including in the Manchester Town Hall's floor mosaics. In the 1970s it was added to the city's traffic bollards, and in 2014 a variant of the Town Hall bee started to be used on the city's bins (Hacking, 2020). In turn, local musicians , street artists and businesses started to use the bee more (Naylor, 2017). However, by May 2017 the city's official use of the bee had waned, eclipsed by the I♥MCR branding campaign that was established after the 2011 UK-wide riots with the support of Manchester City Council. The success of this campaign led the Lord Mayor's Manchester Charity Appeal

Trust to rebrand as the WE♥MCR Charity. Both were pronounced within the public response to the bombing but were already in a position of brand dominance at that time. In contrast, the impact of the bombing on the bee was more transformative. It became, as one journalist put it: 'the perfect unifying symbol: secular, non-tribal, peaceful, community-focused but, ultimately not to be messed with' (Naylor, 2017).

Our analysis of the bee's memetic spread after the bombing is methodologically underpinned by the exercise of 'following' – tracking its more or less digital appearance across a range of corporeal, urban and media spaces via the combination of machine learning and manual methods (Lindgren, 2020; Merrill, 2020b). This effort shares similarities with 'iconographic tracking', which explores the digital flow and transformation of images and how this impacts social life (Gries, 2013; Pearce et al., 2020).

We 'follow' the bee primarily via its appearance on Instagram – selecting this social media platform due to its popularity and emphasis on image-based communication. Much research has addressed the visual social media cultures of Instagram and its specific architectures, affordances and vernacular practices (Leaver et al., 2020). Less interested in these specificities, we chose Instagram as a departure point and source of material that could help us understand how the bee spread memetically in an 'extended social media context' (Highfield & Leaver, 2016, p. 51; Pearce et al., 2020) and in more or less digital ways across even wider 'infrastructures of connection' with broader social consequences (Couldry, 2020, p. 13).

We used Instaloader (2020) to collect 69,441 extant public Instagram posts featuring #manchesterbee(s) from the period between 12 February 2013 and 23 October 2020.[3] The distribution of these posts confirmed the impact of the bombing on the wider adoption of the bee and its hashtag and also revealed the effect of the bombing's anniversaries on its use (Figure 1). Based on the distribution of these posts we selected the 18-month-period between 23 April 2017 and 23 October 2018 for further analysis. This led to a sub-sample of 35,738 posts and 52,974 images (Instagram posts can contain up to 10 images).[4] This period was chosen because it contained a number of events likely to have influenced the bee's memetic spread and because similar research to date has focused primarily on shorter periods immediately following terror attacks (e.g., Al Nashmi, 2018).

Instaloader retrieves posts that have a given search term in its caption or in its associated comments. This means that not all original posters in the sample intended

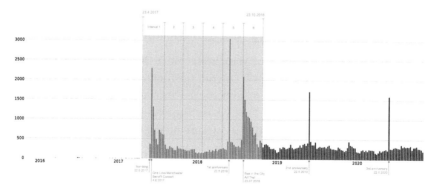

Figure 1. Weekly Frequency of #Manchesterbee(s) Instagram Posts between 23/04/2015 and 23/10/2020.[5]

their posts to contribute to #manchesterbee(s) (Highfield & Leaver, 2016). Still, the entire sub-sample was retained for analysis and approximately 91% (32,658) of its posts featured the search term in their actual captions. The sub-sample was then split into six three-month intervals (Table 1). We then used a machine learning mode of image classification called img2vec (He et al., 2018) to create plots of visually similar images posted during each interval. The exact workflow used to create the plots is detailed in an online open-science repository that accompanies this article.[6] The clustered structure of these plots is conveyed by their silhouettes, which appear as insets (Figure 2).

The plots were then visually analysed on the basis that the content of different clusters of images during different intervals conveyed when and to where the bee spread memetically. Thereafter key clusters of the bee's memetic use, namely those in which images of bees featured most prominently, were analysed in terms of their relation to forms of hybrid togetherness, as supported by reference to the bee's appearance in other material.

A second analytical step involved the closer reading of the sub-sample of Instagram posts and their captions. This was contextualised and complemented by earlier research into the public response to the bombing (see Closs Stephens et al., 2021; Merrill et al., 2020) and, again, the targeted analysis of additional relevant sources. This analytical step focused specifically on how and for whom the bee became a brand, and the impact that this brandification process had for the politics of post-terror togetherness discernible after the bombing. Here, critical visual methodologies (Rose, 2016) were employed to read the sub-sample 'against the grain' in order to discern the political tensions that were hidden by the bee's wider memetic and brand adoption.

For ethical reasons, usernames were removed from the posts and the analysed content consisted only of that which was publicly available through Instagram at the time it was collected. To further mitigate concerns about the content's unsolicited use, we present the plots in low-resolution and high-level aggregate form. We also minimise the use of direct quotations, with only one post caption partially reproduced below. We deemed this ethically permissible because the limited possibilities to search Instagram captions reduce the chances of identifying the original poster. The detailed analysis of individual images justifies their reproduction under the copyright terms of fair use.

Analysis I: making sense of the swarm

Between 23 April 2017 and 23 October 2018 there were three peaks in the hashtag's use (Figure 1). The first corresponds to the bombing's initial aftermath, cresting in Interval 1,

Table 1. Overview of img2vec models.

Img2vec model	Date range	Number of images
Interval 1	23/04/2017–23/07/2017	7,247
Interval 2	24/07/2017–23/10/2017	4,676
Interval 3	24/10/2017–23/01/2018	3,798
Interval 4	24/01/2018–23/04/2018	3,957
Interval 5	24/04/2018–23/07/2018	11,085
Interval 6	24/07/2018–23/10/2018	22,211

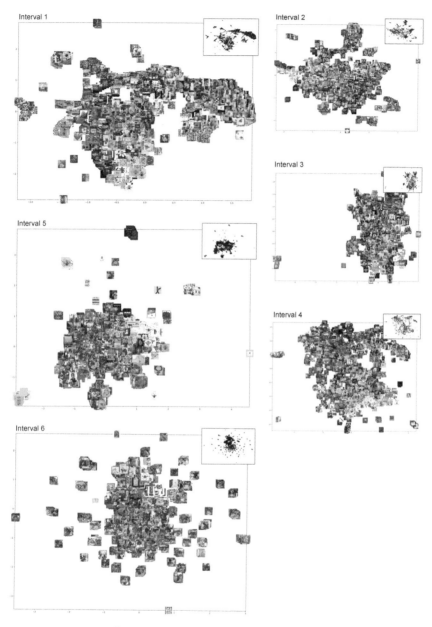

Figure 2. The img2vec plots.[7]

during the week ending 4 June 2017, the day 50,000 people attended *One Love Manchester*, a benefit concert organised by Grande to raise money for the bombing's victims and their families. The second peak correlates with the first-year anniversary commemorations, during Interval 5, which again drew large crowds. The third, during Interval 6, coincides with the *Bee in the City* art trail which opened on 23 July 2018. The impact of the art trail is indicated by the elevated, though subsequently diminishing, number of #manchesterbee(s) posts across the nine weeks that it ran. The image plots allow a finer-grained analysis of the images that accompanied the hashtag during different periods and further convey the timing but also the extent of the bee's memetic spread (Figure 2).

Across the top of the first interval's plot, clusters of images featuring actual bees blend with those featuring flowers and landscapes. These then converge into clusters featuring groups of people, including at *One Love Manchester*, connecting in turn with those of individuals. The latter, which include selfies, connect in succession with body art images including, most pervasively, bee tattoos.

The dense bee tattoo cluster on the right of the first plot conveys the memetic impact of the *Manchester Tattoo Appeal*. The appeal, launched via Facebook by a local tattoo artist on the day after the bombing, saw tattooists across and beyond Manchester offer bee tattoos for a £50 charitable donation. It garnered considerable attention on social media and then in the broadcast and printed press, leading to long queues outside many tattooists in the city's Northern Quarter. By late June 2017, an estimated 10,000 people world-wide had been tattooed with bees (Perraudin, 2017). Many explained their motivations for getting bee tattoos in commemorative and solidaric terms (BBC, 2017). Bee tattoos allowed people to show support for the bombing's victims and their families but also to signal their membership to a resilient Mancunian community and, in doing so, created feelings of togetherness between those sporting them on their bodies and sharing them online. They facilitated forms of hybrid togetherness that were experienced in less digital ways while in the copresence of others when waiting in the queues to get a tattoo and thereafter in more digital ways when browsing images of similar tattoos on social media platforms. The Instagram posts featuring the tattoos thus indexed the embodied energy behind efforts to connect with others via digitally mediatised commemorative activities. In turn, the tattooed bees were more than digital and more than corporeal because their up-take-and spread illustrated the entanglement of both more and less digital activities, artefacts and spaces (see also Brennan, 2019).

On the lower left of the first interval's plot several clearly delineated clusters relate to street artworks featuring the bee. These include the works created by local street artist Qubek in response to the bombing. Particularly prominent are two smaller works finished two days after the bombing and a large mural commissioned by the Manchester Evening News featuring a bee for each of the 22 victims – all in the city's Northern Quarter. Announcing the two smaller pieces on his Facebook page, Qubek wrote:

> Here is my tribute to Manchester ... share this and use it as your profile pic if you like, share the bee love!![8]

> ... the vibe in the city is incredible, we forget that we are all part of the same tribe, it's a shame something so tragic has to happen for us to realise our sense of togetherness and community, big up Manchester and its amazing community.[9]

Qubek's comments indicate again how the bee facilitated post-terror togetherness and reveal additional hybrid pathways of its memetic spread. Here, the more or less digital qualities of street art exceeded just its 'instagrammability' and the tendency for it to be increasingly viewed online and related also to synergies between Instagram's and, in this case, Qubek's pursuit of viewers' attention (MacDowall, 2019).

The street art cluster blends with a looser cluster, in the centre of the first interval's plot, featuring images of the bee used in arts and crafts, and, in the plot's lower reaches,

Figure 3. Our Manchester and Manchester Together.

the bee – a symbol deeply connected with Manchester's industrial, and predominantly white working-class past – might have been expected to struggle to carry this otherness. Certainly, during its memeification after the bombing the bee, through its association with feelings of togetherness, was deployed towards these cosmopolitan ends. But if via this process it approached becoming a vehicle for 'actually existing cosmopolitanism' (Robbins, 1998), through its brandification it arguably came to represent a narrower consumerist and aesthetic cosmopolitanism (Bookman, 2013; Regev, 2007) connected to Manchester's aspirations to further brand itself as a 'glocal city' (Paganoni, 2012).

In short, the memeification of the bee via tattoos and street art, but also vernacular crafts, fed into a process of city branding – partly characterised by participatory branding and partly by 'memejacking' – that was driven by the public attention generated around these phenomena thanks to their appearance on social media platforms like Instagram. While symbols more generally have historically often achieved elasticity in their political meaning, the case of the bee highlights the impact of social media on the selection of which symbols become political in the first place. Herein lies some of the more conflictual politics of post-terror togetherness insofar as social media platforms afforded greater visibility to some grassroots responses to the bombing than others. Those responses that were more digital in character could more easily achieve digital virality and in turn were more likely to gain broader media coverage, boosting their spread further. The less digital responses of other actors or sectors of society were meanwhile less likely to gain visibility via social media and scale-up. Subsequently, it must be acknowledged that social media platforms are associated with particular demographics with, for example, access to and use of Instagram known to be stratified by gender, class and race (van Haperen et al., 2020). Illustrative of this, the bee tattoos in the sub-sample mostly adorn white skin.[13] Anchoring an urban branding effort to those grassroots responses to terror that gained visibility via social media elevates these social media demographics in taking them to – and making them – represent the whole, while obfuscating other responses originating from other groups and quarters.

Indicative of this, the prominence of tattooists and street art in the bee's memetic spread foregrounded the city's gentrifying Northern Quarter as the epicentre of the city's cosmopolitopia. This is borne out by an analysis of the hashtags that co-occurred with #machesterbee(s) over the 18-month-period which revealed #NorthernQuarter to be among the top 25 co-occurring hashtags, the only specific part of the city to achieve this status. These associations fed into Manchester City Council's later brand adoption of the bee which, in emphasising Mancunian industriousness, craft and community, pitched towards 'creative city' marketing strategies as exemplified by the *Bee in the City* art trail. This trail did help the bee to spread beyond the Northern Quarter. But, in also allowing a myriad of organisations to sponsor individual statues and thereby harness the bee's advertising and branding potential, it also flattened the political tensions evident between community and local sponsors and those international corporate and urban development organisations who sponsored the trail at the same time as contributing to social inequality across the city (Lammes & Wilmott, 2020). This sort of brand adoption thus arguably relied on hollowed-out forms of consumerist and aesthetic cosmopolitanism rather than actually existing cosmopolitanism.

Others besides Manchester City Council created political tensions by using the bee to rebrand themselves a year after the bombing. Around the first anniversary the bee also appeared on flyers distributed by the far-right Democratic Football Lads Alliance (DFLA) and Veterans Against Terrorism (VAT), which promoted these groups' own, notionally commemorative, *Manchester Unity March* on 2 June 2018 (Figure 4). These groups adopted the bee brand because it provided an open action frame (see Poell et al., 2016) and in an attempt to take advantage of its memetic spread and popularity in order to mobilise people to join their march. The *Manchester Unity March* was estimated to have attracted 1000–2000 attendees, outnumbering the 500–600 anti-racist protestors that turned up to counter it.[14] On the day of the march, 56 Instagram posts featured #manchesterbee(s). None of them addressed these political tensions. Instead they mostly promoted leisure events and bee-related products. Even though there was a 500% increase in Islamophobic attacks in Manchester in the month after the bombing (Halliday, 2017), just 16 posts from the 18-month sample referenced racism directly. All were anti-racist in nature, including one, posted soon after the bombing, with an image containing the *Our Manchester* poem (Figure 3).

Figure 4. The DFLA/VAT Flyer.

The author of this post wrote in its caption: 'Can we please stop with the racist comments ... It is heartwarming to see the response and strength of the North West as a collective community of all races and religions towards the attack'. This might be read as exemplifying an actually existing cosmopolitanism. And yet, that 'we' still stubbornly accommodates those who responded to the bombing with racism. Herein lies another tension within the political becoming of the bee. In being taken to mean togetherness almost at any cost, the interrogation of the terms of and tensions within this togetherness were side-lined and it was rarely acknowledged that some used the bee in pursuit of more exclusionary rather than inclusionary forms of post-terror togetherness. The poem and the flyer sported near-identical bees, but their political messages could not have contrasted more strongly.

Conclusion

In this article, we have demonstrated how the somewhat neglected civic symbol of the Manchester worker bee was memetically rejuvenated within grassroots political responses to the 22 May 2017 bombing of the city's arena leading it to increasingly appear on Mancunian bodies and streets, and across social media platforms. These more or less digital responses were political in the capacity they attributed to the bee to emphasise hybrid forms of togetherness as evidenced by the bee's elastic adoption by different individuals and groups. At the same time, and as also illustrated in this article, the remixing of bee created and hid political tensions especially as the city's council sought to take advantage of its memetic spread by adopting it as a brand. The increasing official use of the bee to place-brand Manchester indexed political tensions related to the gentrification, commercial development and glocal marketing of certain parts of the city. Its branding use by far-right activists meanwhile highlighted some of the limits placed on the city's post-terror togetherness by some actors. Highlighting, in this way, how the bee became 'political' through interconnected processes of memeification and brandification, we have endeavoured – in the spirit of this special issue – to help broaden current research on the politics of memes by moving beyond the regular focus placed on the self-evident actors of 'politics'. In doing so, we hope we have highlighted the potential, but also need, for more politically orientated (and not only commercially motivated) research into the relationship between memes and brands.

Beyond illustrating the value of empirically exploring the relationship between memes and brands within broader and longer-term responses to terrorism and specifically the politics of post-terror togetherness that it gives rise to, we have also made two further contributions with this article. First, we have conceptualised memes in terms of their 'more or less digital' composition, and secondly, we have demonstrated one method for 'following' memes that is suited to this conceptualisation. Both contributions have relevance for future studies of memes whether these studies target the political, cultural or commercial capacities of memes after terrorism or otherwise.

Notes

1. Later investigations found that the man had largely acted alone but also led to the March 2020 conviction of his brother for 22 counts of murder in connection to the bombing.

2. As illustrated by the creation, in response to the Manchester bombing, of a new UK government agency called The Commission for Countering Extremism.
3. Collected on 24 October 2020.
4. Video posts and Instagram Stories were not analysed.
5. Only posts from this five-year period have been plotted because, as with prior to the bombing, their number before this period (to 12 February 2013) was negligible.
6. See: https://github.com/simonlindgren/manchesterbee
7. Those intervals analysed in more detail are enlarged. Larger versions of the plots are available at: https://github.com/simonlindgren/manchesterbee.
8. https://www.facebook.com/RussMeehanMuralistAndGraffitiArtist/photos/919364091539539/
9. https://www.facebook.com/RussMeehanMuralistAndGraffitiArtist/photos/919370454872236/
10. Twitter launched its own worker bee emoji to coincide with this match.
11. A second *Bee in the City* art trail ran between late October and late December 2020.
12. A £500 licence fee is now charged to use the bee. Commerical uses must still pay royalties to a designated charity.
13. Although skin colour is not indictive of faith and the methods used here do not allow for this observation to be quantified, it should be noted that certain faiths are often interpreted as forbidding tattoos. Henna and transfer bee tattoos provided an alternative to permanent tattoos but were not adopted to the same extent.
14. https://www.rs21.org.uk/2018/06/02/opposing-the-racist-dfla-in-manchester-2-06-18-a-photo-report/

Acknowledgements

The authors are indebted to Shanti Sumartojo, Angharad Closs Stephens and Martin Coward for discussions had within the context of the project entitled 'The Digital and Spatial Affects' of the 2017 Manchester Bombing (funded by Swansea University's CHERISH-DE Centre through its Escalator Fund). The authors would also like to acknowledge the productive conversations had with Paul Dobraszczyk and the work done by Anna Pigott during the earliest stages of that project.

Disclosure statement

No potential conflict of interest was reported by the author(s).

ORCID

Samuel Merrill http://orcid.org/0000-0002-9572-5922
Simon Lindgren http://orcid.org/0000-0001-6289-9427

References

Alexander, J, C. (2012). *Trauma: A social theory*. Polity Press.
Al Nashmi, E. (2018). From selfies to media events: How Instagram users interrupted their routines after the Charlie Hebdo shootings. *Digital Journalism*, 6(1), 98–117. doi:10.1080/21670811.2017.1306787
Bakardjieva, M. (2003). Virtual togetherness: An everyday-life perspective. *Media, Culture & Society*, 25(3), 291–313. https://doi.org/10.1177/0163443703025003001
Bayerl, P. S., & Stoynov, L. (2016). Revenge by photoshop: Memefying police acts in the public dialogue about injustice. *New Media & Society*, 18(6), 1006–1026. https://doi.org/10.1177/1461444814554747
BBC. (2017). Manchester attack: Hundreds queue for bee tattoos. *BBC*. https://www.bbc.com/news/uk-england-manchester-40060657
Beattie, A. R., Eroukhmanoff, C., & Head, N. (2019). Introduction: Interrogating the 'everyday' politics of emotions in international relations. *Journal of International Political Theory*, 15(2), 136–147. https://doi.org/10.1177/1755088219830428
Beck, U. (2003). Rooted cosmopolitanism: Emerging from a rivalry of distinctions. In U. Beck, N. Sznaider, & R. Winter (Eds.), *Global America?* (pp. 15–29). Liverpool University Press.
Bolter, J. D., & Grusin, R. (1999). *Remediation: Understanding new media*. MIT Press.
Bookman, S. (2013). Branded cosmopolitanims: 'Global' coffee brands and the co-creation of 'cosmopolitan cool'. *Cultural Sociology*, 7(1), 56–72. https://doi.org/10.1177/1749975512453544
Brems, C., Temmerman, M., Graham, T., & Broersma, M. (2017). Personal branding on twitter: How employed and freelance journalists stage themselves on social media. *Digital Journalism*, 5(4), 443–359. https://doi.org/10.1080/21670811.2016.1176534
Brennan, M. (2019). Why materiality in mourning matters. In Z. Newby & R. E. Toulson (Eds.), *The materiality of mourning: Cross-disciplinary perspectives* (pp. 222–242). Routledge.
Cassinger, C., Ekell, J., Mansson, M., & Thulfvesson, O. (2018). The narrative rhythm of terro: A study of the Stockholm terrorist attack and the 'last night in Sweden' event. *International Journal of Tourism Cities*, 4(4), 484–494. https://doi.org/10.1108/IJTC-04-2018-0030
Chagas, V., Freire, V., Rios, D., & Magalhães, D. (2019). Political memes and the politics of memes: A methodological proposal for content analysis of online political memes. *First Monday*. http://dx.doi.org/10.5210/fm.v24i2.7264
Closs Stephens, A. (2007). 'Seven million Londoners, one London': National and urban ideas of community in the aftermath of the 7 July 2005 bombings in London. *Alternatives*, 32(2), 155–176. https://doi.org/10.1177/030437540703200201
Closs Stephens, A., Coward, M., Merrill, S., & Sumartojo, S. (2021). Affect and the response to terror: Commemoration and communities of sense. *International Political Sociology*, 15(1), 22–40. https://doi.org/10.1093/ips/olaa020
Closs Stephens, A., & Vaughan-Williams, N. (2009). *Terrorism and the politics of response*. Routledge.
Couldry, N. (2020). *Media – why it matters*. Polity.
Dawkins, R. (1976). *The selfish gene*. Oxford University Press.
Denisova, A. (2019). *Internet memes and society: Social, cultural and political contexts*. Routledge.
Edkins, J. (1999). *Poststructuralism and international relations: Bring the political back in*. Lynne Rienner.
Eriksson Krutrök, M., & Lindgren, S. (2018). Continued contexts of terror: Analyzing temporal patterns of hashtag co-occurrence as discursive articulations. *Social Media+Society*. https://doi.org/10.1177/2056305118813649
Eroukhmanoff, C. (2019). Responding to terrorism with peace, love and solidarity: 'Je suis Charlie', 'Peace' and 'I Heart MCR'. *Journal of International Political Theory*, 15(2), 167–187. https://doi.org/10.1177/1755088219829884
Gries, L. E. (2013). Iconographic tracking: A digital research method for visual rhetoric and circulation studies. *Computers and Composition*, 30(4), 332–348. https://doi.org/10.1016/j.compcom.2013.10.006

Hacking, G. (2020). The Manchester Bee Timeline. Manchester Bees. http://manchesterbe.es/index.php/the_manchester_bee_timeline/

Halliday, J. (2017, Jun 22). Islamophobic attacks in Manchester surge by 500 after arena attack. *The Guardian.* https://www.theguardian.com/uk-news/2017/jun/22/islamophobic-attacks-manchester-increase-arena-attack

He, L., Zhang, D., Tian, L., Han, F., Luo, M., Chen, Y., & Wu, Y. (2018). Visual-based character embedding via principal component analysis. In Q. Zhou, Y. Gan, W. Jing, X. Song, Y. Wang, & Z. Lu (Eds.), *Data science. ICPCSEE 2018. Communications in computer and information science* (Vol. 901, pp. 212–224). Springer.

Highfield, T., & Leaver, T. (2016). Instagrammatics and digital methods: Studying visual social media, from selfies and GIFs to memes and emoji. *Communication Research and Practice, 2*(1), 47–62. https://doi.org/10.1080/22041451.2016.1155332

Hsu, C. (2018). The 'borrowed interest' appeal: Brands riding the wave of popular events and memes in the digital age. *Journal of Brand Strategy, 7*(3), 258–270.

Hutchison, E. (2013). Affective communities as security communities. *Critical Studies on Security, 1*(1), 127–129. https://doi.org/10/1080/21624887.2013.790227

Instaloader. (2020). *Instaloader.* GitHub repository, https://github.com/instaloader/instaloader

Jenkins, H. (2006). *Convergence culture: Where old and new media collide.* NYU Press.

Kavada, A., & Poell, P. (2020). From counterpublics to contentious publicness: Tracing the temporal, spatial, and material articulations of popular protest through social media. *Communication Theory, 0*(0), https://doi.org/10.1093/ct/qtaa025

Kinsley, S. (2014). The matter of 'virtual geographies'. *Progress in Human Geography, 3893*(3), 364–384. https://doi.org/10.1177/0309132513506270

Knobel, M., & Lankshear, C. (2007). *A new literacies sampler.* Peter Lang.

Lammes, S., & Wilmott, C. (2020). Mobile mapping and play. In L. Hjorth, A. de Souza e Silva, & K. Lanson (Eds.), *The Routledge companion to mobile media art* (pp. 202–213). Routledge.

Leaver, T., Highfield, T., & Abidin, C. (2020). *Instagram: Visual social media cultures.* Polity.

Lentin, A. (2019). Charlie Hebdo: White Context and Black Analytics. *Public Culture, 31*(1), 45–67. http://dx.doi.org/10.1215/08992363-7181835

Lindgren, S. (2014). *Hybrid media culture: Sensing place in a world of flows.* Routledge.

Lindgren, S. (2017). *Digital media and society.* SAGE.

Lindgren, S. (2020). *Data theory.* Polity.

Lunenfeld, P. (2014). Barking at memetics: The rant that wasn't. *Journal of Visual Culture, 13*(3), 253–256. https://doi.org/10.1177/1470412914544517

MacDowall, L. (2019). *Instafame: Graffiti and street art in the Instagram era.* Intellect.

Marsh, D., & Fawcett, P. (2011). Branding, politics and democracy. *Policy Studies, 32*(5), 515–530. https://doi.org/10.1080/01442872.2011.586498

McCrow-Young, A. (2021). #Love and terrorism: Instagram mourning and phatic templates in a crisis. *Cyborgology. The Society Pages.* https://thesocietypages.org/cyborgology/2021/03/09/love-and-terrorism-instagram-mourning-and-phatic-templates-in-a-crisis/

Merrill, S. (2018). The dead are coming: Political performance art, activist remembrance and dig (ital) protests. In A. Breed & T. Prentki (Eds.), *Performance and civic engagement* (pp. 159–186). Palgrave Macmillan.

Merrill, S. (2019). Walking together? The mediatised performative commemoration of 7/7's tenth anniversary. *Journalism, 20*(10), 1360–1378. https://doi.org/10.1177/1464884917738414

Merrill, S. (2020a). Sweden then vs. Sweden now. *First Monday, 25*(6), https://doi.org/10.5210/fm.v25i6.10552

Merrill, S. (2020b). Following the woman with the handbag: The activist appropriation of an iconic historical photograph. In S. Merrill, E. Keightley, & P. Daphi (Eds.), *Social movements, cultural memory and digital media: Mobilising mediated remembrance* (pp. 111–139). Palgrave Macmillan.

Merrill, S., & Lindgren, S. (2020). The rhythms of social movement memories: The mobilization of Silvio Meier's activist remembrance across platforms. *Social Movement Studies, 19*(5-6), 657–674. https://doi.org/10.1080/14742837.2018.1534680

Merrill, S., Sumartojo, S., Closs Stephens, A., & Coward, M. (2020). Togetherness after terror: The more or less digital commemorative public atmospheres of the Manchester Arena bombing's first anniversary. *Environment and Planning D: Society and Space, 38*(3), 546–566. https://doi.org/10.1177/0263775819901146

Murray, N., Manrai, A., & Manrai, L. (2014). Memes, memetics and marketing: A state of the art review and a lifecycle model of meme management in advertising. In L. Moutinho, E. Bigné, & A. Manrai (Eds.), *The Routledge companion to the future of marketing* (pp. 328–344). Routledge.

Naylor, T. (2017, May 24). 'Peaceful but not to be messed with' – how the bee came to symbolize Manchester. *The Guardian.* https://www.theguardian.com/uk-news/shortcuts/2017/may/24/peaceful-but-not-to-be-messed-with-how-the-bee-came-to-symbolise-manchester

Paganoni, M. C. (2012). City branding and social inclusion in the glocal city. *Mobilities, 7*(1), 13–31. https://doi.org/10.1080/17450101.2012.631809

Payne, R. (2018). 'Je suis Charlie' : Viral circulation and the ambivalence of affective citizenship. *International Journal of Cultural Studies, 21*(3), 277–292. http://dx.doi.org/10.1177/1367877916675193

Pearce, W., Özkula, S. M., Greene, A. K., Teeling, L., Bansard, J. S., Omena, J. J., & Teixeira Rabello, E. (2020). Visual cross-platform analysis: Digital methods to research social media images, information. *Communication & Society, 23*(2), 161–180. https://doi.org/10.1080/1369118X.2018.1486871

Perraudin, F. (2017, June 23). 10,000 get bee tattoo to raise money for victims of Manchester bombing. *The Guardian.* https://www.theguardian.com/uk-news/2017/jun/23/bee-tattoo-raise-money-victims-manchester-bombing

Pitimson, N. (2016). Coming to terms with digital grief: Hashtags and emojis are here to stay, *The Conversation,* https://theconversation.com/coming-to-terms-with-digital-grief-hashtags-and-emojis-are-here-to-stay-57087

Poell, T., Abdulla, R., Rieder, B., Woltering, R., & Zack, L. (2016). Protest leadership in the age of social media. *Information, Communication, and Society, 19*(7), 994–1014. https://doi.org/10.1080/1369118X.2015.1088049

Poell, T., & Van Dijck, J. (2016). Constructing public space: Global perspectives on social media and popular contestation. *International Journal of Communication, 10,* 226–234.

Regev, M. (2007). Cultural uniqueness and aesthetic cosmopolitanism. *European Journal of Social Theory, 10*(1), 123–138. https://doi.org/10.1177/1368431006068765

Robbins, B. (1998). Introduction Part 1: Actually existing cosmopolitanism. In P. Cheah & B. Robbins (Eds.), *Cosmopolitics: Thinking and feeling beyond the nation* (pp. 1–19). University of Minnesota Press.

Rose, G. (2016). *Visual methodologies: An introduction to the interpretation of visual materials.* Sage.

Shifman, L. (2013). Memes in a digital world: Reconciling with a conceptual troublemaker. *Journal of Computer-Mediated Communication, 18*(3), 362–377. https://doi.org/10.1111/jcc4.12013

Shifman, L. (2014). *Memes in digital culture.* MIT Press.

Thelander, Å, & Cassinger, C. (2017). Brand new images? Implications of Instagram photography for place branding. *Media and Communication, 5*(4), 6–14. https://doi.org/10.17645/mac.v5i4.1053

van Haperen, S., Uitermark, J., & van der Zeeuw, A. (2020). Mediated interaction rituals: A geography of everyday life and contention in Black Lives Matter. *Mobilization, 25*(3), 295–313. https://doi.org/10.17813/1086-671X-25-3-295

Zenker, S., & Erfgren, C. (2014). Let them do the work; a participatory place branding approach. *Journal of Place Management and Development, 7*(3), 225–234. https://doi.org/10.1108/JPMD-06-2013-0016

Memetising the pandemic: memes, covid-19 mundanity and political cultures

Maria Francesca Murru and Stefania Vicari

ABSTRACT
It was late February 2020 when part of Northern Italy entered the first Covid-19 lockdown of the West. While stories of people fleeing quarantined areas soon made national headlines, the international news was suddenly reporting of coronavirus patients connected to Italy all around the world. Against this background, Italian social media started thriving with Covid-19 humour. On 9 March the lockdown turned nationwide and became one of the strictest in Europe. This article addresses everyday memes of quarantined Italy as an instance of *mundane* memetics at a time of crisis. It investigates the leading discourses emerging from these memes to provide insight into the political culture that surfaces at the intersection between the ordinary of everyday social media uses and the extraordinary of crisis events. We combined digital methods and netnographic techniques to generate and analyse a dataset of over 9,000 Covid-19 memetic instances produced on Twitter by Italian publics during the first national lockdown. Our findings show that in early everyday pandemic memes the political stake did not manifest itself in the explicitness of values, attitudes, and knowledge tightly packaged in a purposeful and self-aware political culture. It rather surfaced in the form of a *mundane* political culture – one that was primarily performative, irrespective of any future political action, and marked by populist values.

Introduction

On 22 February 2020 part of Northern Italy entered the first Covid-19 lockdown of the West. Among the 11 municipalities placed under quarantine was Codogno, hometown of the country's 'patient 1'. While stories of people fleeing quarantined areas soon made national headlines, the international news was suddenly reporting of coronavirus patients connected to Codogno all around the world. Against this background, Italian social media started thriving with Covid-19 memes, multimedia remixes and jokes (Vicari & Murru, (2020). On 9 March the Northern lockdown turned nationwide and became one of the strictest in Europe, only to be fully lifted on 3 June 2020.

This article focuses on everyday Covid-19 memes of quarantined Italy during the first wave of the pandemic. Whether reflecting univocal ideological stancing or enabling polyvocal discourse (Milner, 2013), memes are often cultural capital (Nissenbaum & Shifman, 2017) talking politics. But how does every day social media memetics acquire political significance during extraordinary events?

Studies interested in the political significance of memes have so far privileged grassroot memetic production happening on specialised sites (e.g., 4chan's/b/board, see Rintel, 2013) or within ideologically defined groups (e.g., The Proud Boys, see DeCook, 2018). In fact, while media and cultural studies have widely addressed media practices as charged with the rhythms and creativity of everyday life (Silverstone, 1999) research into everyday or – as we call it – *mundane* memetics is still underdeveloped. In this article, by focusing on the Covid 19 crisis, we explore the politics of memes emerging at the interplay between everyday social media practices and extraordinary events. The paper advances a twofold contribution. Firstly, it introduces the concept of 'mundane memetics' to shed light on everyday memetic practices that escape subcultural connotations and proliferate within hybrid discursive contexts populated by highly heterogeneous content. Secondly, it uses the lens of political culture to provide insight into the political emerging at the intersection of the ordinary of mundane memetics and the extraordinary of critical events.

Memes between humour and nonsense

The core definition of 'Internet meme' as 'a group of digital items sharing common characteristics of content, form and/or stance', created with awareness of each other, and circulated, imitated, and/or transformed via the Internet (Shifman, 2014a, p. 41) proves to be still able to grasp the foundational qualities of this protean form of vernacular creativity (Burgess, 2007). Memes should not be considered as singular cultural units that propagate well, but as a family of content items drawn together by the replication of at least one of the three primary memetic dimensions: form (layout and physical components), content (ideas and ideologies), and stance (the positioning of the author in relation to the message being delivered) (Shifman, 2014a, p. 40). While their subcultural roots still represent a source of inspiration, memes have now gained mass propagation, appealing to the general population and becoming a lingua franca (Milner, 2013) that spans vast geography and multiple purposes. Because of the balance between memes' individual uniqueness and the popular templates that animate their replication, Nissenbaum and Shifman (2018) suggest considering Internet memetics in light of De Saussure's (1959) linguistic model. As socially constructed repertoires of expressive possibilities, meme templates are seen as a parallel to *langue*, while meme instances – specific items created and shared on the web – are seen as the *parole* in their being personalised appropriations of a binding and pre-patterned structure for expression.

Memes embody three central features of contemporary digital environments: multimodality, remix culture, and phatic communication (Katz & Shifman, 2017). They combine visual and verbal dimensions, producing multi-layered compositions whose paths of signification spring not only by each of the involved codes of expression but also by their 'centrifugal' or 'centripetal' convergence (Boxman-Shabtai & Shifman, 2014). By including parody of, tributes to, or quotations from pre-existent texts, memes weave an intertextual web of meanings that mix the familiar with the unfamiliar while leveraging social memory and sense of belonging. According to Laineste and Voolaid (2017), this type of intertextuality – in its relying on both the cultural memory of a particular community and global cultural influences – produces hybrid cultural texts whose interpretations may be more or less open or accessible to different audiences. Finally, phatic communication includes all those exchanges where generating a sense of commonality is more important than delivering a message.

As indigenous lingua franca of digital environments, memes are flexible enough to carry out numerous social roles. They enhance social capital and collective identities by 'establishing common ground and kinship among bickering sides' (Nissenbaum & Shifman, 2017, p. 498). When shared on social media, they become a repository of connotations, values, and judgements that can be used more or less consciously for identitarian purposes (du Preez & Lombard, 2014) or to construct 'memetic authenticity' in coordinated political protests that rely on the formulation of truth-related values (Shifman, 2018). Memes can also be used as a means of indoctrination, as it has been shown to happen with the alt-right affiliate movement 'the Proud Boys', where they worked not only to increase visibility but also 'as a way of classifying and recreating a version of the world that they seek to change' (DeCook, 2018, p. 487).

Beyond this vast and multifaceted variety of social functions, memes generate meaning in different ways. One of them is certainly humour, whose ubiquity and cultural relevance has been appreciated since the dawn of the internet (Baym, 1995). According to Gal (2019), ironic humour on social media carries out a boundary work consisting of consolidating groups' identity by excluding those who don't share the same symbolic frames, linguistic codes, and values. Another relevant dynamic of meaning-making activated by memetic engagement is nonsense. This category has been recently explored by Katz and Shifman (2017) as a mode of communication fully systematised in digital environments and emblematically actualised by some very common memetic genres, like, for instance, those containing 'linguistic silliness' (when standardised language is playfully altered to fit a new creative jargon) and 'dislocations' (the subversive association of characters and setting). Seiffert-Brockmann et al. (2018) underline that what counts in memetic playfulness is not the game per se, rather is the idea of playing a game and, more specifically, the enjoyment coming from arbitrarily establishing a set of rules that can be complied to or abandoned by a spontaneously summoned group of people. This creates a partial suspension of the *cognitive* meaning and a parallel opening of the wide field of *affective* meaning, consisting of those emotional responses that appear prior to the consolidation of sense (Katz & Shifman, 2017, p. 837). Despite its subconscious nature, the kind of affect put into play by memes is inherently social in its being aimed at building, reproducing or dissolving social ties. This suspension of cognitive and referential meaning-making to the advantage of the affective significance is what makes memetic creations a repository of social values, political emotions, representative types and collective frames that have not yet found a formal recognition within the public sphere. From this perspective, we can understand why pandemic memes can be read as snapshots of underlying generational conflicts, as recently done by MacDonald (2020). The cluster of memes identified in MacDonald's study shows a very rich intertextuality, where references to popular culture are used as generational identity markers able to express Generation X's frustration against neoliberal norms (MacDonald, 2020). The emergence of 'the political' in its nursery stage is also evidenced in Seiffert-Brockmann et al.'s (2018) mapping of the memetic variations of the Obama Hope Poster, where political discourses are shown to emerge in a format that is still far from the consciousness of the public sphere.

The politics of memes

The political resonance that memes can acquire in various circumstances has been widely researched and variously interpreted. Beyond the dissonance opposing those who see memetic culture as an opportunity for political participation and those who consider it as an unprecedented strategy for propaganda or a self-absolving and low-cost commitment, literature has identified two main ways in which memes can be political. Firstly, memes can be used wittingly and strategically to persuade and summon publics, to carry out public advocacy and coordinate political protest (see Bayerl & Stoynov, 2016; Rentschler & Thrift, 2015). Secondly, as a cheap, accessible, and enjoyable route for personal expression, memetic creativity can translate into polyvocal expression where multiple opinions and identities can gain visibility and be negotiated (Shifman, 2014a).

Beyond these explicit functions, memes appear to be connected to the political, intended as the constitutive antagonism underlying our society and its dynamics of power (Mouffe, 2005). This becomes clearly visible when we consider that in the two prevailing forms of meaning-making, humour and nonsense, the interactional function of tracing boundaries between in-group and out-group members is fundamental. As a participatory mode of communication, memes perform boundary work by relying upon participants' ability and eagerness to play for the sake of play and to properly adhere to the collectively established rules of the game. This means that when nonsense apparently lacks significance, and affective meaning alone works as a pre-cognitive phatic marker of affiliation (Katz & Shifman, 2017, p. 837), memes can acquire political relevance by triggering dynamics of proximity or detachment. It is likely that these political implications do not become visible in the serious discursive practices of taking a stance or 'participating in a normative debate about how the world should look and the best way to get there' (Shifman, 2014a, p. 120). They may rather take the shape of playful and silly practices that implicitly point to the emotional and value-related logic that guide them in their stages of emergence (Seiffert-Brockmann et al., 2018).

The politics of memes at times of crisis

Scholars have widely explored how Twitter in general and memetic creativity in particular work at times of crisis and during challenging events (Cho et al., 2013; Jensen et al., 2020; Rintel, 2013). This body of work has shown that the rituality established especially through irony is particularly effective in spreading emotional support. One of the keys of this emotional support resides in the templatability of memes, that is, in the possibility of creating new meanings by replacing and recombining pre-existent elements and through the contextual manipulation of the relationship between variable content and fixed structures (Rintel, 2013). As underlined by Rintel (2013, p. 266), the combination of timeliness, timelessness and seriality allowed by templatable memes is particularly relevant at times of crisis since it allows a collective narration of challenging events through an already experienced and familiar format. For instance, by analysing the kitten memes in #Brusselslockdown on Twitter, following the Brussels security lockdown in November 2015, Jensen et al. (2020) observe how the *lolcat* template followed a path of progressive politicisation that transformed an ephemeral form of participation into an act of symbolic resistance against the terrorists as well as the police. In fact, in a context that we might define as of 'everyday politics' (Highfield, 2016), 'the mundanity of a picture displaying a cat looking sternly into a book of military strategy' (Jensen et al., 2020, p. 72) initially helped people understand and engage with the events and ultimately bolstered a personalised but collective processing of the ongoing societal crisis.

Among the several abnormal conditions brought about by the Covid-19 crisis, the unusual interplay between the ordinary and the extraordinary established in people's life is particularly striking. With the pandemic outbreak, national and regional lockdowns and all the measures restricting physical contact and freedom of movement, together with the distressing feeling of constant threat, suddenly impacted everyday life and its reassuring taken for granted. While daily routines were radically upset in their spatial, temporal and relational coordinates, social media platforms acquired new centrality in their being almost exclusive bridges between the now isolated domestic spaces and the temporarily suspended life outside. Research into the initial phase of the Covid-19 crisis shows that irony, humour and memes soon started to populate everyday social media practices, with an increasingly frequent reference to political values and identities (Vicari & Murru, 2020). Both existing research into memetics in crisis situations (e.g., Jensen et al., 2020) and initial work on the Covid-19 pandemic (Vicari & Murru, 2020) seem then to point to a – still underexplored – political emerging with the intertwining of 'silly' expressions of citizenships, everyday practices, and extraordinary events.

Silly citizenship, the everyday, and political cultures

Research has largely underlined how social media, as highly personalised spaces, have an elective affinity with the everyday politics consisting of extemporaneous contributions by 'individuals who are loosely connected (if at all), but who have their own personal interests, perspectives and issues of importance' (Highfield, 2016, p. 15). This kind of engagement with public debate or issues is often mediated by irreverent satire and whimsical humour leading to what Hartley (2010) defines as 'silly citizenship'. The political usually surfaces here as the unexpected outcome of playful practices that naturally belong to an off-topic domain, potentially crossed by multiple narrative trajectories and exposed to tangents and deviations (Highfield, 2016). Despite being uninterested in producing long-lasting effects on political decision-making, the everyday politics of the irreverent internet (Highfield, 2016) finds its civic value in being a fabric of signifying practices where citizenship is deployed as in constant and evolving relational identities. These identities take shape in the midst of discursive struggles between contested meanings, conflicting subjectivities and differing power relations (Hartley, 2010).

Social media 'everyday politics' (Highfield, 2016) and related expressions of 'silly citizenship' (Hartley, 2010) align with what Merelman (1998) has described as 'mundane political culture', a manifestation of citizenship that is essentially discursive and whose definition is shaped in contrast to the political culture as specified by Inglehart: a 'system of attitudes, values, and knowledge that is widely shared within a society' (1998, p. 18). The notion of Inglehartian political culture has a prescriptive nature in orienting people towards particular public policies, political institutions, and political leaders. It denotes a form of accomplished and explicit political culture, characterised by stable connections between values, attitudes and well-acknowledged political objects, like public policies, candidates or elected politicians (Merelman, 1998). Conversely, mundane political culture identifies those forms of cultural citizenship that can acquire political resonance but are entirely performative, consisting of discursive manifestations that primarily pertain to the domain of entertainment, proliferate just for the sake of playful conversation, and are originally conceived as irrespective of any future and purposeful political action.

Mundane political culture provides the symbols, terms, and ideas through which people interpret the public space and their engagement with it but it does not require the actions and communication typical of formal politics. It is implicit since its ideas and symbols contain unresolved and multivalenced meanings that remain undetermined and tacitly referenced as in the Wittgensteinian language games (Merelman, 1998, p. 517).

While political participation has surfaced in some of the work interested in the use of memes in crisis situations (e.g., Jensen et al., 2020), most meme research directly focused on the political has so far privileged grassroot memetic production happening on specialised sites (e.g., 4chan's/b/board) or dedicated Twitter accounts, where memes work as a contested subcultural capital within specific collective identities (see Nissenbaum & Shifman, 2017; Rintel, 2013). In this article, instead, we seek to advance scholarly work interested in the politics of memes by exploring memetics emerging (1) from 'mundane forms of social media communication' (Highfield, 2016, p. 19), understood as everyday social media practices and (2) at the interplay between these forms and extraordinary events. We do so by specifically drawing upon the ideal types of Inglehartian and mundane political culture.

The case study: everyday memetics in quarantined Italy

Italian pandemic memes make for a relevant case study for a number of reasons. Research shows that Italy's popular culture has provided a fertile ground for the emergence of online irony, humour and satire. This fertile ground is often traced back to the political cartooning used to oppose the Fascist regime and, more recently, both to satire against Silvio Berlusconi and to the history of the political party Five Star Movement (Movimento Cinque Stelle), founded by former comedian Beppe Grillo (Ferrari, 2018). While no existing research has specifically focused on memetic practices in the context of Italy, the work by Vicari, Iannelli, and Zurovac on political hashtag publics (2020) and Ferrari (2018)'s exploration of 'user-generated satire' and 'political fakes' point to the existence of a lively terrain for cultural jamming. In particular, the combination of symbols derived from televised popular culture with the digital and social affordances of contemporary social media (see Iannelli & Giglietto, 2015), seems to have favoured the emergence of online satire fed by visual content in general (Vicari et al., (2020) and memes in particular (Ferrari, 2018, p. 2214).

Existing research exploring Italian Twitter at the outbreak of the Covid-19 pandemic shows that Covid-19 irony, humour and memes soon became a key element of everyday social media practices, often hinting at local political values and identities (Vicari & Murru, 2020). To explore the political significance of the memes emerging in this context and provide insight into the politics of memes surfacing at the interplay between ordinary practices and extraordinary events, we explored the political culture of Italian pandemic memes during the first national lockdown. Against the theoretical background detailed above and the contextual dynamics discussed here, in our empirical work we operationalised the notions of 'political culture' and 'everyday social media practices' as follows.

While the term 'political culture' is still marked by problems of definition that have turned it into an overused buzzword (Formisano, 2001), we circumscribed it to point to those expressive and creative practices of meaning-making that variously articulate the cultural and social preconditions of civic and political participation (Dahlgren, 2006). Considering the multifarious manifestations that political culture can assume in mediatic environments, we explored Italian pandemic memes as *discursive practices* that express some kind of political culture. Drawing on Merelman (1998), we considered the notion of Inglehartian political culture as denoting a form of accomplished and explicit political culture, namely one expressed by memes strategically used with propaganda aims and as building blocks of ideological frames directly linked to well defined political projects. An example here would be the incorporation of the 'Pepe the Frog' meme into alt-right politics, where the memetic imaginary reinforcing a specific politics of othering was purposefully used to reappropriate discursive positions pertaining to public affairs issues (Peters & Allan, 2021). We then used the notion of mundane political culture to identify all those forms of memetic practices where the political primarily arises as an off-topic outcome of irreverent satire. Discourses constructed through these memes do not point to a recognisable and distinct ideological frame, nor are they explicitly connected to specific political projects. They nevertheless acquire political significance in their apparently disengaged humour by dragging up the values and conflicting identities through which people interpret their place in the public space.

As a proxy for 'everyday social media practices', we looked at practices we had identified in a previous explorative exercise (see Vicari & Murru, 2020) – dispersed within the wider Twitter stream exclusively marked by the use of top trending Covid-19 event hashtags and keywords (Bruns & Hanusch, 2017) and mixed up with heterogeneous content as breaking news, useful information and political commentary (more information about this is provided in the next section).

Ultimately, our study addresses the following research question:

Taking the ideal types of mundane and Inglehartian political culture into account, how did the political emerging at the interplay between the ordinary of mundane social media memes and the extraordinary of early pandemic life express itself via discursive practices on Italian Twitter?

Data and methods

Data collection

The study presented in this paper focuses on Covid-19 memes produced in the context of mundane Twitter practices during Italy's first lockdown. The sample period spans from

28 February – a week into the country's Northern lockdown – to 3 June – when most of the national restrictions were lifted. Digital methods (Rogers, 2019) were key to the data collection phase of the study. We used the Twitter Capture and Analysis Tool (TCAT) to implement a keyword query strategy relevant to the pandemic in Italy[1] and launch a live data capture of tweets – comprehensive of their metadata. Our query design did not follow a 'programme and anti-programme approach' (Rogers, 2019, p. 27): as specified earlier, we identified as everyday Twitter practices those practices marked by top trending pandemic hashtags and their correspective keywords. The rationale behind this choice was that these hashtags – as top-trending – were more likely than others to be used in 'mundane forms of social media communication' (Highfield, 2016, p. 19) relevant to the pandemic. Choosing Twitter – whose Streaming API is currently more accessible and reliable than the APIs of other mainstream social media (e.g., Facebook, Instagram) (see Rogers 2019, pp. 156–157) – and using computational techniques to delimit our data site, allowed us to gather a vast amount of information on cultural objects, values and structures that we would have been unlikely to reach on other mainstream platforms and via non computational means. The live data capture returned 608,316 tweets containing at least one of the keywords used in our queries (as a word or as a hashtag).

Data filtering

Since we chose to only focus on Italian language memetics that included visual content, we used TCAT to filter tweets by language (i.e., Italian) and based on whether they incorporated image media urls. Ultimately, this automated filtering returned 101,776 Italian tweets containing images. We extracted these tweets and archived them in Google sheets where we used the IMAGE ('url') function to display image content. Based on Shifman's definition of memes, we then manually scanned the archive to identify tweets that showed characteristics of memetics, namely, tweets delivering 'units of popular culture that are circulated, imitated, and transformed by individual Internet users, creating a shared cultural experience' (2013, p. 367). In the process, we considered the entire tweet as our unit of analysis, comprehensive of its text and image components (see Figure 1). This decision was informed by the fact that in many tweets the text component could be read as part of the meme, whether or not their image component incorporated superimposed text (e.g., in image macros).

Ultimately, the study presented in this paper is based on the exploration of 9,548 tweets incorporating visual memetics – 20% of which are original tweets and 80% retweets – selected through the manual filtering described in this section and still live on Twitter at the time of writing. We decided to include retweets in our analysis as this would allow us to quantitatively assess the overall appeal of each discourse to their publics.

Data coding and analysis

While the live data capture progressed via TCAT, we – both Italian citizens – regularly observed and engaged with local cultural dynamics emerging on Italy's social and mainstream media in relation to the pandemic: author A from within the country and author B from the UK. This insider/outsider reflexive and dialogical process gave us a privileged

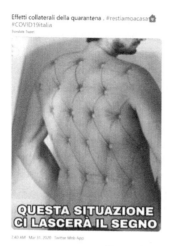

Text component: 'Quarantine's side effects'

Image component: image macro incorporating text 'This situation will leave a mark on us'

Figure 1. Tweet as a memetic unit of analysis.

cultural *entrée* (Kozinets, 2010) into Italian pandemic memes – one based on our diverse familiarity with national and subnational 'symbolic boundaries' (Friedman & Kuipers, 2013). It was this unique cultural entrée that provided us with the means to identify and reflect upon the cultural subtleties – like subtexts or domestic forms of intertextuality – that characterise memetic cultures (Laineste & Voolaid, 2017).

Drawing from Nissenbaum and Shifman (2018), we coded and analysed our final dataset developing a grounded theory approach (Bryant & Charmaz, 2007). We used open coding to identify and mark inductively the stance and content formulated in the memes in our dataset (e.g., stance: supporting, content: political leader; stance: delegitimizing, content: professional authority), with each author reading and coding half of the dataset. We then dialogically reflected on the coding we each had done, identified and merged overlapping coding categories and discarded those no longer relevant. With our initial coding categories having been fine-grained, we traced the emergence of clusters of semantically related memes (see also Segev et al., 2015) based on their stance/content combinations. We then grouped these clusters based on their feeding into one of five types of discourse that accounted for the vast majority of the memes in our datasets. Finally, to assess the political emerging at the interplay between the ordinary of everyday social media memes and the extraordinary of early pandemic life, we reflected on the extent to which these discourses showed, mixed, or were devoid of connections with explicit political projects (e.g., political parties, movements, or figures).

Pandemic memes as local politics

It is in generating, repurposing, or endorsing content/stance combinations that meme users – consciously or unconsciously – position themselves (stancing) in relation to specific objects (content). Political expression emerges there, at the intersection of memes' content and stance. In the following sections, we discuss the five leading discourses that shaped the political culture emerging from early everyday pandemic memes on Italian Twitter.

We are all in this together

About 40% of the tweets in our dataset showed evidence of memetic production that built on the shared feeling of experimenting the new life in the pandemic, with three fourth of this production happening during the first month of lockdown. Memes emerging in this context acted as a sounding board for the whirlwind of emotions generated by the pandemic outbreak. The kick-off of pandemic memes consisted of the humorous manifestation of all those feelings of dismay, disorientation and fear for the future that unavoidably accompanied an epochal transition such as a global epidemic could be. Memetics allowed this affective wave to flow and perhaps be normalised and streamlined. This could happen because memes, as peculiar combinations of standardised scripts and original variations on the theme, act as social rituals connecting individual practices to collective meanings and can therefore serve solidarity functions for both individuals and communities (Yang & Jiang, 2015).

In early pandemic memes, the effect of normalisation and emotional relief was achieved through a peculiar combination of content – primarily collective parodies – and stance. Initially, the leitmotiv was the daily life in lockdown, radically turned upside down in its habits, rhythms and spatial references. The tone exploited the full essence of irony as 'enjoyment of incongruity' (Morreall, 2009), as laughter that derives from realising the striking contrast between the expectations of what once was taken for granted and the reality of the pandemic. Irony was most often the self-irony of self-defeat memes (Ask & Abidin, 2018), which expresses the conscious but playfully surrenders to loss and powerlessness. Leaving home to go grocery shopping was thus represented through the popular imagery of apocalyptic movies, as a brave endeavour in a dangerous world (see first meme in Figure 2).

References to popular imagery worked as a comforting way back to the already known, and as a counterpoint to the disorienting irruption of the unexpected produced by the

Picturing a new apocalyptic daily life	Building a communal gaze	Mocking the fathering Prime Minister	Reversing stigma
Here is a picture of me and my daughter getting ready to go to the grocery	We are getting close	Nothing left to do but laugh	Libya's Coast Guard has spotted the first inflatables with Lombard migrants from Codogno
	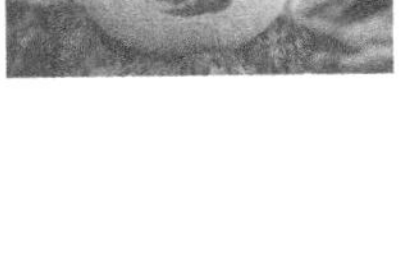		
		(Keep doctoring my pictures, and I won't let you out until 15 August)	(Coronavirus Italy. Here are the first boats towards African coasts)

Figure 2. 'We are all in this together.'

pandemic. In this first period, memes often took a first-person plural point of view, building a communal bewildered gaze (see second meme in Figure 2).

In some cases, the 'us' evoked by these memes started to embody the 'us' of citizens fearfully waiting to learn about the new rules dictated by the Prime Minister in his – soon ritual – daily press conference. The ironic hyperbole transformed the Prime Minister into an inflexible father threatening and punishing his children-citizens (see third meme in Figure 2).

The pandemic also dug up pre-existing dichotomies 'us/them'. In some cases, irony arose from the twisting of pre-existing juxtapositions, like in memes parodying the requests to close Italian harbours to stop migratory flows – a long lived slogan of the Italian right and far right, especially the League political party. As shown in the fourth meme of Figure 2, it was now Africa to close its borders, with stigma suddenly targeting those globally considered as the first Western spreaders of the virus.

Good citizens and rule breakers

An alternative discourse to 'we are all in this together' emerged where meme's political resonance went beyond the creation of a space of commonality and started to be concretised through 'making a point' (Shifman, 2014a). A first instance of this politicisation became evident when collective parodies turned adversarial: a normative judgment started to be exercised from the point of view of an ordinary citizen towards their fellow citizens, expressing normative positions on what was right and what was wrong. These memetic practices emerged in around 25% of our dataset and first surfaced when the atavic hostility between Northern and Southern regions of Italy was revived by the enactment of lockdown measures. In these early instances, mockery was often used against those who, shortly after the announcement that restrictions of movement would come in place, crowded the train stations and airports in Northern Italy to move South and reach holiday homes or families of origin.

While certain memes offered a seemingly benign, while ironic, representation of the events (see first meme in Figure 3), in others sarcasm started telling a different story. There, those travelling South, often to rejoin their families of origin, could be pictured as a 'migrant underclass' (see second meme in Figure 3) or as guided by egotistical cowardice and lacking any sense of responsibility towards the public interest and the interest of their very families (see third memes in Figure 3). Ultimately, these memes marked the first step towards a new kind of politicisation that became more pervasive in the following weeks.

In fact, past the first month of lockdown, the tone of pandemic memes often consisted of offensive and mocking irony (first meme in Figure 4) or moral reproach (second meme in Figure 4). In these instances, the 'us' acquired a prescriptive posture that broke the horizontal links between citizens experiencing the same astonishing circumstances by instituting normative boundaries between insiders and outsiders.

Down with the leader

While normative memes redefined right and wrong doings in the pandemic society, a different type of political expression emerged in memetic practices involving individual

Ironic take on the flee towards the South	Picturing a 'Southern migrant underclass'	Picturing the 'egoistic Southerner'
Inhabitants of Codogno and Lombardy who meet in the South of Italy for a peaceful aperitivo.	A picture of Frecciarossa [train] leaving Milan.	STAY AT HOME

		(Southerners at the station welcome their relatives arriving from Milan)

Figure 3. 'Good citizens and rule breakers' (1).

Offensive and mocking irony targeting rule breakers	Moral reproach targeting rule breakers
Why can't I run?	Muted tweet

(MAN, WOMAN, GAY, YELLOW, WHITE, BLACK, RICH, POOR, TALL, SHORT, UGLY, WHY CAN'T I GO RUNNING?)	(From Bergamo. Dedicated to those who still go for walks or train in the streets, to those who travel South, to those who don't use gloves, to those who think 'better one day as a lion')

Figure 4. 'Good citizens and rule breakers' (2).

parodies of politicians. Around 12% of the tweets in our dataset showed stancing that drew upon derisive comments and/or destructive criticisms, mainly through two discursive strategies: ridicule and delegitimization. Ridiculing often took place through a degradation of politicians as decision-makers. Particularly emblematic of this category is the first meme shown in figure 5. This meme derided Luigi Di Maio, Minister of Foreign Affairs and member of the Five Star Movement, by picturing him in conversation with 'Uan' (read 'Wuhan'), a famous puppet from a 1980s children's TV show.

The second strategy consisted of questioning the authoritativeness of politicians through their delegitimization, mainly relying on moral evaluation (Ross & Rivers, 2017). The moral principle of coherence was most often evoked here, principally through memes that schematically listed statements made by politicians at different times of the pandemic and in clear mutual contradiction. An example of this is provided by the second meme in Figure 5, focused on Matteo Salvini, leader of the League political party.

Down with the experts

While individual parodies thrived in ridiculing and/or delegitimizing political leaders, similar stancings were used in the collective parodies delivered in about 5% of our dataset, where the traditional authority of entire categories of experts was dismantled. This often-implied collapsing political and scientific expertise.

The focus on virologists, and their authority, derives from the complex relationship between Italian publics and a number of 'celebrity' virologists. This relationship partially comes as a legacy of the long-lasting public dispute between Professor of Virology

Ridiculing the leader	Delegitimising the leader
+++ANSA - 23.03.20; 15.47+++ Talks continue between Wuhan and the Foreign Minister di Maio.	It could have gone better
	 (Let's listen to the scientific community: lockdown, close our borders; It is about the health of millions of people; Let's reopen! Everything that we can open! Reopen, relaunch!; So, open, open open! Going back to run, going back to work!)

Figure 5. 'Down with the leader'.

Roberto Burioni and the Italian anti-vaccination movement and politicians aligning with it. Burioni, a figure who has received international praise as 'an outspoken advocate for scientific evidence on vaccines and other medical topics' (Starr, 2020, p. 16), is extremely active on both social media platforms and TV channels, public and private ones. Burioni is a very popular figure in Italy but also a polarising one, not least for his unapologetic rhetoric. The 'Burioni effect', combined with the sudden presence of a number of – often disagreeing – virologists on Italian legacy media (Nadotti, 2020, p. 16), most likely contributed to the emergence of collective parodies comparing virologists' failing authority to that of politicians. The second meme in Figure 6, for instance, equates early claims made by virologists Roberto Burioni and Massimo Galli (top row) with those made by political leaders from the left (centre row) and the right (bottom row).

The (Italian) model does not work

In a small number of memes (i.e., less than 5% of our dataset), policies, especially those enforced during lockdown, also became the target of strong criticism, often via sarcastic or ironic stancing. It was not uncommon for these memetic instances to frame bureaucratic complexity as an 'Italianism', re-enacting self-stereotypes that in a way aligned with the 'we are all in this together' memetics thriving at the start of the pandemic.

The second meme in Figure 7, for instance, presents a fake version of the form Italians were required to use to self-certify the reasons for leaving their house during lockdown. The official form went through several iterations, often leaving citizens unsure as to what version they were supposed to use. The questions in the fake form presented in this meme recall an iconic scene of the 1984 cult comedy movie 'Non ci resta che piangere'

Ridiculing 'the experts'	Delegitimising (and collapsing) 'the experts'
Collect all the picture cards of Italy's new commanders.	Reminder for forgetful #jackhall.
 (Virologists The full collection)	 (It was February and they said: it is unlikely that the virus will reach Italy. don't worry, go out and have aperitivo open, open, open...foreigners should come on holiday, everything is fine March: '[PM] CONTE UNDERESTIMATED THE VIRUS')

Figure 6. 'Down with the experts'.

Sarcastic take on Covid-19 furlough scheme	Ironic take on bureaucratic practices
Contradictions Italian style	Available online a draft of the new self-certification form
 [CASSA INTEGRAZIONE / TASK FORCE jars image] (Furlough scheme Task force)	 Ultimo modello di autocertificazione [form image] (Latest self-certification form Who are you?____ What are you doing?____ What are you bringing?____ Yes, but how many are you?____ 1 florin Date, time and location. Signature of the certifying individual; Police officer)

Figure 7. 'The (Italian) model does not work'.

(Nothing left to do but cry), where the protagonists, in Medieval Italy, were repeatedly – and nonsensically – halted by a customs official requiring them to pay 'one florin'.

Discussion and conclusion

In this article, we analysed early everyday Covid-19 memetics of Italian Twitter to explore the political emerging at the interplay between the ordinary (i.e., everyday Twitter practices) and the extraordinary (i.e., early pandemic life).

Existing research into the politicisation of memes has primarily focused on specialised sites inhabited by subcultural communities whose structure, membership and status are constantly performed and discussed. In this article, we redirected the focus towards memetic practices that escape subcultural connotations and that proliferate within hybrid discursive contexts populated by highly heterogeneous content. We addressed ordinary and undefined memetic practices as part of the mundane domain of everyday life, where people mix together routines and improvisations to deal with contingencies, domesticate the unexpected, and make sense of the surrounding world. The specific social circumstances of the pandemic, with the obligatory segregation into domestic spaces and the subsequent limitation of the variety of work and leisure activities that had previously filled and organised daily life, allowed us to investigate how the mundanity of memetic practices works within an extraordinary context and makes space for manifold processes of politicisation.

We assumed that the political significance of mundane memes can be more adequately grasped in their being connected pieces of wider political cultures. Hence, drawing on the ideal-typical opposition between mundane and Inglehartian political culture, we investigated the political culture expressed by Italian pandemic memes during the first Covid-19 lockdown.

The five leading discourses emerging in our analysis show that the familiar ordinariness of memetic practices acted as a counterpoint to the destabilising emergency brought by the pandemic. Reading the new daily life through the lens of templatable memes (Rintel, 2013) paved the way to a sort of attempted 'normalisation' of the extraordinary. At the same time, the activation of mutual processes of recognition led to the symbolic emergence of a sympathetic 'us', ideally including all the people equally affected by the crisis. Coherently with the scope and tone of silly citizenship (Hartley, 2010), pandemic memes then gradually became political by establishing a collective 'us', firstly characterised by inclusiveness and then progressively connotated by conflictual differences. In fact, the supportive togetherness implied by the commonality so often expressed in very early pandemic memes, soon started to be crossed by intransigent moral boundaries, like the one opposing responsible and law-abiding citizens to reckless and selfish citizens. An even deeper contrast opposed ordinary citizens against political and scientific élites, with the latter being sketched in their erroneous predictions and as falling short of their institutional prestige. By identifying good or bad civic behaviours and exhibiting criticism against politicians, experts and institutions, pandemic memes drew upon the values and symbols through which public spaces and public subjectivities are commonly articulated. They undeniably expressed pieces of wider political cultures, but they did it in a peculiar way that is worth understanding.

Where political expression did emerge, namely, in pandemic memes that were 'making a point' (Shifman, 2014a), this 'point' was never particularly innovative or new, probably because it was there to mark previously established communal belonging more than to initiate activist or social change (Mina, 2014) practices. In fact, Italian pandemic memes did develop the ridiculing and delegitimizing techniques typical of political memetics (Ross & Rivers, 2017), but they did so primarily relying on anti-elitist narratives. This was evidenced by the frequent targeting of well-known political leaders via pre-existing schemata adopted to attack them (e.g., inexperience for Di Maio and the Five Star Movement and hypocrisy for Salvini and the League). Similarly, the mockery towards experts who had previously acquired mediatic visibility expressed the erosion of public trust and the underlying delegitimization of scientific authority.

Considering the ideal types discussed by Merelman (1998), the content observed in our study suggests that the mundanity of the memetic practices here mapped was coherently mirrored in the mundane political culture they expressed. This content consisted mainly of symbols, with political leaders or experts becoming representative of wider and unreliable elites, and basic values, namely compliance with laws and coherence in politicians' statements, turning into criteria to trace new boundaries between 'us' and 'them'. Critical stances fell short of depth, addressing the institutional pandemic response or the 'other' misaligned citizens without explicitly advancing viable alternatives in the form of public policies, governmental acts or political projects. Similarly, the limited spectrum of values addressed in the memes – and the absence of clear mutual connections between these values – did not compose an ideological frame endorsing clear positions about the goals government, democracy or policies should aim to achieve. What we see can thus be referred to as a primarily performative mundane political culture, apparently irrespective of future political outcomes insofar as it appears to be devoid of any cohesive discursive frame and lacking explicit references to recognisable political projects or subjects.

In this vague domain of ideas and symbols that evoke without explaining, an affinity can nevertheless be identified between populism as thin-centered ideology (Mudde & Kaltawasser, 2017) and the values and identities highlighted by the five leading discourses that characterised the mundane political culture of the memes in our study. The generic criticism expressed by memes that were 'making a point' recalls populism as a common and minimal set of ideas relying on a few topoi, like anti-elitism and anti-scientism, a fierce opposition of 'us' versus 'them' and an emotionally charged appeal to a communal belonging where any outlying voice is harshly blamed. A similarity can also be found in relation to discursive structures. As shown by the ideational approach (Hawkins & Kaltwasser, 2017), populism is less conscious and programmatic than a fully articulated ideology and for this reason can be easily combined with other ideological features indifferently coming from right-wing or left-wing allegiances. Similarly, the mundane political culture emerging from the pandemic memetics analysed in our study took the shape of a loosely connected set of values and symbols, unable to systematically interpret the political challenges brought about by the Covid-19 pandemic through clearly defined political stances.

In conclusion, our work contributes to research considering memetic outputs as a repository of social values, political emotions, representative types, and collective frames in a nursery stage, namely before entering the consciousness of the public sphere (Seiffert-Brockmann et al., 2018). We argue that these unconscious or unfledged parts of the political can be reframed as expressions of mundane political cultures: they are performed through fragmentary discourses that remain devoid of any clear connections with publicly recognisable political projects or subjects.

Future research could explore how the political cultures arising from pandemic memetics evolved past the first wave of the pandemic, when a wider set of defined contentious issues started to dominate the public debate, like protests against lockdown or vaccine passports. For instance, if we studied memes following the summer of 2020, would we find a more varied spectrum of values, less generic expressions of criticism and more clearly articulated political positions? The highlighted proximity between populism and the mundane memetics emerging from the extraordinariness of the pandemic also points to the need for future research into how the political significance of apparently disengaged social media practices can interplay with and support populist ideologies as macro-political projects.

Note

1. We selected keyword queries (i.e., 'COVID19italia', 'codogno', 'coronavirusita', 'coronavirusitalia', 'coronavirusitalianews', 'coronaviruslombardia', 'coronavirusnontitem', 'coronaviruspiemonte', 'covid19ita') based on pandemic hashtags trending in Italy on 20 February 2020.

Disclosure statement

No potential conflict of interest was reported by the author(s).

ORCID

Maria Francesca Murru ⓘ http://orcid.org/0000-0002-6992-4397
Stefania Vicari ⓘ http://orcid.org/0000-0002-4506-2358

References

Ask, K., & Abidin, C. (2018). My life is a mess: Self-deprecating relatability and collective identities in the memification of student issues. *Information, Communication & Society*, 21(6), 834–850. https://doi.org/10.1080/1369118X.2018.1437204

Bayerl, P. S., & Stoynov, L. (2016). Revenge by photoshop: Memefying police acts in the public dialogue about injustice. *New Media & Society*, 18(6), 1006–1026. https://doi.org/10.1177/1461444814554747

Baym, N. K. (1995). The performance of humour in computer-mediated communication. *Journal of Computer-Mediated Communication*, 1(2). https://doi.org/10.1111/j.1083-6101.1995.tb00327.x

Boxman-Shabtai, L., & Shifman, L. (2014). Evasive targets: Deciphering polysemy in mediated humor. *Journal of Communication*, 64(5), 977–998. https://doi.org/10.1111/jcom.12116

Bruns, A., & Hanusch, F. (2017). Conflict imagery in a connective environment: Audiovisual content on Twitter following the 2015/2016 terror attacks in Paris and Brussels. *Media, Culture & Society*, 39(8), 1122–1141.

Bryant, A., & Charmaz, K. (2007). *The Sage handbook of grounded theory*. Thousand Oaks: Sage Publication.

Burgess, J. (2007). *Vernacular creativity and new media*. Doctoral dissertation. Queensland University of Technology, Brisbane, Australia.

Cho, S. E., Jung, K., & Park, H. W. (2013). Social media use during Japan's 2011 earthquake: How Twitter transforms the locus of crisis communication. *Media International Australia*, 149(1), 28–40. https://doi.org/10.1177/1329878X1314900105

Dahlgren, P. (2006). Doing citizenship. *European Journal of Cultural Studies*, 9(3), 267–286. https://doi.org/10.1177/1367549406066073

DeCook, J. R. (2018). Memes and symbolic violence: #proudboys and the use of memes for propaganda and the construction of collective identity. *Learning, Media and Technology*, 43(4), 485–504. https://doi.org/10.1080/17439884.2018.1544149

De Saussure, F. (1959). *Writings in general linguistics*. Columbia University.

du Preez, A., & Lombard, E. (2014). The role of memes in the construction of Facebook personae. *Communicatio*, 40(3), 253–270. https://doi.org/10.1080/02500167.2014.938671

Ferrari, E. (2018). Fake accounts, real activism: Political faking and user-generated satire as activist intervention. *New Media & Society*, 20(6), 2208–2223. https://doi.org/10.1177/1461444817731918

Formisano, R. P. (2001). The concept of political culture. *The Journal of Interdisciplinary History*, 31(3), 393–426. https://doi.org/10.1162/002219500551596

Friedman, S., & Kuipers, G. (2013). The divisive power of humour: Comedy, taste and symbolic boundaries. *Cultural Sociology*, 7(2), 179–195. https://doi.org/10.1177/1749975513477405

Gal, N. (2019). Ironic humor on social media as participatory boundary work. *New Media & Society*, *21*(3), 729–749. https://doi.org/10.1177/1461444818805719

Hartley, J. (2010). Silly citizenship. *Critical Discourse Studies*, *7*(4), 233–248. https://doi.org/10.1080/17405904.2010.511826

Hawkins, K. A., & Kaltwasser, C. R. (2017). The ideational approach to populism. *Latin American Research Review*, *52*(4), 513–528. https://doi.org/10.25222/larr.85

Highfield, T. (2016). *Social media and everyday politics*. Polity Press.

Iannelli, L., & Giglietto, F. (2015). Hybrid spaces of politics: The 2013 general elections in Italy, between talk shows and twitter. *Information, Communication & Society*, *18*(9), 1006–1021. https://doi.org/10.1080/1369118X.2015.1006658

Jensen, M. S., Neumayer, C., & Rossi, L. (2020). "Brussels will land on its feet like a cat": motivations for memefying #brusselslockdown. *Information, Communication & Society*, *23*(1), 59–75. https://doi.org/10.1080/1369118X.2018.1486866

Katz, Y., & Shifman, L. (2017). Making sense? The structure and meanings of digital memetic nonsense. *Information, Communication & Society*, *20*(6), 825–842. https://doi.org/10.1080/1369118X.2017.1291702

Kozinets, R. V. (2010). *Netnography*. Sage.

Laineste, L., & Voolaid, P. (2017). Laughing across borders: Intertextuality of internet memes. *The European Journal of Humour Research*, *4*(4), 26–49. https://doi.org/10.7592/EJHR2016.4.4.laineste

MacDonald, S. (2020). What Do You (really) meme? Pandemic memes as social political repositories. *Leisure Sciences*, *43*(1-2), 143–151. https://doi.org/10.1080/01490400.2020.1773995

Merelman, R. M. (1998). The mundane experience of political culture. *Political Communication*, *15*(4), 515–535.

Milner, R. M. (2013). Media lingua franca: Fixity, novelty, and vernacular creativity in internet memes. *AoIR Selected Papers of Internet Research*, *3*(IR14).

Mina, A. X. (2014). Batman, pandaman and the blind Man: A case study in social change memes and internet censorship in China. *Journal of Visual Culture*, *13*(3), 359–375. https://doi.org/10.1177/1470412914546576

Morreall, J. (2009). *Comic relief. A comprehensive philosophy of humour*. Wiley-Blackwell.

Mouffe, C. (2005). *On the political*. Routledge.

Mudde, C., & Kaltawasser, C. R. (2017). *Populism: A very short introduction*. Oxford University Press.

Nadotti, C. (2020, November 30). Coronavirus, dagli esperti italiani troppe informazioni spesso incoerenti. La Repubblica. https://www.repubblica.it/cronaca/2020/11/30/news/coronavirus_dagli_esperti_italiani_troppe_informazioni_spesso_incoerenti-276305771/

Nissenbaum, A., & Shifman, L. (2017). Internet memes as contested cultural capital: The case of 4chan's/b/board. *New Media & Society*, *19*(4), 483–501. https://doi.org/10.1177/1461444815609313

Nissenbaum, A., & Shifman, L. (2018). Meme templates as expressive repertoires in a globalizing world: A cross-linguistic study. *Journal of Computer-Mediated Communication*, *23*(5), 294–310. https://doi.org/10.1093/jcmc/zmy016

Peters, C., & Allan, S. (2021). Weaponizing Memes: The Journalistic Mediation of Visual Politicization. *Digital Journalism*.

Rentschler, C. A., & Thrift, S. C. (2015). Doing feminism in the network: Networked laughter and the 'binders full of women' meme. *Feminist Theory*, *16*(3), 329–359. https://doi.org/10.1177/1464700115604136

Rintel, S. (2013). Crisis memes: The importance of templatability to internet culture and freedom of expression. *Australasian Journal of Popular Culture*, *2*(2), 253–271. https://doi.org/10.1386/ajpc.2.2.253_1

Rogers, R. (2019). *Doing digital methods*. Sage.

Ross, A. S., & Rivers, D. J. (2017). Digital cultures of political participation: Internet memes and the discursive delegitimization of the 2016 US Presidential candidates. *Discourse, Context and Media*, *16*, 1–11.

Segev, E., Nissenbaum, A., Stolero, N., & Shifman, L. (2015). Families and networks of internet memes: The relationship between cohesiveness, uniqueness, and quiddity concreteness. *Journal of Computer-Mediated Communication, 20*(4), 417–433.

Seiffert-Brockmann, J., Diehl, T., & Dobusch, L. (2018). Memes as games: The evolution of a digital discourse online. *New Media & Society, 20*(8), 2862–2879. https://doi.org/10.1177/1461444817735334

Shifman, L. (2013). Memes in a digital world: Reconciling with a conceptual troublemaker. *Journal of Computer-Mediated Communication, 18*(3), 362–377. https://doi.org/10.1111/jcc4.12013

Shifman, L. (2014a). *Memes in digital culture*. MIT Press.

Shifman, L. (2018). Testimonial rallies and the construction of memetic authenticity. *European Journal of Communication, 33*(2), 172–184. https://doi.org/10.1177/0267323118760320

Silverstone, R. (1999). *Why study the media?* Sage.

Starr, D. (2020). Fighting words. *Science, 367*(6473), 16–19. https://doi.org/10.1126/science.367.6473.16

Vicari, S., Iannelli, L., & Zurovac, E. (2020). Political hashtag publics and counter-visuality: A case study of #fertilityday in Italy. *Information, Communication & Society, 23*(9), 1235–1254. https://doi.org/10.1080/1369118X.2018.1555271

Vicari, S., & Murru, M. F. (2020). One Platform, a Thousand Worlds: On Twitter Irony in the Early Response to the COVID-19 Pandemic in Italy. *Social Media + Society, 6*(3). https://doi.org/10.1177/2056305120948254

Yang, G., & Jiang, M. (2015). The networked practice of online political satire in China: Between ritual and resistance. *International Communication Gazette, 77*(3), 215–231. https://doi.org/10.1177/1748048514568757

Boris Johnson and US President Donald Trump. During the pandemic, the political decisions and personal health choices of Johnson and Trump became a frequent motif in memes that contested their ability to steer the national and international community through the pandemic. In the following section, we introduce our methodological set-up: a qualitative, thematic analysis (Hawkins, 2017; Nowell et al., 2017) of these memes. The ensuing analytical section presents the main findings along three thematic paths pertaining to populism – ideology, communication and style – which show how memes simultaneously circumvent and reaffirm populist logics. Finally, the conclusion points to the implications of this conflation of the critical and affirmative.

Populist political leaders: ideology, communication and style

Academic literature on political populism is vast and multifaceted, covering various political actors, groups and projects (Diehl, 2017; Nai & Coma, 2019). Moreover, as argued by Mudde and Kaltwasser (2018, p. 1668), ' … populism is often poorly defined and used in wrong ways.' However, the literature singles out ideology, communication and style as key perspectives to understanding populist political leaders. We link these perspectives to the genre conventions of political memes to identify shared traits and establish a framework for analyzing the ways in which memes both satirize and potentially reaffirm populist political leaders.

First, political populism is seen as an ideology (Diehl, 2017; Mudde, 2004), characterized by people-centrism and anti-elitism (Mény & Surel cited in Ernst et al., 2019). Oft-quoted is Mudde's definition of populism as a 'thin-centred' ideology:

> … that considers society to be ultimately separated into two homogeneous and antagonistic groups, 'the pure people' versus 'the corrupt elite', and which argues that politics should be an expression of the *volonté generale* (general will) of the people (Mudde, 2004, p. 543, emphasis in original).

As a thin-centred ideology, populism constitutes a 'loose complex of ideas' (Krämer cited in Sorensen, 2017) that may be combined with other ideologies (Mudde, 2004, p. 544). For this reason, populism is seen across the political spectrum. 'The people', key to populist ideology, is defined in opposition to 'the elite', which is typically associated with established political parties. 'The people' constitutes a more broadly defined group, or 'an imagined community', as Mudde contends (2004, p. 546) in reference to Anderson's concept about the nation in nationalism. Populist political leaders project authenticity and an outsider position as key strategies for connecting with 'the people' and constructing their image as that of vox populi (Mudde & Kaltwasser, 2017).

Second, populists 'need the 'oxygen of publicity'' that the media provide (Aalberg et al., 2017, p. 4). This explains why communicative strategies are repeatedly highlighted in media and communication studies as key constituents of populist politics. Some see populism as a communicative framework in itself (Nai & Coma, 2019); others argue that particular communicative styles facilitate rather than define populism (Mudde, 2004, p. 454), thereby distinguishing between populism as ideology and populism as style (see also Diehl, 2017; Ernst et al., 2019; Esser et al., 2017). Applying a communication perspective means shifting the focus from '*what populism is* to *what it does* and *how it does it*', Sorensen argues (2017, p. 138, emphasis in original), i.e., from content to form. Changes in the interplay between media and politics, including media systems and media technologies as well as the structures of political parties, are seen to further the progress of populism (Sorensen, 2017). While research has devoted most attention to the performance of populists in and through news media (e.g., Esser et al., 2017; Mazzoleni, 2008), studies increasingly center on populists' use of social media such as Facebook and Twitter. Scholars stress the ways in which populist logics and social media logics interact when populists bypass the professional gatekeepers of institutionalized media and communicate directly in a popular and emotionally engaging manner with 'the people' (e.g., Bracciale & Martella, 2017; Engesser et al., 2017; Ernst et al., 2019). Digital communicative *genres* such as memes are less in focus, however (see also Wagner & Schwarzenegger, 2020). Similarly, scholarship on political memes, to which we shall return, does not consider memes in the context of populist political communication.

Third, populism is seen as a performative style of political leaders (Diehl, 2017; Mudde & Kaltwasser, 2017; Nai & Coma, 2019). Mudde and Kaltwasser (2018, p. 1668) argue that 'there is no such thing as the prototypical populist leader' because no universal traits render populist leaders successful, and variations emerge due to cultural specificity and changing contexts. At the same time, other scholars repeat a range of performative characteristics that populist leaders seem to share. These include bombastic, spectacular, provocative behavior; acting at odds with the social norms that otherwise apply to politicians' more or less institutionalized role performances; aggressive, exaggerated and polarizing rhetoric; and deliberately not trying to be agreeable (e.g., Diehl, 2017). For example, Nai and Coma (2019, p. 1351) conclude, based on an empirical study, that populist leaders 'score lower on agreeableness, emotional stability and consciousness' but higher on 'extraversion, narcissism, psychopathy and Machiavellianism'. They see this as:

> … a pattern of 'populist reputation' which portrays them as disagreeable, narcissistic and potentially unhinged, yet extrovert and socially bold – in short, bad-tempered and provocative, but charismatic. (Nai & Coma, 2019, p. 1359)

Donald Trump is highlighted as a key incarnation of these traits. This suggests that the issue of communicative strategy indeed overlaps with the issue of performative or political style, which, according to Pels (2003, p. 45), includes 'speaking, acting, looking, displaying, and handling things, which merge into a symbolic whole that immediately fuses matter and manner, message and package, argument and ritual'. The mediated physical appearance of populist political leaders is especially significant as producer of such symbolic meaning in visual culture. Central to political performance and style, their bodily staging 'enables the politician to speak, to gesticulate and to produce facial expression' (Diehl, 2017, p. 361), thus stimulating identification and evoking emotions in voters – or 'the people'. With this mediated public staging, populists distance themselves from the traditional, professional bodily appearance of politicians, which includes moderate body language, rhetoric and dress codes. Especially important to populists is a bodily performance which signals 'strong-man style of political leadership' (e.g., Mudde & Kaltwasser, 2017).

The ideology, communication and style of populist political leaders obviously overlap and mutually reinforce one another. According to Diehl (2017, p. 148), 'the source of populist authenticity is its ability to maintain consistency between style and ideology in all sites of mediation'. Ernest et al. (2019, p. 10) similarly see 'populist communication as the outcome of a political strategy that uses both ideological key messages and certain stylistic elements.' Be that as it may, we treat the three perspectives separately in this paper as a framework for the thematic analysis because we found that memes tend to zoom in on one of these key aspects to satirize the polarizing outsider status, communicative strategies, and style of populist political leaders.

Political memes

Political memes have turned into a 'significant means of information, interaction and political deliberation' (Denisova, 2019, p. 2) to the degree that researchers have pointed to 'the memefication of political discourse' (Bulatovic, 2019, p. 250). They have joined the many genres included in political humor (see Hariman, 2008 for overview), bearing the strongest resemblance to political cartoons. The most important difference between political memes and traditional political cartoons is that the interpretation of the latter hinges on the cartoonist, the newspaper or magazine in question as well as underlying commercial, cultural and political contexts (Chen et al., 2017). Political memes do not have these fixed points. Metadata about who made them, when, where and how is often not available. Memes are spread according to social media logics such as programmability and popularity, depending on both algorithms, commercial interests and human agency (van Dijck & Poell, 2013). Engaging with political actors or issues, they are created bottom up by an often unspecific group of media users as part of participatory digital culture (Wiggings & Bowers, 2014). In this sense, memes do not lean on the institutional authority in the way that political cartoons do and can be understood as a democratizing genre. While political memes in this way break from traditional political cartoons, the boundaries between the two genres are still blurred. It goes beyond the confines of this article to account for this in detail, so suffice it here to mention that political cartoons are now uprooted from their institutional and industrial origin when disseminated on social media or re-mediated in memes (Chen et al., 2017, p. 147).

When and how are memes political? According to the definition proposed by Wiggins (2019, p. 65), '… there must be some argument or purpose (contained within the meme) for it to be political'. He further contends that this:

> … must be constructed with regard to a particular political view, how to respond to a political actor or other entity, the proposal or rejection of or support for legislation, the advocacy for and exercise of force and security, the promotion of peace or war, or simply to accuse political agents of maleficence, corruption, incompetence, etc. (Wiggins, 2019, p. 65)

Following this definition, political memes constitute a broad category, encompassing all memes with a political claim or content. Whether or not memes have been produced with deliberate political intent is often difficult to determine since, as already mentioned, information about the creator and the original context is often not retrievable. But they may be interpreted politically regardless of their objective (Bulatovic, 2019, p. 251) as a key genre convention is to mock or expose the professional and personal actions of politicians, including, in the case of populist leaders, challenge their performances of authenticity and outsider status.

As stated in the introduction, the central question raised by scholars concerning political memes pertains to whether or not they challenge prevalent political discourses. Do they serve as a vernacular, political communicative tool to contest or change the political agenda, or do they merely confirm established, hegemonic discourses? This question resonates with classic hi-low culture discussions and also reflects debates concerning internet cultures, which have been framed as a 'site of struggle between dominant and alternative discourses' (Denisova, 2019, p. 40).

Arguments in favor of the political potential of memes contend that they humorously and critically deconstruct political power by subverting dominant visual representations of this power (Boudana et al., 2017; Ibrahim, 2016; Jensen et al., 2020; Mortensen, 2017). Memes work as 'discursive weapons', performing the double role of creating 'social distortion and a sense of community' (Nissenbaum & Shifman, 2015, p. 484), which is particularly vital during times of crisis and uncertainty. Moreover, Chagas et al. (2019) assert that memes' humorous mode of address may stimulate the public's otherwise shrinking engagement in politics:

> Some note that public disengagement, lack of popular mobilization and lack of interest in collective matters are seen as threats to the legitimacy of democratic institutions and democracy as a whole. This has led some to search for answers about this 'crisis' and ways to revitalize political participation […]. Humor has been a relatively recurring aspect of these debates. (Chagas et al., 2019, no page number)

While some scholars argue that memes enable media users to express and negotiate political viewpoints and values, others maintain that they do not contain enough nutrition to substantially influence political debates. In a study of memes spread during the 2016 US presidential election, Denisova infers that memes constitute the 'fast food' of social media:

> As the fast-food communication of the social media, memes convey the ideas from the media discourse in an unreflective and subjective manner. Rarely a meme can be neutral – it is the emotional appeal of a meme that becomes the quick trigger to make you 'like' or 'share' it (…) They serve as sensitive monitors of the public opinion – they shed light on the topics that people endorse and the styles of communication that they favour (lad, vulgar, sarcastic, etc.). (Denisova, 2019, p. 194)

If we follow the argument that memes only prompt media users to endorse existing political views, they also, as Denisova (2019, p. 193) further contends, contribute to the polarized political climate. This is ascribable to the emotional mode of address, which, according Denisova, hardly triggers reflection beyond quick likes and shares (ibid.).

Existing scholarship, in sum, presents clear-cut fronts between arguments for and against memes creating a space for political deliberation. However, we argue that the viral mass dissemination of memes makes general claims about their political potential futile. This potential depends on the case and context in question as well as the theoretical and methodological approach. Accordingly, we propose that instead of making general claims, theoretical nuances and empirical perspectives should be added to the overall question based on delimited studies of meme subgenres, in particular historical contexts such as the one explored in this article of populist political leaders during the COVID-19 crisis.

Even though memes of populist political leaders have not drawn much scholarly attention so far, they constitute a large subgenre within political memes. There may be several reasons why. First, populist leaders lend themselves to memes because, as mentioned, they communicate in a polarizing and simplifying way and often do so by taking advantage of the swift, ephemeral form and style of social media. Their one-liners and mannerisms may easily be converted to memes. Second, memes easily pick up on populism because this ideology feeds into the personalization of politics, i.e., the media's tendency to reduce major political and societal challenges to the level of individual actors and their interplay as opposed to focusing on the social and political structures and interests undergirding these challenges (e.g., Bennett, 2012; Hjarvard, 2013). Personalization is closely tied to the emotionality distinguishing today's mediatized politics; emotions influence political and moral judgements, motivate participation, and contribute to constructing collective identities (e.g., Pantti, 2010). While memes criticize populist political leaders, including their tendency to turn to personalized and emotional forms, they still contribute to this discourse by focusing on actors and appealing to emotions. In sum, populist politicians use a mode of address similar to that of memes and other social media genres, and, conversely, the social media genre of memes parodies populist political leaders.

Context and cases

The COVID-19 pandemic was ongoing when we embarked on the present study. The pandemic presented enduring and disruptive political, communicative and performative challenges for leaders around the globe. It seemed an obvious choice to explore if this extraordinary situation potentially magnified tendencies regarding the political potential of memes. Critical deliberation might feed into memes in response to this extreme situation that politicians had to solve, and citizens had to cope with. This point is particularly applicable to populist political leaders, whose handling of the crisis was commonly perceived to be highly problematic and to have grave consequences for their populations.

In early 2020, the COVID-19 virus quickly spread around the world, including Europe and the US. The World Health Organization declared it a pandemic in March 2020. The pandemic developed differently, but most countries experienced several waves of intense spread of the virus, resulting in multiple lockdowns of large parts of society. By early February 2021, the UK had the highest death toll in Europe, the virus claiming more than 110,000 lives. More than 460,000 Americans had died with the virus at this point in time.[1] The first vaccines were given one year into the pandemic, in December 2020.

As the analysis focuses on populist political leaders, we chose two complementary Western cases of male political heads of state commonly considered to be populists: British Prime Minister Boris Johnson and US President Donald Trump. Language and culture were a primary reason for this choice. Memes are often difficult to decode due to their viral nature. Humor does not easily translate in the first place, and memes refer to particular national, cultural, social and political circumstances, traditions and sayings, which are not necessarily known to foreign scholars. This also manifested itself here. Sampling relevant memes turned out to require thorough knowledge of the pandemic in specific countries as well as the political distribution of responsibility for the handling of the crisis in these national settings. But this, of course, also created an Anglo-Saxon bias.

A second explanation for our choice was that Trump and Johnson exemplify how 'populism is a matter of degree' (Diehl, 2017, p. 363). Not 'all political actors are (at every time) populist ... and many of the quintessential contemporary 'populists' do not always use a populist discourse', Mudde argues (2004, p. 545). As already mentioned, Trump is often highlighted as a key example of a populist political leader (e.g., Nai & Coma, 2019), using polarizing rhetoric and projecting bombastic and provocative behavior as well as a 'strong-man' style of political leadership. Hodson (2021) argues that Trump has long cultivated this image by taking advantage of options for visual mise-èn-scene. This visual politics has played an important part in him being elected President and in continuously connecting with his supporters (ibid.). Johnson does not constitute an equally clear-cut case with his Eton and Oxford background and less confrontational style. However, Johnson's similarities with Trump are frequently emphasized, and he is often labelled a populist by news commentators and pundits due to his use of 'the people' versus 'elite' discourse; his powerful, simple political communication, such as the 'Get Brexit Done' slogan; and his atypical physical appearance in public, earning him the public nickname of a 'lovable buffoon' (Bale, 2019; Carr, 2019; Grise, 2019; Landler, 2019; Sullivan, 2019).

In terms of the COVID-19 crisis, both Johnson and Trump were met with heavy criticism for their handling of the pandemic, not least after they both contracted the virus following what appeared to be careless behavior in March 2020 (Johnson) and October 2020 (Trump). Johnson's COVID-19 strategy was also criticized for being implemented too late, involving insufficient testing, and striving for herd immunity. Similarly, Trump was condemned for neither taking the pandemic seriously nor implementing a national strategy as well as for reacting too slowly and lying about the severe health risk. Johnson and Trump thus constitute complementary cases. They share populist political traits and were targets of heavy criticism during the pandemic, which was expressed in memes (along with many other communicative forms).

Methodology

Our study is based on a thematic analysis of political memes of Johnson and Trump during the COVID-19 pandemic to explore our main research question: *How did memes thematically address and criticize these populist political leaders and their handling of the crisis in 2020?*

To prepare for the thematic analysis, a research assistant purposively sampled and collected memes from September 2020 to November 2020 via manual micro-archiving (Brügger, 2005). Archiving digital material involves lifting the text from its original context. This may pose a challenge in some studies but was less problematic here. In accordance with the thematic analysis, we focused on how certain themes manifested themselves in the memes rather than when and where they first appeared, and how they spread. In any event, the fleeting virality of memes would have made it difficult to trace the original source or context. The micro-archiving relied on still images and screen dumps, using Google as main entry point for the sampling. As Google algorithms may personalize search results, the research assistant cross-checked with the search engine DuckDuckGo, which shows the same results for given searches to all users. The DuckDuckGo search added a few memes without significantly altering the sample.

When sampling memes, it is impossible to reach saturation since, as mentioned, ephemerality is a key genre trait. We aimed for a sample of memes covering part of 2020 and of a certain quantity, using a criterion-based sampling strategy (Miles & Humberman cited in Punch, 2014, p. 162). The sampling was based on the search terms 'Boris Johnson meme COVID 19' and 'Donald Trump meme COVID 19',[2] and three criteria were applied: The memes should include (1) textual and visual components; (2) presence in photos, cartoons, drawing or other visual forms of Johnson or Trump's face and/or body; and (3) implicit or explicit reference to the COVID-19 pandemic in text or images. The sample contains 27 memes with Boris Johnson and 64 memes with Donald Trump that circulated between March and November 2020. It is difficult to explain with certainty why Trump is featured in more than twice as many memes as Johnson; it seems likely that differences in population sizes and amount of global attention to the two leaders play a part. Moreover, making a total or representative sample was not our ambition in the first place.

We chose the thematic strategy. This enabled us to synthesize our analytic observations as this is a qualitative method for 'for identifying, analyzing, organizing, describing, and reporting themes found within a data set' (Braun & Clarke cited in Nowell et al., 2017, p. 2). As argued by Hawkins, this is the strength of a thematic analysis (2017, no page number):

> Themes go beyond topical reporting, to provide depth of understanding within an interaction, text, or message, often revealing information about a process or processes that are occurring. Thematic analysts make sense of recurring observations found within data in (sic!) effort to interpret what is occurring within communication.

We followed the phased procedure for thematic analysis suggested by Nowell et al. (2017). A first step involved familiarizing ourselves with the data inductively, noting observations and theoretical reflections. A second step was to generate initial topical codes, for example, 'Johnson and the elite', 'Imitation of social media communication', 'Herd immunity strategy' and 'Fake news'. Based on these initial overviews, we searched for themes across the identified topics. While this phase often requires several steps, going back and forth between initial observations and defining/naming themes (ibid.), it turned out to be relatively straightforward to reach consensus in our case. Three themes were prevalent across the two cases, enabling us to condense our observations and provide in-depth understanding beyond their immediate denotations: (1) the *ideology* of Johnson and Trump was addressed in memes reversing the people-centrism and anti-elitism characteristic of populists; (2) memes commented on their mis-managed COVID-19 *communication strategies*; and (3) the populist *style* was thematized in memes putting a spotlight on their distinctive bodily representations and performances. These themes resonate with the key traits of populist political leaders presented above.

Only a few topics did not fit within these themes. For example, in the case of Johnson, memes coupled the challenges relating to Brexit (the UK leaving the EU) with COVID-19. In particular, one Trump meme stood out for supporting the Republican President and poking fun at Democrat protesters holding up signs with statements such as 'CURING CORONAVIRUS IS RACIST'.

Countering populist ideology, communication and style

The thematic analysis shows that during the COVID-19 pandemic, memes served as 'sensitive monitors of public opinion' (Denisova, 2019) about the populist leaders' handling of the crisis. The three overriding themes – ideology, communication strategy and style – resonate with the traits of populism and populist leaders. This indicates that the memes thematizing Trump and Johnson's handling of the COVID 19-crisis center on conspicuous characteristics of populist political leaders as opposed to the wider implications of their policies for public health, social security, etc., or seeing them as leaders of government and representatives of a political system. While this approach could work in theory to explore and criticize the public persona of these populist leaders from within, our thematic analysis reveals that the memes tend to reaffirm a polarized political approach, populist modes of communication and individualized visual politics.

Populists versus the people

Memes recurrently challenge the leadership of Johnson and Trump on a cornerstone of populism, their self-proclaimed people-centrism and anti-elitism. They criticize these leaders for neither representing the people nor serving their best interests, and they portray them as well-known popular cultural villains to emphasize this distance to their populace. In this manner, the memes within the first theme confirm the simplified populist understanding of the relationship between politicians and citizens.

Johnson is positioned as part of the established political elite, which populists typically frame themselves in opposition to. The main example is a collage of British politicians' faces grinning in a smirky manner with Johnson in the center, while the superimposed text states: 'It's one rule for us. Another for the Plebs'. Plebs is an abbreviation of Plebeians, a term traditionally designating 'the general citizenry in ancient Rome as opposed to the privileged patrician class'.[3] The term here refers to the British population, suffering from the pandemic and the restrictions imposed by Johnson's government. By framing him in opposition to the people, the meme exposes the hypocrisy of Johnson's populist strategy of authenticity and outsider status. Exemplifying the cultural specificity of memes, the British aristocracy emerges as an additional elite group in the Johnson memes. In particular, the Prime Minister is shown with the royal family. These memes signal a contradictory and hierarchical relationship, however, by illustrating Johnson as the henchman of the Queen, her husband or her oldest son, and also by insinuating the royal family's disdain for the Prime Minister. For example, a meme has the Queen state: 'Does your arse get jealous of all the shit that comes out of your mouth?'

Memes of Trump criticize the gap between the President and the people he claims to represent by exposing his conspicuous wealth and luxurious lifestyle. A recurring theme is to make fun of loss of taste as a symptom of COVID-19 as 'taste' is associated with both the sensory apparatus and esthetic preferences. Another widespread theme is Trump playing golf during the crisis, which again sets him apart from the people. Such memes couple Trump's excessive wealth and lifestyle with him contracting COVID-19 and not taking the pandemic seriously on a personal or political level.

Numerous visual references to popular culture, a key genre convention of memes (Wiggings & Bowers, 2014), reiterate this inverted anti-elite/people-centrism relation.

While no particular references dominate, Johnson and Trump are associated with iconic movie villains, indicating that they are indeed part of 'the corrupt elite', which populists typically position themselves in opposition to. These villains include the fictional Russian boxer Ivan Drago from *Rocky IV*, who makes the iconic quote: 'IF HE DIES, HE DIES', here referring to Johnson himself becoming severely ill with COVID-19. Dark-side characters from the *Star Wars* movies, corrupting the good side, and Squidward Tentacles from the cartoon *SpongeBob SquarePants*, known for being bad tempered, pretentious and despising his fellow characters, are also featured. Another recurring reference is to Lord Maximus Farquaad from the animated movie *Shrek*. Farquaad bears physical resemblance to Machiavelli, who also seems to inspire his leadership. Memes of both Trump and Johnson quote the Lord Farquaad line: 'SOME OF YOU WILL DIE, BUT IT IS A SACRIFICE I AM WILLING TO MAKE', alluding to their indifference and failed corona strategies causing high death tolls. The implicit reference to Machiavelli might be read as a comment on the Machiavellianism and anti-democratic traits ascribed to populist political leaders (e.g., Nai & Coma, 2019).

In sum, the memes discredit the political authority of Johnson and Trump by uncovering their staged anti-elitist strategies. At the same time, they reduce both leaders to somewhat dark, ridiculous or incapable figures, which potentially moderates or curbs the memes' critical edge. The memes put critical spotlight on their populist strategy of signaling authenticity and a position outside of established party politics when trying to connect to 'the people'. They do so by exposing Johnson's elite background and Trump's excessive lifestyle and by criticizing the restrictions imposed on the population, hinting at power abuse and lack of respect. Still, reducing the interplay of politicians and citizens to 'us' versus 'them' is to reproduce the simplistic populist logic of polarization. The political argument or purpose, fundamental for memes to be political (Wiggins, 2019), becomes clouded when memes replicate the dichotomous and simplistic ideology of populism to expose the populist leaders' performances of anti-establishment.

Populist crisis (mis)communication

The second theme in the memes concerns the (unsuccessful) populist communication strategies of Johnson and Trump. In particular, these memes thematize how their public communication is a smokescreen for lack of political and personal responsibility, and also how these populist leaders contribute to misinformation about the pandemic.

The British 'Stay at Home' campaign and ambition to reach herd immunity are recurring references in Johnson memes. They repeat a main visual depiction of the communication campaign: a yellow sign, bordered by red or green stripes. The campaign was introduced in March 2020 under the slogan 'Stay home. Protect the NHS. Save lives' (NHS = National Health Service) but soon changed to 'Stay Alert. Control the Virus. Save Lives' and similar warning slogans. The memes ridicule the many alternating catchphrases presented at press conferences by inserting mock slogans on the yellow warning sign. Several memes showcase the dissatisfaction with Johnson, who disregards the hygienic recommendations himself and thus communicates one message in words and another in actions. These memes once again individualize and personalize the handling of the crisis at the expense of the broader political and societal dimensions.

The Trump memes play on the President's hazardous and undocumented claims about the virus. They center on how he, after contracting COVID-19 himself, ought to take his own proposed medicine against the virus. Several memes represent Trump drinking or being injected with disinfection to parody his suggestion that such remedies might cure COVID-19 and to expose his public staging of power relations and authority on medical questions. As in Johnson's case, Trump memes also frequently feature still images from press conferences or other public appearances, showing signs held up as illustrations referring to his ignorance, shallowness and populist disrespect for science by means of phrases such as 'I'm with stupid', below which is an arrow pointing towards Trump, or 'He touches US send Help Please!!!' (US being both a pronoun and the nation).

In both cases, the memes seem to be intentionally political as they parody and deconstruct Johnson and Trump's communicative handling of the COVID-19 crisis. The memes highlight how the populist leaders expose their countries to danger due to their lacking understanding of and control over the grave situation. Nonetheless, they mainly seem to reverse the simple political slogans that are part of Johnson's communicative style and the relatively unreflective, often personalized, subjective or emotional outbursts that Trump is (in)famous for. A Trump meme sums up this communicative strategy: 'Don't panic people! Trump will tweet the virus away'. The irony is, however, that the meme is itself distributed on social media and follows the same communicative logics of the bold, quick statement.

Reproducing populist style

The memes amplify the performances of the populist leaders whose key trademark is their counter-establishment staging. This third theme feeds into the personalization of politics central to populist logics. Memes typically reduce the major political and societal challenges posed by the pandemic to the populist leaders as individual actors, focusing mainly on Johnson's distinct, unorthodox style and Trump's overtly expressive and masculine body language.

The representations of Johnson in the memes are quite homogeneous. They are typically from one of his televised addresses to the nation or from Parliament, showing his upper torso and face in relative close-up. He maintains a professional appearance in so far as he wears the political 'uniform' of male, Western political leaders: a dark blue suit, white or light-blue shirt and a blue or red tie. However, this is contradicted by his facial expressions and hair. Johnson is typically caught in awkward moments. He looks goofy, strained or tense, closes his eyes, does over-exaggerated thumbs up, or is shown with his distinct, fluffy blond hair, thus reproducing his public 'buffoon' image.

The representations of Trump's body play on his projection of 'strong man' by visually deconstructing his masculinity. A characteristic example is a meme of Trump as an anti-superhero: Under the headline 'SUPERSPREADER', is a drawing of Trump opening his suit, revealing a superman-like costume. However, replacing the Superman emblem is a drawing of the corona virus, connoting the dangers of the strong-man syndrome: Instead of superpowers to save mankind, the President is represented as a threat by (super)-spreading the virus. Memes also invert Trump's 'strong-man' style by representing him as a child or a woman. Several memes, for example, picture him as Marie Antoinette, the French queen who allegedly suggested just before the Revolution that the starving people should eat cake. The caption to one of these memes reads: 'NEED MONEY AND SUPPLIES FOR YOUR STATE? TELL ME I'M PRETTY', thereby portraying Marie Antoinette/Trump as leaders whose vanity stand in the way of them tending to the urgent needs of their populace.

These contrasting and ridiculing bodily representations of Johnson and Trump seem overtly simplified in accordance with the communicative logics of both memes and populism. In the case of Johnson, the memes basically reproduce his appearances and performances in the public space, while the memes of Trump reverse his strong-man syndrome, one of his most striking populist characteristics. In this sense, they might be said to reveal little new and to confirm more than challenge the leaders' public performances and visual staging.

Conclusion: who gets the last laugh?

Based on an empirical study of memes that places British Prime Minister Boris Johnson and former US President Trump in the spotlight during the COVID-19 pandemic in 2020, the present study set out to achieve two goals: On the one hand, to contribute to the scholarly literature on *populist political leaders* by studying a popular social media genre, which places populist leaders at the center of attention in both critical and affirmative ways, but which has not so far been a center of attention in the literature on political populism and populist political leaders. On the other hand, this study also had the objective of adding to scholarly literature on *political memes* by analyzing how the generic features and communicative logic of memes are partially in accordance with key traits of populist political leaders. The empirical study, confined to those particular cases and contexts, has provided nuances to the main, often dichotomous, question raised in meme scholarship as to whether memes serve as a tool for political contestation or mainly reiterate established power discourses.

Our thematic analysis in several ways points to the paradoxical intersection of populist political leaders and political memes as a social media genre: First, the memes reveal that populist leaders do not necessarily serve the people as they claim to; it is rather the other way around. They display their elite connections and how they undermine their own populist strategy of showcasing authenticity and a position outside of established party politics when trying to connect with 'the people'. Second, the memes demonstrate that populist leaders' communicative strategies are simplistic and sources of misinformation and misconceptions, disclosed by inconsistencies between facts and their public statements as well as between political objectives and personal actions. Finally, the memes challenge the bodily appearances of populist leaders, including their counter-establishment staging, i.e., unorthodox or overtly expressive and masculine body language. Such contestations may appear to be critical at first sight as the memes typically lay bare the paradoxes of both memes and populist leaders when turning their messages and actions into jokes and satire.

And yet, our analysis shows that memes employ the double strategy of criticizing and reproducing populist discourse and ideology. Populist leadership lends itself perfectly to memes due to the distinctive traits presented in this paper that are easy to recognize and parody. Populism shares not only communicative traits with memes but also communicative system. Populist leaders communicate in a simple, controversial and personalized

Carr, R. (2019, July 23). Boris Johnson: populists now run the show, but what exactly are they offering? *The Conversation*. Retrieved Feb 9, 2021, from https://theconversation.com/boris-johnson-populists-now-run-the-show-but-what-exactly-are-they-offering-120808

Chagas, V., Freire, F., Rios, D., & Magalhães, D. (2019). Political memes and the politics of memes: A methodological proposal for content analysis of online political memes. *First Monday, 24*(1). https://doi.org/10.5210/fm.v24i2.7264

Chen, K. W., Phiddian, R., & Stewart, R. (2017). Towards a discipline of political cartoon studies: Mapping the field. In J. M. Davis (Ed.), *Satire and politics: The interplay of heritage and practice* (pp. 125–162). Palgrave Macmillan.

Denisova, A. (2019). *Internet memes and society: Social, cultural, and political contexts*. Routledge.

Diehl, P. (2017). The body on populism. In C. Heinisch, C. Holtz-Bacha, & O. Mazzoleni (Eds.), *Political populism: A handbook* (pp. 261–372). Nomos.

Engesser, S., Ernst, N., Esser, F., & Büchel, F. (2017). Populism and social media: How politicians spread a fragmented ideology. *Information, Communication & Society, 20*(8), 1109–1126. https://doi.org/10.1080/1369118X.2016.1207697

Ernst, N., Blassnig, S., Engesser, S., Büchel, F., & Esser, F. (2019). Populists prefer social media over talk shows: An analysis of populist messages and stylistic elements across six countries. *Social Media + Society, 5*(1), 1–14. https://doi.org/10.1177/2056305118823358

Esser, F., Stepinska, A., & Hopmann, D. N. (2017). Populism and the media. In T. Aalberg, F. Esser, C. Reinemann, J. Strömbäck, & C. H. de Vreese (Eds.), *Populist political communication in Europe* (pp. 365–380). Routledge.

Grise, A. (2019, Dec 13). Boris Johnson's triumph of populism comes straight from the Trump playbook. *The Independent*. Retrieved Feb 9, 2021, from https://www.independent.co.uk/voices/boris-johnson-general-election-december-2019-a9244811.html

Hariman, R. (2008). Political parody and public culture. *The Quarterly Journal of Speech, 94*(3), 247–272. https://doi.org/10.1080/00335630802210369

Hawkins, J. M. (2017). Thematic analysis. In M. Allen (Ed.), *The SAGE encyclopedia of communication research methods* (pp. 1757–1760). Sage.

Hjarvard, S. (2013). *The mediatization of culture and society*. Routledge.

Hodson, D. (2021). The visual politics and policy of Donald Trump. *Policy Studies*, DOI: 10.1080/01442872.2021.1926445

Ibrahim, Y. (2016). Tank Man, media memory and yellow duck patrol. *Digital Journalism, 4*(5), 582–596. https://doi.org/10.1080/21670811.2015.1063076

Jensen, M. S., Neumayer, C., & Rossi, L. (2020). 'Brussels will land on its feet like a cat': Motivations for memefying #Brusselslockdown. *Information, Communication & Society, 23*(1), 59–75. https://doi.org/10.1080/1369118X.2018.1486866

Landler, M. (2019, Sep 27). Trump and Boris Johnson: Populist Peas in a Pod? Not Really. *The York Times*. Retrieved Feb 9, 2021 from https://www.nytimes.com/2019/09/27/world/europe/trump-johnson-populism.html

Mazzoleni, G. (2008). Populism and the media. In D. Albertazzi, & D. McDonnell (Eds.), *Twenty-first century populism: The spectre of Western European democracy* (pp. 49–66). Palgrave Macmillan.

McCrow-Young, A., & Mortensen, M. (2021). Countering spectacles of fear: Anonymous' meme 'war' against ISIS. *European Journal of Cultural Studies*, 136754942110050. https://doi.org/10.1177/13675494211005060

Mortensen, M. (2017). Constructing, confirming, and contesting icons: The Alan Kurdi imagery appropriated by #humanitywashedashore, Ai Weiwei, and Charlie Hebdo. *Media, Culture & Society, 39*(8), 1142–1161. https://doi.org/10.1177/0163443717725572

Mudde, C. (2004). The populist zeitgeist. *Government and Opposition, 39*(4), 541–563. https://doi.org/10.1111/j.1477-7053.2004.00135.x

Mudde, C., & Kaltwasser, C. R. (2017). *Populism: A very short introduction*. Oxford University Press.

Mudde, C., & Kaltwasser, C. R. (2018). Studying populism in comparative perspective: Reflections on the contemporary and future research agenda. *Comparative Political Studies, 51*(13), 1667–1693. https://doi.org/10.1177/0010414018789490

Nai, A., & Coma, F. M. (2019). The personality of populists. *West European Politics, 42*(7), 1337–1367. https://doi.org/10.1080/01402382.2019.1599570

Nissenbaum, A., & Shifman, L. (2015). Internet memes as contested cultural capital: The case of 4chan's /b/ board. *New Media & Society, 19*(4), 483–501. https://doi.org/10.1177/1461444815609313

Nowell, L. S., Norris, J. M., White, D. E., & Moules, N. J. (2017). Thematic analysis: Striving to meet the trustworthiness criteria. *International Journal of Qualitative Methods, 16*(1), 1–13. https://doi.org/10.1177/1609406917733847

Pantti, M. (2010). The value of emotion: An examination of television journalists' notions on emotionality. *European Journal of Communication, 25*(2), 168–181. https://doi.org/10.1177/0267323110363653

Pels, D. (2003). Aesthetic representation and political style: Re-balancing identity and difference in media democracy. In J. Corner, & D. Pels (Eds.), *Media and the restyling of politics: Consumerism, celebrity and cynicism* (pp. 41–66). Sage.

Punch, K. (2014). *Introduction to social research*. Sage.

Sorensen, L. (2017). Populism in communications perspective: Concepts, issues, evidence. In R. C. Heinisch, C. Holtz-Bacha, & O. Mazzoleni (Eds.), *Political populism: A handbook* (pp. 137–151). NOMOS.

Sullivan, A. (2019, Dec. 6). Boris's blundering brilliance Brexit has given the U.K's self-seeking Prime Minister the opportunity to show he actually knows what he's doing. *Intelligencer*. Retrieved May 28, 2021, from https://nymag.com/intelligencer/2019/12/boris-johnson-brexit.html

van Dijck, J., & Poell, T. (2013). Understanding social media logic. *Media and Communication, 1*(1), 2–14. https://doi.org/10.17645/mac.v1i1.70

Wagner, A., & Schwarzenegger, C. (2020). A populism of lulz: The proliferation of humor, satire, and memes as populist communication in digital culture. In B. Krämer, & C. Holtz-Bacha (Eds.), *Perspectives on populism and the media* (pp. 313–332). Nomos.

Wiggings, B. E., & Bowers, B. G. (2014). Memes as genre: A structurational analysis of the memescape. *New Media & Society, 17*(11), 1886–1906. https://doi.org/10.1177/1461444814535194

Wiggins, B. E. (2019). *The discursive power of memes in digital culture : Ideology, semiotics, and intertextuality*. Routledge.

'#OkBoomer, time to meet the Zoomers': studying the memefication of intergenerational politics on TikTok

Jing Zeng and Crystal Abidin

ABSTRACT
TikTok, a short video platform featuring content between 15 and 60 seconds long, has become a popular and rapidly growing social media application around the world. As a platform catering for light entertainment, TikTok champions virality and encourages memetic remixes. Meme videos, mostly featuring lip-syncs, dance routines, and skits, have become one of the defining features of the platform. These seemingly trivial videos have been utilised by young TikTokers to advocate for various causes. This paper uses #OkBoomer memes as a case study to examine the political culture of young people and Gen Z in particular. By analysing how intergenerational politics has been 'memefied', this study delineates how Gen Z imagines and expresses a generational sentiment towards 'Boomers' as the imagined other. They do so through short video cultures and practices on TikTok, drawing upon the networked experiences of their peers. Specifically, the paper considers the key controversial issues, meme forms and meme functions across the #OkBoomer memes on TikTok, and its eventual mainstreaming in society.

Introduction

(Boomer)
Back in my day, we walked uphill both ways /
(Zoomer)
Maybe because of you we won't have any more snow days /
Ok Boomer, time to meet the Zoomers /
Generation of humour, while you stay the accusers /

This is an excerpt of the lyrics from 'Ok Boomer', a rap song created by @james.bee, a Gen Z TikToker. The first line depicts 'Zoomers' mimicking 'Boomers' who often claim to be tougher than younger generations (i.e., 'walked uphill both ways'), and the next three lines reflect a snappy retort from 'Zoomers'. He uploaded this audio clip (@james.bee, 2019[1]) on TikTok in December 2019 and it has since been viewed a few millions times, and also hailed by some as a 'generation anthem'. @james.bee's viral video was a milestone contribution to the #OkBoomer meme trend on TikTok, which was initiated by Gen Z, or the self-proclaimed cohort of 'Zoomers'. In general, 'Boomers' refers to people born during the post-World War II baby boom between 1946 and 1964, while Gen Z refers to those born between 1997 and 2012 (Dimock, 2019; Fingerman et al., 2012).

The tagline 'Ok Boomer' epitomises Gen Z's 'discursive activism' (Shaw, 2012, p. 2016) against Boomers—a strategy of using 'conflict or provocation' as a way to have 'productive' discussions, where a 'community is able to define itself in opposition to others' (Shaw, 2016, p. 9)—and the ideological tension between the two generations (Meisner, 2020; Parker et al., 2019). The phrase emerged as Gen Z's 'verbal dismissive eye roll' to the critical rhetoric that accuses their generation of being 'snowflakes,' delusional, and unable to grow up (Gerhardt, 2019; Gonyea & Hudson, 2020). It has also become an all-purpose retort used by young people to disarm the older generation when they dispense what is perceived as presumptive, condescending, or politically incorrect viewpoints (Roberts, 2019).

While it has been observed that Millennials are mostly allied with Gen Z in their advocacy for social change (Roberts, 2019), the #OkBoomer campaign on TikTok—deployed via the playful use of pop cultural references, digital paralanguages like stickers and emoji, TikTok vernacular like audio memes and canon gestures, and youthful parlance and lingo—should be understood as a quintessential part of Gen Z's political activism because it constitutes a significant 'cue to heightened generational awareness' for the cohort (White, 2013, p. 219).

#OkBoomer memes have been circulated in various contexts and media platforms, but it truly gained its memetic momentum on TikTok (Gonyea & Hudson, 2020; Roberts, 2019). TikTok has become a popular and rapidly growing social media application around the world, and memetic videos have become one of its defining features. These seemingly trivial visual formats should not be categorically overlooked as isolated social media artefacts, because 'visual social media content can highlight affect, political views, reactions, key information and scenes of importance' (Highfield & Leaver, 2016, p. 48). In this paper, we perceive such memes as manifestations of Gen Zs' politics—specifically a 'small p', 'everyday politics' where political interests, pursuits and discussions can be 'framed around our own experiences and interests' in the 'highly personalised spaces' of social media (Highfield, 2016, p. 3). In these modes, everyday politics are intimately expressed through highly personable and personalised ways, and are intertwined with the display of identity politics. Using #OkBoomer as an example, this study examines how the political identities of young people are constructed and communicated in the form of video memes. The analysis focuses on the primary issues and topics in which intergenerational politics are identified, the main meme forms through which Gen Z's generational sentiments are expressed, and the major communicative functions therein.

Literature review

Intergenerational politics and Boomer grievances

We define 'intergenerational politics' as the tendency of people from a particular cohort to form shared political consciousness and behaviours, and their corresponding tendency to clash with the political attitudes of other cohort groups (Braungart & Braungart, 1986;

Kagwanja, 2006). Based on this definition, our discussion of young people's intergenerational politics focuses on both their political culture and their cross-generational resentment toward older generations.

The intergenerational politics between Boomers and Gen Zs have a powerful impact on the framing of public debates about social injustice and inequality (Bristow, 2020; White, 2013). The perceived social and economic power of Boomers and their conservative viewpoints have contributed to 'anti-Boomer sentiment' in Western societies (Bristow, 2020; MacDonald, 2020). For instance, Boomers have been the subject of ire from younger generations who blame the cohort for ushering in several societal issues including Brexit and the election of Donald Trump in 2016 (Bristow, 2020), generational economic inequality (Meisner, 2020; White, 2013) and climate change (Lim, 2020).

We take a sociological approach to understanding 'generations' as a *symbolic* and *dynamic*, rather than a *biological* and *static*, existence (Bolin, 2017; Bristow, 2020; Mannheim, 1970). As a form of social identity, a 'generation' comes into being through collective identification (Turner, 1975), or through creating the 'generational we-sense' (Bolin, 2017, p. 92). Gen Z TikTokers' engagements with generational politics can be understood as their articulation of such a *we-sense*. In this context, the platform TikTok itself also plays an important role in fostering this collective identity. Firstly, TikTok was made for and dominated by teenagers and preteens, especially in its early days (Savic, 2021). This makes TikTok itself a 'formative component' (Bolin, 2017, p. 4) in these Gen Zs' collective identities. Secondly, TikTok also serves as a locale wherein the *we-sense* of Gen Zs is constructed. A group's collective self-representation is increasingly intertwined with, as well as facilitated by, their engagement with social media (Humphreys, 2018; Rettberg, 2018). Although collective identity, such as being Gen Z, mostly comes into being through an invisible process, social media makes it visible and tangible (Milan, 2015, p. 893). #OkBoomer video memes exemplify such tangible artifacts of Gen Z's 'generationing', wherein the process centres on collectively drawing 'generational borders'.

By objecting to a perceived set of 'Boomer mentalities and ideologies', Gen Zs draw generational borders that can be ambiguous. As such, whether the TikTokers partaking in 'Boomer vs. Zoomer' banter are actually age-aligned members of each generation is secondary to our analysis, as we focus on how these TikTokers partake in self-identification and construct what it means to be a 'Boomer' and 'Zoomer' through cultural and political alignments.

We wish to note that, while highlighting the generational differences and tensions between Boomers and Gen Z, we do not intend for this comparison to commit 'generationalism', which refers to the oversimplified viewpoints on a generation that are then used to explain socio-political problems (Bristow, 2020; Purhonen, 2016). Rather than using the notion of a 'generation' as an *explanation* of societal issues, we consider young people's collective generational identification as a *symptom* of being subjected to specific societal inequities and oppressions. The generational tensions observed can be useful to explore how young people are constructing and contesting their everyday politics and identity politics, as a cohort who share generational sentiments, which they express and share through new communication platforms like TikTok. To this end, we utilise the #OkBoomer meme trend on TikTok as a case study, with our first research question being:

RQ1: What are the key controversial issues covered in #OkBoomer memes?

Political memes on TikTok

In the context of internet culture, memes are online artefacts that are circulated through imitation, competition and transformation (Ask & Abidin, 2018; Milner, 2016; Shifman, 2013). Despite often being dismissed as pointless and trivial, internet memes can have significant social, cultural and political merit. For instance, internet memes are effective communicative devices for alignment building and for stimulating socio-political discussion. Prior research has demonstrated that internet memes function as collective symbols for community identification around specific political causes, such as human rights advocacy (Vie, 2014), the #MeToo movement (Zeng, 2020) and anti-racism campaigns during COVID-19 (Abidin & Zeng, 2020).

Memes can take on varied formats, and the vast majority of existing literature about internet memes focuses on static images with humorous captions. More recently, short videos on TikTok have become another popular vehicle for political memes. TikTok memes are characterised by digital media scholars Kaye et al. (2020, p. 18) as 'circumscribed creativity'. Circumscribed creativities are creative potentials that are afforded, as well as restrained, by the features and logics of platforms. In the context of TikTok, the platform offers a technological infrastructure that celebrates and encourages memetic content.

For instance, content discovery on TikTok is largely algorithm- and trend-based. On its 'For you' page, the default interface where content is offered, users often scroll through a large volume of trendy videos that are automatically recommended to them, based on the platform's proprietary algorithm that generates tailor-made selections for each user. From the user's perspective, this continuous flow of videos across a variety of content genres and topics requires them to be attuned to very specific memes by quickly learning their templates and then being literate enough to recreate the memetic content in order to achieve visibility. However, there are often contestations around the primary reading and intonations of emerging memes on TikTok that often result in 'competitive ranking' and 'chart jacking' (Abidin, 2021, pp. 80–81), in part due to the multi-layered interpretations afforded by the intertextuality of 'audio memes' (Abidin, 2021, p. 80).

In terms of functionality, TikTok has introduced a variety of standardised templates and features that streamlines meme re-creation. For instance, TikTok's 'duet feature' allows users to directly respond to one another's videos by appending a new video to the left of the original. This function has become a widely used feature in the creation of meme videos (Zeng et al., 2021). Reusable special effects, sound clips and background sounds are other examples of affordances that facilitate seamless meme re-creation.

This meme-friendly and streamlined video production process, together with its young user base, makes TikTok a fertile ground for observing young people's creative engagements with various social-political issues (Hautea et al., 2021). By focusing on the popular TikTok meme #OkBoomer, we study how the circumscribed creativities of TikTok interplay with Gen Z's memefication of intergenerational politics through two further research questions:

RQ2: How are intergenerational politics expressed through #OkBoomer memes on TikTok?

RQ3: What are the communicative functions of #OkBoomer memes on TikTok?

Methods

To build our corpus of data, we used TikTok's online archive to retrieve videos hashtagged with '#OkBoomer' (Figure 1). In July 2020, we used a web-crawler to obtain publicly available metadata of the 1,755 unique videos published between August 2019 and July 2020 that were returned in this search. Retrieved metadata includes the video IDs, duration, caption, name of the background music or audio meme, publishing time and view/share/comment counts.

As shown in Figure 1, the #OkBoomer challenge became viral on TikTok in November 2019; around 50% of videos in the dataset were published during this month. In Table 1, the key metrics of all 1,755 videos are summarised.

We contextualise our analyses and understanding of these meme videos through both authors' long-term immersions as active users on TikTok, and through independent participant observations of TikTok culture from early-2019 to late-2020. From our corpus, we filtered out a random sample of 300 #OkBoomer related TikTok clips for closer study through content analysis. Our coding scheme was developed based on communications scholar Shifman's (2013) 'meme dimensions' and Zeng et al.'s (2021) analytical framework for TikTok 'meme categorisation'. We annotated all sampled videos according to three content levels: 'controversial issue', 'meme form', and 'communication function'.

We define 'controversial issues' as matters of shared concern wherein the intergenerational tensions between the old and the young are most visible. 'Meme form' refers to the content style through which memes are delivered in each video. In the context of TikTok, meme forms are largely shaped by the platform's technological features. 'Communicative function' refers to the explicit purpose that each meme video intended to convey. To study meme forms, we annotated each video's form according to three aspects: an audio feature, visual feature and performance feature. Complete categories are presented in Table 2. Subcategories under the 'controversial issues' and 'communicative function' dimensions were developed through multi-step open coding. In the first step, lower-level labels were assigned to randomly selected videos based on the aforementioned subjects and their meme functions. In the second step, all labels were organised into higher-

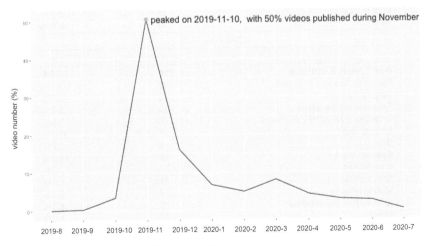

Figure 1. Monthly distribution of #OkBoomer videos.

Table 1. Summary of key metrics from all 1,755 videos.

	Min	Median	Mean	Max
Length (sec)	3	15	20	62
Views	42,300	486,700	966,200	32,500,000
Likes	6,764	79,600	150,200	2,900,000
Shares	6	1,254	3,733	139,500
Comments	0	379	1,030	45,800

Table 2. Summary of results from content analysis.

CONTROVERSIAL ISSUES	n	%
Gen Z Lifestyle & Wellbeing	120	40.0%
Appearance	52	17.3%
Work	14	4.7%
Technology usage	33	11.0%
Mental state	23	7.7%
Conservative Politics	59	19.7%
Environment	19	6.3%
Immigrants/Racial issues	15	5.0%
Donald Trump	12	4.0%
Abortion	5	1.7%
Other political topics	6	2.0%
Gender & Sexuality	31	10.30%
MEME FORMS	n	%
Audio feature		
With sound template	135	45.0%
With original sound clip	165	55.0%
Visual feature		
Stickers	123	41.0%
Duet	17	5.7%
Greenscreen	16	5.3%
All other effects	13	4.3%
Performing features		
Lip-synching	109	36.3%
Acting skit	132	44.0%
Dancing	6	2.0%
Music sharing	8	2.7%
Craft in making	25	8.3%
Other	50	16.70%
MEME FUNCTION	n	%
Gen Z retort & Criticism	210	70.0%
Targeting Boomers in general	82	27.3%
Targeting parents	32	10.7%
Targeting grandparents	16	5.3%
Targeting other family members	9	3.0%
An encounter	63	21.0%
Other	8	2.7%
Boomer react	34	11.3%
Complaining	21	7.0%
Self-mocking	13	4.3%
Merchandising	7	2.3%
Informative Educational	19	6.3%
Other	24	8.0%

Note: subcategories under each coding dimension are not mutually exclusive.

level groups based on their semantic relationship. Through this process, a codebook was developed for further systematic content analysis by two coders. The average inter-coding reliability was .78, as calculated with Cohen's Kappa. A detailed explanation of the coding scheme with examples can be found in Appendix 1.

We wish to note that Gen Z's generational sentiments are situated in both historical and cultural contexts. This study of #OkBoomer memes on TikTok has likely reflected the spirit of Gen Z in an Anglo-centric context, with the predominance of White-presenting young people with American accents. As young people's engagement with politics on social media manifests differently across race and ethnicity (Auxier, 2020), and the mentality of Gen Z also varies by region (Kim et al., 2020), findings from the current study should not be generalised to understand Gen Z cultures in other non-White and/or non-Anglo-centric contexts.

Results and discussion

Results of the content analyses of the sample videos are summarised in Table 2. In the following sections, these findings will be discussed in relation to the three research questions of this study.

Controversial issues

The first aim of this study is to identify key issues around which the intergenerational discordance between Gen Z and Boomer intensifies. Through content analysis, we identified the three most mentioned controversial issues: young people's lifestyles and well-being, Boomers' views on gender and sexuality norms and conservative politics.

Young people's lifestyles and well-being

The first controversial issue that was widely featured in #OkBoomer memes was young people's lifestyles and well-being. Among the videos analysed in this study, 40% of content conveyed Boomer's criticisms on the way Gen Z live and look. Videos covering this issue are often paired with titles like 'what are the most Boomer things that you have heard' or 'some of my most Ok Boomer moments'. Some frequently criticised aspects of Gen Z include their preferred fashion styles, their lack of motivation and their being too soft or sensitive. Regarding the first aspect mentioned, TikTokers share stories of how they are admonished by Boomers because of their ripped jeans, unnatural hair colour or for wearing too much makeup. Another recurring topic is the older generation lecturing Gen Z for spending too much time on the phone and not having a job. In such videos, adolescent appearing TikTokers reenact conversations in which their parents or grandparents lecture them about how hardworking they used to be, and that young people these days 'are too lazy to get a job'. In some cases, the 'Boomers' dismiss young people's professions, such as tattoo artists or e-sport players, as not being 'real jobs' (Figure 2).

The mental health and well-being of Gen Z is another memetic topic in the #OkBoomer stories shared on TikTok. Content surrounding these topics often mentions depression, anxiety and other mental health issues that commonly afflict members of Gen Z, and how 'Boomers'—in most cases their parents—are dismissive of such issues.

Figure 2. Example of a 'Boomer aunt' commenting on gaming as a job.
Source: @overtimegg (2019).

In these videos, Gen Z TikTokers reenact how their parents attribute their mental health problems to stereotypical causes such as 'spending too much time on the phone', 'not drinking enough water' or 'sleeping too little'.

Early adolescence is a period of vulnerability for the development of mental health issues (McLaughlin & King, 2015). Although the use and presence of social media can be a source of mental health strain for young people (Hendry, 2020), it can also be used to express their struggles with mental well-being. In our data, many adolescent-appearing TikTokers convey feelings of insufficient support from their parents or feelings of complete neglect. As one TikToker wrote, 'It is our cry for help, but they never listen'. Through the use of TikTok videos, these young people channel their dissatisfaction from subpar mental health conversations with their parents and guardians into short comedy clips to which many of their TikTok peers can relate. For example, across various comment sections, young people often respond to relatable TikTok memes by sharing experiences with their own parents (Figure 3).

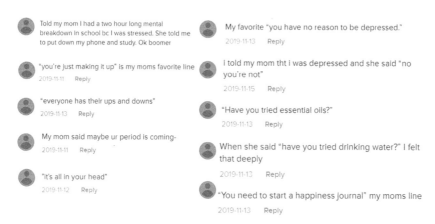

Figure 3. Examples of comments from TikTok users in response to 'depression' memes. User profile pictures and names have been omitted.

Gender and sexuality norms

Gender norms can be defined as expectations about the way males and females should behave, think and feel (Gilbert & Scher, 1999). In #OkBoomer memes, this topic appears in 10.3% of all coded videos within this study's corpus. Firstly, meme videos within this category challenge the gender-normative expectations of older generations about how 'boys' and 'girls' should appear and behave. As mentioned in the previous section, the fashion styles of young people are often commented upon by negatively the older generation, and such criticisms are closely linked to a larger generational disagreement about identity exploration and expression.

Along with ripped jeans and unnatural hair colours, a large number of Boomers' complaints regarding Gen Z's self-presentation are based on gender normative and binary views on 'what a girl or boy should look like'. For example, in videos featuring stories of Gen Z being 'dress-coded by a Boomer', some commonly found remarks from Boomers include hair being too 'short' for a 'girl', not 'sitting' like a 'lady' and looking too 'sporty' for a 'female'. However, such dress code condemnation was not exclusively made about 'girls'. Male-presenting Gen Z TikTokers also shared Boomer discourse on 'boys', and how they have experienced criticism for their long hair, and for wearing nail polish, jewellery and makeup (Figure 4).

Aside from boycotting Boomers' gender normative views on young people's appearances, young TikTokers also use the #OkBoomer trend to shed light on the older generation's conservative views on homosexuality and transgender issues. Review studies have identified the 'enduring significance' (Robards et al., 2018) of platforms and social media for queer young people to express their feelings, air grievances, and seek community. Unsurprisingly, this is similarly the case on TikTok where most videos on queer issues and topics are created by young TikTokers who self-identify as members of the LGBTQIA+ community. In these videos, young TikTokers reveal comments from their parents who deny, or even condemn, their sexual orientation and identity. These

Figure 4. Example of Gen Z being 'dress-coded' by a Boomer.
Source: @occultic (2019).

TikTokers recall experiences of being admonished by their parents for being 'too young to know' they are gay, that they are gay 'because of the internet', that being gay 'is a sin' or that they are simply 'going through a phase'. Transgender Gen Z TikTokers share frustrations that their identities are constantly being denied by others, including their parents. Although the vast majority of these videos are made to be humorous, they reveal a great sense of resignation. Through sharing and watching similar stories, these #OkBoomer video clips allow young TikTokers to commiserate with and console one another (Ask & Abidin, 2018).

Conservative politics

Approximately 20% of videos surveyed relate to the topic of conservative politics, which include comments about policies on immigration, abortion, gun rights and Donald Trump's election campaigns. However, the topic that generated the most intergenerational tension was climate policies and environmental conservation.

In most of the #OkBoomer memes that addressed environmental issues, the resentment expressed by Gen Z TikTokers highlighted the older generations' failures to respond to the climate crisis. Unlike conventional climate campaigns, Gen Z's climate activism is more than just environmental messaging, but also a fight against intergenerational injustice that 'catalysed public debate on what society owes to the young' (Thew et al., 2020, p. 1). For example, in @ditshap's (2020) clip, she acts out a dialogue with a judgemental 'Boomer' who comments on the holes in her jeans. However, she retorts by pointing out that Boomers are responsible for the 'holes in the ozone layer' (Figure 5).

In 2020, in the wake of the COVID-19 pandemic, the virus became another meme element in Gen Z's climate change jokes. In these videos, the pandemic was framed either as Earth's 'revenge' for the environmental damage caused by the Boomer generation or as a weapon for teenagers to 'punish' Boomers for long ignoring their requests for environment protection (Figure 6). In some clips, COVID-19 was even labelled as a 'Boomer remover'.

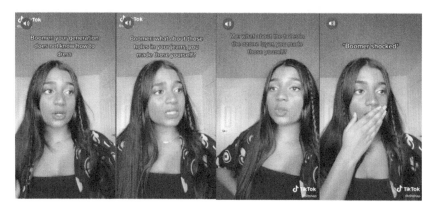

Figure 5. Example video of Gen Z commenting on Boomers' role in climate change.
Source: @ditshap (2020).

Figure 6. Example of TikToker joking about using COVID-19 to punish Boomers.
Source: @originalkontent (2020).

Meme forms

Having established the key controversial issues in #OkBoomer TikTok memes, the second objective of the study is to understand how these intergenerational tensions are memefied in short videos. As previously mentioned, the vernacular styles of videos on TikTok are shaped by both youth creativity and TikTok's platform affordances. Focusing on these aspects, this section assesses the meme forms in our corpus, comprising meme cues, reacts via duets and craft activism.

Lip-sync activism

Sound is a crucial element in the meme-making ecology of TikTok. Digital anthropologist Abidin has posited that sound is privileged over image on TikTok, serving as both a 'driving template' and 'organising principle' for content (2021, p. 80). In our corpus, lip-syncing was a prominent performance style across the #OkBoomer memes, and was featured in 36.3% of videos. The most widely used audio clip for lip-syncing is 20-year-old college student @peterkuli's (2019) remix 'Ok Boomer'. The sound clip is a two-minute-long rap that repeats the 'Ok Boomer' catchphrase throughout, while criticising Boomers for being condescending, being racist and supporting Trump.

After @peterkuli uploaded this audio clip to TikTok, it quickly went viral in October 2019, turning 'Ok Boomer' into a viral catchphrase on the platform (Noyes, 2019). In the most memetic format of this music's use, the song plays in the background as the creator acts out (with the help of text stickers) an anecdote involving a Boomer, with the punchline 'Ok Boomer' being timed to coincide with the performer's impression and lip-sync of angry yelling.

Inspired by the viral meme, more #OkBoomer-related original music was made by TikTokers and shared on the platform. This included @james.bee's (2019) version of 'OkBoomer', which was introduced at the beginning of this study. With its catchy lyrics, the audio meme was reused by thousands of TikTok content creators and inspired a series of meme sub-genres. One such niche is the 'Super Mario & Boomer' meme, wherein videos of Mario Kart characters riding over various obstacles are paired with a line from @james.bee's rap which goes, 'Back in my days we walked uphill both ways' (Figure 7). This line refers to the stereotype of Boomers dramatising and lording their hardships over younger generations who allegedly have it 'easy' these days.

Figure 7. Screenshots of game-streaming videos using @james.bee's OkBoomer music.
Source: @xdnube(2020), @somestupidvideos (2020), @scoopydoop43 (2020).

Although most of the original #OkBoomer-themed music uses rap to express grievance through dismissive rhetoric, some TikTokers take a softer-toned approach. For instance, 22-year-old comedic pianist @mrbeardofficial (2019) introduced his 'romantic' version of an #OkBoomer song, which included a twist of the #OkBoomer slogan, and was titled '*Boomer, I'm not ok*'. The TikToker introduced it as 'a Boomer love song', with lyrical lines like 'Ok Boomer, why can't you hold me as close as you hold your belief that climate change isn't real/ Ok Boomer, why can't you carry me like you carry your handgun in public/'. TikToker @mrbeardofficial's remix describes a love story in which Gen Z begs for love from Boomers, with the latter refusing to return their affections.

Audio memes are central to the affective expressions of Gen Z TikTokers' memetic storytelling. Epitomising the cohort's collective generational sentiments, #OkBoomer-themed songs are the ambient spirit with which TikTokers create their own personal narratives. Like @peterkuli's 'Ok Boomer', many of these short audio clips only include an excerpt from the chorus featuring the phrase 'Ok Boomer'. This form of audio clip provides great interpretive flexibility for other TikTokers to fill the narrative gap. As Abidin (2021, p. 80) points out, the 'templatability' of sound is central to viral trends on TikTok and is one of the app's most novel features. In the context of discursive activism on TikTok, such templatability enables users to have one united 'voice' to which they can creatively add their personal storyline and/or visual narrative. This synchronised yet personalised meme advocacy can be understood as 'lip-sync activism', which is not restricted to actual performances of lip-synchronisation but is extended as a metaphor to demonstrate the networked participation of users delivering a united message through individualised narration.

Reacts via duets

The 'duet' feature is one of the most popular features of TikTok, allowing users to 'react' or build on another clip by recording their own videos alongside the original as it plays (TikTok, 2020). This function has been widely and creatively applied to show TikTokers following tutorials (e.g., cooking receipt, experiments), to add to long chains of collaborative content (Abidin, 2021) and to react to meme content (Zeng et al., 2021). In the context of #OkBoomer memes, the duet feature was most often used by Gen Z to respond to Boomers' condemnations of young people.

In early 2019, TikTok user @old_school_is_not_so_bad posted a video in which he proudly self-identified as a 'Boomer'. In the post, he called out the young generations for 'having Peter Pan syndrome', for not wanting to 'grow up' and for 'wanting to create a utopian society in which everything is equal'. In response to his criticisms of the entire generation, Gen Z TikTokers used the duet feature to refute this narrative. In these duets, some TikTokers responded with their thoughts on the Boomer generation, while others pointed out why young people defy these stereotypes and still others simply replied with 'Ok Boomer' (Figure 8). While this may not be the first time that the #OkBoomer retort was first introduced on the internet, this video is widely considered to be one of the triggers of the viral #OkBoomer content on TikTok (Adem, 2020; Lorenz, 2019).

In a similar example, another older user (@irishmanalways) was so offended by the #OkBoomer trend that he posted a TikTok video that expressed his irritation with the use of expletives. At the end of the video, he implied that young people were addicted to technology by challenging them to go one week without the use of common technological devices and services, like cell phones and the internet. In response to the video, some younger TikTokers dueted the original video with clips of themselves taking up the challenge, while others dueted back by proposing new 'challenges' back to @irishmanalways. Witty but hard-hitting proposals included trying one week with 'no racism, no homophobia, no transphobia, no misogyny, no xenophobia' (Figure 9).

Craft activism

The third form of #OkBoomer memes examined in this study is that of craft activism, which involves TikTokers displaying the process of making 'Ok Boomer'-themed objects or pieces of art. The majority of these videos are devoted to the object's creation process and culminate in the unveiling of the 'Ok Boomer' tagline. Often, the true nature of the objects being created is not clear until the final unveiling. Examples of such craft-making include in-progress clips of 3D printing, embroidery and laser cutting (Figure 10).

TikTok is known as a platform where young people share their DIY (Do It Yourself) projects and demonstrate their creative processes (Zeng, 2020), so it is not surprising to see young users responding to the #OkBoomer meme trend with art and craft videos. Craft is often associated with imitation and recreation, which reflects the core elements of meme production. What makes crafting videos on TikTok interesting is their dual function as both the creators' own form of artistic expression and a tutorial for other

Figure 8. Examples of duets to @old_school_is_not_so_bad's video.

Figure 9. Examples of duets to @irishmanalways's TikTok.

Figure 10. Examples of 'Ok Boomer'-themed crafts.

users. Unlike comedic content on TikTok that reaches virality through relatable humour, viral crafting videos on TikTok require a nuanced balance between skill and relatability. Therefore, the majority of viral crafting videos on TikTok focus on inspiring others by demonstrating craftwork that can be imitated and recreated, rather than solely impressing them.

The prevalence of crafting videos also signifies the inclusiveness and diversity of participants in the #OkBoomer memetic trend. As the examples of crafting videos demonstrate, participants in a memetic campaign on the platform are not limited to TikTokers with performative talents like dancing, singing and acting, but the scope of content also accommodates artistic talents and handiwork.

Meme functions

In the previous two sections, we discussed the prominent controversial issues embodied in #OkBoomer videos and how Gen Z creatively memefied them. As the third objective of the study, we explored how these memes were used to convey generational sentiment, or these memes' communicative functions. In this final section, #OkBoomer memes' communicative functions that have emerged from the corpus are considered, with the three main functions being retort and criticism; self-defence and self-mocking; and merchandising and bandwagoning.

Retorts and criticism by Gen Z

Gen Z's use of #OkBoomer memes to rebut and criticise Boomers was evident in 70% of the videos sampled. In the analysis of this sample, descriptions of the perceived Boomer were annotated. 27% of videos were found to address the Boomer generation in general, while the majority of these rebuttals and criticisms targeted specific individuals in the lives of young TikTokers. In the coded sample data, 19% of videos featured young Tik-Tokers referring to a family member as a 'Boomer'. While grandparents were commonly featured, parents appeared twice as frequently in the sample. In 20% of the videos, Gen Z TikTokers categorised strangers that they encountered as 'Boomers', including customers they served at part-time jobs in various shops and eateries and strangers on public transport.

The ambiguity in young people's usage of #OkBoomer shows that they do not use 'age' as the qualifier to determine whether someone is a Boomer. A common refrain that was sighted was, 'It is not your age, it's how you act'. Gen Z TikTokers also qualified whether those they had encountered exuded a 'Boomer vibe', which was not exclusively applied to any specific generation but could apply to anyone of any age. From this study's content analysis, 'Boomer vibes' are detected when people appear to be patronising or express conservative viewpoints on socio-political issues. In other words, being a Boomer is not an age-specific phenomenon but rather a mindset. Furthermore, in the process of calling out 'Boomers', Gen Z TikTokers are simultaneously establishing their own shared identity. In creating and sharing memes of their own 'Boomer moments' or 'Boomer encounters', they are constantly and collectively perpetuating an image of what Boomers are and, in contrast, a vision of what Gen Z should be.

Self-defence and Self-deprecation by Boomers

The second function of #OkBoomer was to counteract young TikTokers' call-outs. Although content with this function only represents a small fraction of videos studied (11.3%), it demonstrates the less visible engagement of older users with the trend. Some popular videos from this category were made by TikTokers to share their experiences being 'Ok Boomered', and to respond in humorous ways. For instance, @tmdad14, a dentist who became famous on TikTok for his dancing videos, shared a video (@tmdad14, 2019) with his 2.2 million fans titled, 'Me realising "Ok Boomer" is actually an insult'. @Tmdad14 began the video by saying 'I am not 65, I am 45. Come on!', then responded with dance moves that he jokingly called 'Boomer Woah'. The 'Woah' is one of the most viral dance moves on TikTok and has also contributed to @tmdad14's TikTok fame. Most of his fans responded kindly by telling him that he passed 'the vibe check'.

As demonstrated by the example of @irishmanalways mentioned in the previous section (Figure 9), there were Boomer TikTokers who were offended by Gen Z's callouts. However, as observed in this data, most Boomer TikTokers' engagement with the #OkBoomer memes adopted a self-deprecating demeanour. On the one hand, some self-labelled Boomer TikTokers have taken the side of Gen Z and acknowledged the various things that the older generation could have done better. For instance, @monw0102 and @billyvsco are two parents who have actively engaged with the #OkBoomer trend. Unlike most young creators who created #OkBoomer memes that were meant to resonate with their fellow Gen Z TikTokers, the content of @monw0102 and @billyvsco mostly addressed parents on the platform. They share tips on how to not behave like a 'Boomer' in front of their children and offer advice to parents on how to be less controlling, to respect their children's private space and to foster better communication.

On the other hand, there are examples of Boomer TikTokers who try to showcase a different kind of 'Boomer' image to young users on the platform. Users within this group proudly adopt the label of 'Boomers' and often succeed in impressing young TikTokers with their energy and sense of humour (Figure 11). By performing some of Gen Z's favourite dance routines, these Boomer TikTokers are well received by the Gen Z community on the platform, with some young people even jokingly commenting that they would grant them a 'Gen Z pass' because they were 'cool'. Similar accounts of elderly influencers who capture the hearts of young audiences by participating in stereotypically youth-oriented internet trends and cultures have been noted on YouTube (Moon & Abidin, 2020).

Merchandising and bandwagoning by TikTokers and brands

As previously discussed, one popular form of participating in the #OkBoomer meme was through the creation of 'Ok Boomer'-themed objects. Some of these objects have been commercialised as merchandise. TikTokers that contributed to such content included independent craft entrepreneurs who participated in the meme by making #OkBoomer artefacts, and who then provided links to Etsy or other e-commerce websites where their followers could purchase such items.

However, a large number of #OkBoomer merchandise creators on TikTok have been 'incidental entrepreneurs' whose art, handiwork or designs became highly sought only after the TikTokers experienced 'accidental celebrity' through virality (Abidin, 2018). A prominent example is @calibronia's launch of the 'Zoomer Sweater'. In December 2019, @calibronia dueted @james.bee's *Ok Boomer* song with a design concept of a hoodie with a slogan inspired by his lyrics: 'Ok Boomer, time to meet the Zoomers' at the

Figure 11. Examples of Boomer TikTokers: @bearded_boomer, @gregrungetv and @tn_tonya.

Figure 12. Screenshots of @calibronia's duet to @james.bee and the product page of the Zoomer Hoodie.

back and 'Gen Z' at the front (Figure 12). The duet went viral with over 2 million views, with many TikTokers commenting that they wanted to purchase the hoodie. Fans of this design include the original music video creator @james.bee, who then gave @calibronia permission to sell the Zoomer sweater.

The overnight success of the Zoomer sweater was swiftly echoed in many craft videos featuring 'Ok Boomer' objects, which were subsequently mass produced to meet the demand from fans. Examples included keychains, T-shirts and stickers. Such merchandising marked a turning point for the 'Ok Boomer' trend, which rapidly evolved from being a subcultural TikTok meme to becoming a generational slogan emblazoned on commodities that young people could adorn to signpost their identity politics. While the mainstreaming of 'Ok Boomer' memes indicates the generational spirit of Gen Z, the rapid commodification also risks a dilution of the original political message, as 'Ok Boomer' merchandise is also adopted as a fashion accessory for virtue signalling. As is common in the lifecycle of internet memes and viral cultures, this eventual erosion of the 'Ok Boomer' meme's significance to Gen Z is also evidenced in the rapid decline of its popularity among internet users (see Figure 1 again), for whom the cooptation by corporations and opportunistic entities invoked their swift discarding of, and distancing away from, the catchphrase.

Furthermore, there were also more obvious commercially driven attempts to bandwagon on the #OkBoomer trend that further alienated the original intention of the meme. For instance, TikTok influencer Charli D'Amelio (@charlidamelio, 2020) participated in a commercial video for a food product which featured the #OkBoomer meme. As a teenage TikToker with the most followers on TikTok, (over 52 million followers at the time of writing), her #OkBoomer commercial video was the most watched (with over 22 million views) and most liked (over 2.9 million likes) video in our dataset. Such corporate brandjacking of what initially began as a young people's vernacular movement is a sad lament of how corporations co-opt socio-political sentiments and affiliations to generate profits.

Conclusion

This study has discussed the intergenerational politics between Gen Z and Boomers, specifically through the case study of #OkBoomer memes on TikTok. Both scholars and commentators have criticised the #OkBoomer trends on social media for expressing antagonistic stereotypes and discrimination against older people (Lorenz, 2019;

Meisner, 2020). However, this study has demonstrated that it is more productive to understand #OkBoomer as a consequence of intergenerational discord, rather than a cause. Informed by this study's findings, Gen Z's #OkBoomer rhetoric is complex and multifaceted.

Firstly, rather than an incendiary remark, #OkBoomer is often used by Gen Z as a response to antagonism from Boomers. As the analysis revealed, in most personal stories embedded in TikTok videos, this catchphrase is most often employed by Gen Z when they are attacked due to their lifestyle, dress code or sexuality. Like most people in their youth, members of Gen Z value their freedom of expression and identity exploration. From hair colour to partner preference, they are averse to the lecturing and judgment of older generations. In this context, the creation of #OkBoomer memes offers a counter-reaction. However, apart from indignation, there is also a sense of desperation. As demonstrated by TikTokers' sharing of their mental health struggles, after failing to get help from their own 'Boomer' parents, they engaged with the #OkBoomer meme to bitterly joke about their shared experiences.

While inter-family tension is widely featured in #OkBoomer memes on TikTok, the intergenerational disparities in political issues are highly visible. Gen Z uses #OkBoomer memes to lambast various conservative political views that are, rightly or wrongly, associated with the Boomer generation. Perceiving the climate crisis as an intergenerational injustice, Gen Z conveys their anger at Boomers, even though controversial jokes about COVID-19 being a 'Boomer remover'.

Furthermore, this study has also shed light on how the platform affordance impacts Gen Z's collective identification and self-representation. TikTok's technological features and platform logics shape not only the vernacular styles of Gen Z's memefied political messages, but also how they form alignment. As earlier iterated, this is most evident through the duet feature on TikTok, that allows users to react through direct callouts and replies to others. Moreover, by using audio memes, TikTokers engage with what we call 'lip-sync activism', a form of platform-enabled advocacy (especially in the case of lip-sync culture on TikTok) that displays a united voice but tells personal narratives.

To conclude, through examining Gen Z's own narrations about their everyday politics and identity politics on TikTok, this study has identified the generational sentiment that encapsulates a widespread attitude and belief shared by this cohort of young users. The intergenerational politics between Gen Z and Boomers are engaged by the former to construct and imagine their own generational consciousness around various social issues, such as the rise of populism and the existential threat of climate change. This study has provided an analytical framework that focuses on the vernacular communicative style of short videos, the specificities of TikTok's affordance, and the particular digital culture of young people, which we hope will be useful for future research to examine the social and political significance of TikTok videos across various (sub)cultures and trends.

Note

1. All cited TikTok videos are listed as multimedia references in Appendix 2.

Disclosure statement

No potential conflict of interest was reported by the author(s).

ORCID

Jing Zeng http://orcid.org/0000-0001-5970-7172

References

Abidin, C. (2018). *Internet celebrity: Understanding fame online*. Emerald Publishing.
Abidin, C. (2021). Mapping internet celebrity on TikTok: Exploring attention economies and visibility labours. *Cultural Science Journal*, *12*(1), https://doi.org/10.5334/csci.140
Abidin, C., & Zeng, J. (2020). Feeling Asian together: Coping with #COVIDRacism on subtle Asian traits. *Social Media + Society*, https://doi.org/10.1177/2056305120948223
Adem, I. (2020). How "OK Boomer" reignited a generational War. *Unaffiliated Press*. https://www.unaffiliatedpress.ca/article/2020/2/7/how-ok-boomer-reignited-a-generational-war
Ask, K., & Abidin, C. (2018). My life is a mess: Self-deprecating relatability and collective identities in the memification of student issues. *Information, Communication & Society*, *21*(6), 834–850. https://doi.org/10.1080/1369118X.2018.1437204
Auxier, B.. (2020). Activism on social media varies by race and ethnicity, age, political party. *Pew Research Center*. https://www.pewresearch.org/fact-tank/2020/07/13/activism-on-social-media-varies-by-race-and-ethnicity-age-political-party/
Bolin, G. (2017). *Media generations: Experience, identity and mediatised social change*. Routledge.
Braungart, R. G., & Braungart, M. M. (1986). Life-course and generational politics. *Annual Review of Sociology*, *12*(1), 205–231. https://doi.org/10.1146/annurev.so.12.080186.001225
Bristow, J. (2020). Post-Brexit Boomer blaming: The contradictions of generational grievance. *The Sociological Review*, *69*(4), 759–774. https://doi.org/10.1177/0038026119899882
Dimock, M. (2019). Defining generations: Where Millennials end and Generation Z begins. *Pew Research Center*. https://www.pewresearch.org/fact-tank/2019/01/17/whe re-millennials-end-and-generation-z-begins/
Fingerman, K. L., Pillemer, K. A., Silverstein, M., & Suitor, J. J. (2012). The baby boomers' intergenerational relationships. *The Gerontologist*, *52*(2), 199–209. https://doi.org/10.1093/geront/gnr139
Gerhardt, M. (2019). The 'OK, boomer' meme hurts Gen Z more than the older generation it's aimed at. *NBC News*. https://www.nbcnews.com/think/opinion/ok-boomer-meme-hurts-gen-z-more-older-generation-it-ncna1079276
Gilbert, L. A., & Scher, M. (1999). *Gender and sex in counselling and psychotherapy*. Allyn & Bacon.
Gonyea, J. G., & Hudson, R. B. (2020). In an era of deepening partisan divide, what is the meaning of age or generational differences in political values? *Public Policy & Aging Report*, *30*(2), 52–55. https://doi.org/10.1093/ppar/praa003
Hautea, S., Parks, P., Takahashi, B., & Zeng, J. (2021). Showing they care (Or don't): affective publics and ambivalent climate activism on TikTok. *Social Media + Society*, https://doi.org/10.1177/20563051211012344
Hendry, N. A. (2020). Young women's mental illness and (in-)visible social media practices of control and emotional recognition. *Social Media + Society*, https://doi.org/10.1177/2056305120963832

Highfield, T. (2016). *Social media and everyday politics*. Polity Press.

Highfield, T., & Leaver, T. (2016). Instagrammatics and digital methods: Studying visual social media, from selfies and GIFs to memes and emoji. *Communication Research and Practice*, 2(1), 47–62. https://doi.org/10.1080/22041451.2016.1155332

Humphreys, L. (2018). *The qualified self: Social media and the accounting of everyday life*. The MIT Press.

Kagwanja, P. M. (2006). 'Power to Uhuru': Youth identity and generational politics in Kenya's 2002 elections. *African Affairs*, 105(418), 51–75. https://doi.org/10.1093/afraf/adi067

Kaye, D. B. V., Chen, X., & Zeng, J. (2020). The co-evolution of two Chinese mobile short video apps: Parallel platformization of Douyin and TikTok. *Mobile Media & Communication*, https://doi.org/10.1177/2050157920952120

Kim, A. P., Smith, T. R., & McInerney, N. Y. (2020). *Gen Zers in the Asia–Pacific region aren't like their older siblings. Here is what you need to know*. https://www.mckinsey.com/business-functions/marketing-and-sales/our-insights/what-makes-asia-pacifics-generation-z-different#

Lim, Y. J. (2020). The PESTEL model application to Ok Boomer and TikTok from a public relations perspective. *Journal of Media Research [Revista de Studii Media]*, 13(37), 94–110. https://doi.org/10.24193/jmr.37.6

Lorenz, T. (2019). 'OK Boomer' marks the end of friendly generational relations. *The New York Times*. https://www.nytimes.com/2019/10/29/style/ok-boomer.html

MacDonald, S. (2020). What do you (really) meme? Pandemic memes as social political repositories. *Leisure Sciences*, https://doi.org/10.1080/01490400.2020.1773995

Mannheim, K. (1970). The problem of generations. *Psychoanalytic Review*, 57(3), 378–404. https://www-proquest-com.ezproxy.uzh.ch/scholarly-journals/problem-generations/docview/1310157020/se-2?accountid=14796

McLaughlin, K. A., & King, K. (2015). Developmental trajectories of anxiety and depression in early adolescence. *Journal of Abnormal Child Psychology*, 43(2), 311–323. https://doi.org/10.1007/s10802-014-9898-1

Meisner, B. A. (2020). Are you OK, Boomer? Intensification of ageism and intergenerational tensions on social media amid COVID-19. *Leisure Sciences*, 43(1), 143–151. . https://doi.org/10.1080/01490400.2020.1773983

Milan, S. (2015). From social movements to cloud protesting: The evolution of collective identity. *Information, Communication & Society*, 18(8), 887–900. https://doi.org/10.1080/1369118X.2015.1043135

Milner, R. M. (2016). *The world made meme: Public conversations and participatory media*. MIT Press.

Moon, J., & Abidin, C. (2020). Online ajumma: Self-presentations of contemporary elderly women via digital media in Korea. In K. Warfield, C. Abidin, & C. Cambre (Eds.), *Mediated interfaces: The body on social media* (pp. 177–189). Bloomsbury Academic.

Noyes, A. K. (2019). 'OK Boomer': Champlain College student behind remix of viral Gen Z comeback. *Vermont Public Radio*. https://www.vpr.org/post/ok-boomer-champlain-college-student-behind-remix-viral-gen-z-comeback#stream/0

Parker, K., Graf, N., & Igielnik, R. (2019). Generation Z looks a lot like Millennials on key social and political issues. *Pew Research Center*. https://www.pewsocialtrends.org/2019/01/17/generation-z-looks-a-lot-like-millennials-on-key-social-and-political-issues/

Purhonen, S. (2016). The modern meaning of the concept of generation. In I. Goodson, A. Antikainen, P. Sikes, & M. Andrews (Eds.), *The Routledge International Handbook on narrative and life history* (pp. 167–178). Routledge.

Rettberg, J. W. (2018). Self-representation in social media. In J. E. Burgess, A. Marwick, & T. Poell (Eds.), *The SAGE Handbook of social media* (pp. 429–443). SAGE.

Robards, B. J., Churchill, B., Vivienne, S., Hanckel, B., & Byron, P. (2018). Twenty years of 'cyberqueer': The enduring significance of the internet for young LGBTIQ+ people. In P. Aggleton, R. Cover, D. Leahy, D. Marshall, & M. L. Rasmussen (Eds.), *Youth, sexuality and sexual citizenship* (pp. 151–167). Routledge.

Roberts, M. (2019). OK, boomer. The kids are fighting back. *The Washington Post.* https://www.washingtonpost.com/opinions/ok-boomer-the-kids-are-fighting-back/2019/11/05/32894688-0011-11ea-9518-1e76abc088b6_story.html

Savic, M. (2021). From Musical.ly to TikTok: Social construction of 2020's most downloaded short-video App. *International Journal of Communication 15*(2021), 3173–3194. https://ijoc.org/index.php/ijoc/article/viewFile/14543/3495

Shaw, F. (2012). The politics of blogs: Theories of discursive activism online. *Media International Australia, 142*(1), 41–49. https://doi.org/10.1177/1329878X1214200106

Shaw, F. (2016). "Bitch I said Hi": The Bye Felipe campaign and discursive activism in mobile dating apps. *Social Media + Society.* https://doi.org/10.1177/2056305116672889

Shifman, L. (2013). Memes in a digital world: Reconciling with a conceptual troublemaker. *Journal of Computer-Mediated Communication, 18*(3), 362–377. https://doi.org/10.1111/jcc4.12013

Thew, H., Middlemiss, L., & Paavola, J. (2020). "Youth is not a political position": Exploring justice claims-making in the UN climate change negotiations. *Global Environmental Change, 61*(2020), 1–10. https://doi.org/10.1016/j.gloenvcha.2020.102036

TikTok. (2020). Trending on TikTok: Duet me. https://newsroom.tiktok.com/en-us/trending-on-tiktok-duet-me

Turner, J. C. (1975). Social comparison and social identity: Some prospects for intergroup behaviour. *European Journal of Social Psychology, 5*(1), 1–34. https://doi.org/10.1002/ejsp.2420050102

Vie, S. (2014). In defence of "slacktivism": The Human Rights Campaign Facebook logo as digital activism. *First Monday.* https://firstmonday.org/ojs/index.php/fm/article/download/4961/3868

White, J. (2013). Thinking generations. *The British Journal of Sociology, 64*(2), 216–247. https://doi.org/10.1111/1468-4446.12015

Zeng, J. (2020). #MeToo as connective action: A study of the anti-sexual violence and anti-sexual harassment campaign on Chinese social media in 2018. *Journalism Practice, 14*(2), 171–190. https://doi.org/10.1080/17512786.2019.1706622

Zeng, J., Schäfer, M. S., & Allgaier, J. (2021). Reposting "till Albert Einstein is TikTok famous": The memetic construction of science on TikTok. *International Journal of Communication 15*(2021), 3216–3247. https://ijoc.org/index.php/ijoc/article/view/14547

Appendices

Appendix 1

Table A1. Coding categories explained with examples.

	CODING DIMENSION ONE: CONTROVERSY ISSUES	
	Definition	Example
1. Gen Z Lifestyle & Well-being	Video featuring Boomers' remarks about Gen Z on the following issues	
1.1 Appearance	Boomer complaining on Gen Z's look, e.g., clothing choices makeup, hair colour	https://www.tiktok.com/@beanieboi7879/video/6760358233694686469?lang=en
1.2 Work	Boomer commenting about Gen Z being lazy, not wanting to have a 'real job'	https://www.tiktok.com/@overtimegg/video/6759629753226906885
1.3 Technology usage	Boomer complaining about Gen Z's relationship with technology, such as spending too much time on the phone	https://www.tiktok.com/@themermaidscale/video/6780969338632555778?lang=en
1.4 Mentality	Boomer commenting on Gen Z's mental health, or criticising them for being too sensitive or soft	https://www.tiktok.com/@mineandhers/video/6760772051193089285?lang=en
2. Conservative Politics	**Videos featuring Boomer's conservative political views**	
2.1 Climate policies	Boomers' view on climate policies	https://www.tiktok.com/@stale.catfood/video/6749557149745122566
2.1 Immigrants/Racial issues	Boomers' view on immigration issues, or on race and ethnicities	https://www.tiktok.com/@haleyrosefergiee/video/6779728321115606278

(Continued)

Table A1. Continued.

	CODING DIMENSION ONE: CONTROVERSY ISSUES	
	Definition	Example
2.3 Donald Trump	Boomers' role in electing Donald Trump to be the US President	https://www.tiktok.com/@sawyermcd/video/6840578128507686149
2.4 Abortion	Boomers view on the legality of abortion	https://www.tiktok.com/@thenillawafers/video/6823834073954340101
2.5 Other political topics	Other opinions expressing political conservatism, such as gun rights etc.	https://www.tiktok.com/@mrbeardofficial/video/6751475347390270726
3. Gender & Sexuality	Boomer's viewpoints on gender/sexuality/transgender/homosexual	https://www.tiktok.com/@guitarguygizmo/video/6778210026940026117?lang=en
4. Other issues	The issue presented in the video is not clear or not listed above	https://www.tiktok.com/@chicken.shake/video/6804188954183732486

CODING DIMENSION TWO: MEME FORMS		
5. Audio feature		
5.1 With sound template	Videos using a sound template from TikTok	https://www.tiktok.com/@elisamson/video/6759907561182432518
5.2 With original sound clip	Videos using the creator's own sound clip	https://www.tiktok.com/@wasildaoud/video/6766754038554938629
6. Visual feature		
6.1 Stickers	Videos with text stickers to add captions to the clip	https://www.tiktok.com/@lowlifemaya/video/6757539988918766853
6.2 Duet	Videos using the duet function to respond to another users' clip by adding a new screen next to the original screen	https://www.tiktok.com/@lexaprofag/video/6764681817497881861
6.3 Green Screen	Videos using the special effect on TikTok that allows users to set a background picture.	https://www.tiktok.com/@jnetmoore22/video/6784922262907800838
6.4 All other effects	Other video creation effects not listed above	
7. Performing features		
7.1 Lip-synching	Video using a background soundtrack to do lip synchronisation; the sound can be music or a dialogue	https://www.tiktok.com/@sophie.helton/video/6796027191248325894?lang=en
7.2 Acting skit	Creators performing a comedy skit or role-playing a conversation	https://www.tiktok.com/@raw.dawg.ryan/video/6749557149745122566
7.3 Dancing	Creators showing dance moves in the video	https://www.tiktok.com/@rusty.fawkes/video/6814375694739524870
7.4 Music sharing	The creator plays music or shares an original song from themselves	https://www.tiktok.com/@mandystroyer/video/6803485122294238469?lang=en
7.5 Craft in making	Video showing the process of making 'Ok Boomer'-related objects	https://www.tiktok.com/@arrizonagt/video/6758808625189260549
7.6 Other	Other video content style	

CODING DIMENSION THREE: MEME FUNCTION		
8. Gen Z retort	Videos serve to criticise boomer generation's behaviours or viewpoints; videos presenting Gen Z's respond to Boomer's judgemental remark on them	
8.1 Targeting Boomers in general	There is no specification; Ok Boomer is used to address the Boomer generation or older people in general	https://www.tiktok.com/@originalkontent/video/6807494385803070725?lang=en
8.2 Targeting parents	'Boomer' refers to either mother/father/both	https://www.tiktok.com/@elisamson/video/6759907561182432518
8.3 Targeting grandparents	'Boomer' refers to grandparents in the video	https://www.tiktok.com/@harleec55/video/6777793905426435333
8.4 Targeting other family members	'Boomer' refers to other family members such as uncle/auntie, or refers to 'family' in general	https://www.tiktok.com/@whyyyyler/video/6756351514865978630?is_copy_url=1&is_from_webapp=v2

(*Continued*)

Table A1. Continued.

	CODING DIMENSION THREE: MEME FUNCTION	
8.5 Targeting a stranger	A specific person the creator encountered, e.g., stranger, customer, neighbour	https://www.tiktok.com/@haleyrosefergiee/video/6779728321115606278
8.6 Other	Refers to other people, or when it is not clear	https://www.tiktok.com/@piper.scout/video/6777844118577024261
9. Boomers react	Videos featuring Boomers respond to Ok Boomer memes	
9.1 Complaining	Videos from Boomers who complain about being called 'Boomer'	https://www.tiktok.com/@24_hr_grandma/video/6779680224549342469
9.2 Self-mocking	Videos from Boomers who label themselves as Boomer in a joking or self-deprecating manner	https://www.tiktok.com/@heardeverything/video/6801287192070098181
10. Merchandising	Videos featuring an Ok Boomer-themed objects that is available to buy from the creator	https://www.tiktok.com/@missnoroooz/video/6767076738410269957?is_copy_url=1&is_from_webapp=v2
11. Informative Educational	Videos providing informative facts about the Boomer generation	https://www.tiktok.com/@jeeshthepeesh/video/6777509195605396742
12. Other	Videos- Function cannot be identified or cannot be placed under items listed above	

Appendix 2

Table A2. List of cited TikTok videos.

@bearded_boomer (2020, August 16). '#inverted #masterroshi #dragonball #dragonballz #dbz #kamehouse #turtlehermit #okboomer'. Available at https://www.tiktok.com/@bearded__boomer/video/6861612104126942469

@calibronia (2019, December 10). '#duet with @james.bee i was inspired … '. Available at https://www.tiktok.com/@calibronia/video/6768669881924685061

@charlidamelio. (2020, January 30). '#SuperBowlLIV? Ok, Boomer, see you there! … ' Available at https://www.tiktok.com/@charlidamelio/video/6787720248645684485

@ditshap (2020, July 18). 'COMBACKS'. Available at https://www.tiktok.com/@ditshap/video/6850588271311998213?is_copy_url=1&is_from_webapp=v1

@gregrungetv (2020, February 28). 'The kids in the bus were going nuts when I was leaving'. Available at https://www.tiktok.com/@gregrungetv/video/6798528401436216582

@james.bee (2019, December 18). 'It is now a sound you can USE!!!'. Available at https://www.tiktok.com/@james.bee/video/6767856644232629509?is_copy_url=1&is_from_webapp=v1

@mrbeardofficial (2019, December 13). 'Boomer, I'm not ok … '. Available at https://www.tiktok.com/@mrbeardofficial/video/6770034516816841990?lang=en

@occultic (2019, November 13). 'basically my life … '. Available at https://www.tiktok.com/@occultic/video/6758929445685415173

@originalkontent (2020, March 23), 'Based on a true story … ' Available at https://www.tiktok.com/@originalkontent/video/6807494385803070725?lang=en

@overtimegg (2019, November 20). '#whirlpool these BOOMERS … '. Available at https://www.tiktok.com/@overtimegg/video/6759629753226906885

@peterkuli (2019, October 31). 'thank you all keep fighting every boomer you see'. Available at https://www.tiktok.com/@peterkuli/video/6754074622305635590

@scoopydoop43 (2020, January 20). '#fyp #boomer #foryoupage #smb1 #tas'. Available at https://www.tiktok.com/@scoopydoop43/video/6783993690881903878

@somestupidvideos (2020, January 18). 'Im stuck in 800 followers … ..' Available at https://www.tiktok.com/@somestupidvideos/video/6783315323555695878

@tmdad14 (2019, November 11). 'Ok boomer' woah. Available at https://www.tiktok.com/@tmdad14/video/6754729234222042374

@tn_tonya (2020, March 5). 'When there's a new version … 'Available at https://www.tiktok.com/@tn_tonya/video/6800553841965223173

@xdnube(2020, January 19). 'He do be kinda speedy doe'. Available at https://www.tiktok.com/@xdnube/video/6783622702478445829

ə OPEN ACCESS

Memetic commemorations: remixing far-right values in digital spheres

Tommaso Trillò and Limor Shifman

ABSTRACT
This paper examines memetic content as a window into the values expressed by far-right constituents. Our main premise was that far-right memes are a site of interaction between two types of values: those of the far-right as a social movement and those characterizing memetic communication on social media. We studied this notion through a case from Italy: the photo-based meme genre of 'alternative calendar commemorations' that memorialize events or figures important to the far-right imaginary. A multi-modal qualitative analysis based on Schwartz's theory of personal and political values yielded mixed results. As expected, we found strong appeals to collectivistic values such as patriotism and tradition. Yet some of the individualistic values associated with memes, such as self-direction and authenticity, were also evident in the corpus. We conclude by discussing how this blend of values challenges both well-established value theories and perceptions about the political work of far-right memes.

Over the past decade, a vibrant popular and academic discourse has connected the success of far-right movements in various countries with their use of memes. Specifically, the literature highlights the role of memes in securing far-right electoral success (e.g., Heikkilä, 2017), mainstreaming white supremacist ideology under the cloak of 'politically incorrect' humor (Greene, 2019; Topinka, 2018), and cementing far-right camaraderie and outgroup antagonism (DeCook, 2018; Tuters & Hagen, 2020). In this study, we shift the focus from the political functions of memes to the ways in which members of the far-right use memes to express their values in digital spheres.

Our research is positioned in a growing corpus of literature that investigates the far-right as a social movement (Klandermans & Mayer, 2005; Caiani & Della Porta, 2018; Castelli Gattinara & Pirro, 2019). This perspective allows for a nuanced interpretation of the action repertoires adopted by far-right organizations to navigate complex socio-political opportunity structures. Values, broadly defined as beliefs about the desirable conduct of individuals and collectives (Schwartz, 1992), are an important component of such action repertoires and fundamental to the signifying

This is an Open Access article distributed under the terms of the Creative Commons Attribution-NonCommercial-NoDerivatives License (http://creativecommons.org/licenses/by-nc-nd/4.0/), which permits non-commercial re-use, distribution, and reproduction in any medium, provided the original work is properly cited, and is not altered, transformed, or built upon in any way.

work of any social movement (Benford & Snow, 2000). While we may not agree with or even deeply resent the values of the far-right, we cannot ignore the fact that group members consider such values to be guiding principles. In light of the systemic challenge that far-right movements represent for democracies across the globe, understanding which values are conveyed in their digital communication is a worthwhile endeavor.

The main premise of this study is that the values expressed by far-right constituents (as well as other ideological groups) are shaped by the techno-cultural environment in which they are articulated. As such, far-right memes may involve the negotiation between two potentially contrasting sets of values: those embraced by far-right constituents in specific national contexts and those intrinsic to digital memes as a trans-national communicative genre. Despite its fragmentation, the political family of the far-right typically shares a commitment to the values of authority, hierarchy, and order (Caiani et al., 2012). Such movements are also founded on the rejection of classical liberal values such as individualism, rationalism, pluralism, and egalitarianism. Although the study of the values embedded in memes is less established, Shifman (2019) has identified authenticity, creativity, communal loyalty, freedom of information, and expressive egalitarianism as core communicative values associated with memetic expression. These values apply to memes based on well-known templates such as stock character macros and rage comics, but also to other formats such as photo-based 'testimonial rallies' (Shifman, 2018) or 'cue card confessions' (Hall, 2016).

We examine this possible intersection between far-right and memetic values through a case study from Italy. Despite a strong anti-fascist legal framework, Italy has not been immune to the rising popularity of the far-right. A tech-savvy far-right movement has entered the political mainstream (Caiani & Parenti, 2013) and presents itself as a viable alternative to traditional political forces. Our study focuses on a photo-based meme genre identified in an exploratory analysis of common social media practices of far-right actors in Italy: 'alternative calendar commemorations' that memorialize events or figures important to the imaginary of the far-right. In contrast to more commonly explored memes of the far-right, alternative calendar commemorations are associated with mainstream social media sites rather than niche platforms, feature identifiable individuals rather than anonymized tropes, and use memory rather than humor as a cloak for nationalist propaganda.

In the first part of the paper, we review the literature on the political roles of far-right memes. We then discuss Shalom Schwartz's (1992) model of personal and political values as the primary theory guiding our analysis. Beyond its centrality in the field, Schwartz's model offers clear definitions and indicators for ten universally relevant values and maps the relationships among them. However, this theoretical clarity comes at the expense of flexibility. Thus, we also seek to critically engage with Schwartz's theory, pointing towards some of its shortcomings and suggesting avenues for future theoretical development. Thereafter, we introduce the case study of the Italian far-right and our methodological approach: a multi-modal analysis of 100 meme instances shared to Twitter or Instagram using Schwartz's model. The results section charts the mix of expected and somewhat surprising values that manifest in alternative calendar commemorations memes. Finally, we discuss the implications of this study for understanding the communication of values and the memetic activity of the far-right.

Literature review

Far-Right memes

In this paper, we use 'far-right' as an umbrella term for politically motivated actors that share a commitment to authoritarianism and reject the egalitarian premises of liberal democracy (Caiani et al., 2012). As this definition suggests, the galaxy of the far-right is wide and varied. It encompasses political parties as well as a complex network of extra-parliamentary actors such as grassroots movements, youth groups, and politicized football (soccer) fan clubs (Castelli Gattinara & Pirro, 2019). Historically relegated to an 'outsider-challenger' role, the far-right has recently expanded its ranks, entered the political mainstream, and stabilized its presence in most political systems across Europe and North America (Mudde, 2016).

The mainstreaming of the far-right has sparked a new wave of scholarly interest in its activities and a growing consensus that far-right actors should be studied as a social movement (Caiani & Della Porta, 2018). This approach conceptualizes the far-right as networked individuals deploying an array of tools to advance their political agendas. While contemporary far-right movements still rely on veteran forms of mobilization such as electoral campaigning, rallying, leafleting, or street violence (Castelli Gattinara & Pirro, 2019), the use of social media is one of the most prominent tactical innovations supporting their recent success (Caiani & Kröll, 2015).

Social media mobilization includes the deployment of memes for campaigning, propaganda, and recruitment. Shifman defines memes as groups of digital items that share common characteristics of content, form, and/or stance, created with awareness of each other, and circulated, imitated, and transformed by many users via the Internet (Shifman, 2013, p. 41). This definition positions memes as groups of texts characterized by variation alongside a shared 'core,' the unique features which tie together the units of a memetic group (Segev et. al., 2015). As such, memes do not adhere to any specific form. While the image-text combination known as 'image macro' has been widely acknowledged as a popular form of memetic expression (Milner, 2016), memes can assume many shapes and communicative stances.

Based on this understanding of memes, Marino (2015) has developed a semiotic model that locates all memetic formats on a continuum between minimal and maximal modes of user intervention. Image macros, for instance, allow for restricted levels of manipulation, while other memes are based on embodied and highly performative modes of imitation that allow for more varied interpretations. These include flash mobs, dance challenges, reaction videos, and photo fads. This lens has been applied to analyze a wide array of video- and photo-based memes. For example, Brantner et al. (2020) have analyzed the feminist photo-based meme #distractinglysexy where scientists across the globe responded to a sexist comment by a Nobel laureate about women in STEM by uploading photos of themselves wearing their lab gear.

The popularization of commercial social media platforms has turned memes into a fundamental component of mainstream digital cultures. Among other uses, memes are regularly adopted for political commentary (Milner, 2016; Rentschler & Thrift, 2015). Initially celebrated for their progressive potential, memes have proven to be a suitable conduit for a broad range of political messages including far-right propaganda and recruitment. Tuters (2017) traces the association between memes and the far-right to 'the deep vernacular web': a diverse set of autochthonous internet subcultures that resent 'mainstream' online culture and feel threatened by social media companies' gentrification of the internet. Members of the deep vernacular web also see the survival of their community as dependent on a culture war to preserve 'the true spirit of the internet' as a space of radical freedom through anonymity (Nagle, 2017). In this war, the individualistic 'face culture' of social media typified by the selfie conflicts with the 'mask culture' of the anonymous web typified by the meme (de Zeeuw & Tuters, 2020).

Memes perform a number of key functions for the far-right, including channeling a dispersed user-base towards far-right movements and fostering in-group belonging among constituents. In this latter sense, core far-right activists use memes to create 'social movement online communities' (Caren et al., 2012). However, the far-right's ability to accrue such a following depends on their ability to tap into the audience of commercial social media platforms. Several studies have explored this aspect of far-right activism (Zannettou et al., 2018; Hokka & Nelimarkka, 2020), with the US and Germany being the most widely investigated national contexts. Literature on the American far-right focuses on the construction of shared identity around coded cues known as 'dog whistles' (Bhat & Klein, 2020); photo-based memes depicting 'violence-gesturing content' such as individuals posing with guns or knives (DeCook, 2018); and novel hate symbols such as Pepe the frog (Hagen, 2018). In Germany, research shows that the far-right constructs a sense of shared identity through image macros offering political commentary (Guenther et al., 2020), the online sale of 'fashionable' consumer goods featuring fascist symbols (Miller-Idriss, 2018), and the production of memetic visuals that use popular social media aesthetics (e.g., 1980s vaporwave style) to modernize Nazi iconography (Bogerts & Fielitz, 2019). Studies beyond these two countries are sparse (e.g., Siapera & Veikou, 2016; Hokka & Nelimarkka, 2020; Klein, 2020; McSwiney et al., 2021) but useful in demonstrating how the far-right uses memetic content as a form of cultural capital and builds community around a system of shared symbols and templates (Nissenbaum & Shifman, 2017).

The far-right also uses memes to construct different strawmen as the designated enemies of the movement. These include new targets such as 'politically correct' culture (Topinka, 2018) and 'social justice warriors' (Massanari & Chess, 2018), alongside veteran marks such as 'the Jewish conspiracy' (Finkelstein et al., 2019). These strawmen collectively construct a vaguely defined 'other' against which the far-right mobilizes. Tuters and Hagen (2020) see this strategic ambiguity as instrumental to a process that they term 'memetic antagonism.' Using memes to define their enemies in nebulous terms, far-right activists of all brands can set aside the rules of constructive political debate and coalesce around violently antagonistic narratives (Mouffe, 2013).

The overall framework in which the far-right embraces the 'mask culture' of the meme, constructs ingroup loyalty through shared subcultural knowledge of obscure templates, mobilizes against a set of nebulous others, and uses humor as a cloak to hide hate speech is extremely useful for understanding a large portion of far-right memes. However, in this study, we wish to explore a type of far-right memetic activity that goes beyond the framework outlined above. We propose alternative calendar commemorations, which feature identifiable individuals and adopt a serious stance, as an illuminating case study. Such commemorations adhere to the general logic governing memes; namely, a group of texts with shared characteristics of content, form, and stance created with awareness of each other. Like other photo-based memes, alternative calendar commemorations also function as 'operative signs' (Shifman, 2014) – recognizable codes that invite others to participate by producing their own iteration of the meme.

By sharing self-portraits from historical locations or portraits of admired figures, members of the far-right participate in a process that we define as 'memetic commemoration.' This ritual is a form of connective memory (Hoskins, 2011) that allows far-right constituents to 'create, articulate, and negotiate their shared memories of particular events' (Fridman, 2015, p. 214). While commemorating the past glory of the nation and its heroes has long been a feature of far-right rhetoric (Falasca-Zamponi, 1997), memetic commemorations add a subversive and activist element to this narrative. In a crowd-sourced process of memory construction, far-right constituents celebrate the revisionist version of history promoted by the movement while also adding a personal touch to the narrative by, for example, including their body in the photograph or adding a personal anecdote in the caption (Zhukova, 2020). Thus, we see these memes as a form of memory activism (Kubal & Becerra, 2014) where far-right constituents directly participate in reassessing ambiguous figures or events that are central to the identity of the movement (Couperus & Tortola, 2019). Posted to mark noteworthy days of the year (anniversaries of key battles, incidents, births, deaths, etc.), such memes collectively produce an 'alternative calendar' (Fridman, 2015) of far-right commemorations that stand in contraposition to mainstream understandings of what ought to be memorialized. Memetic commemorations could therefore be considered as one of the tools through which the far-right attempts to expand their mainstream appeal by re-framing the memory of controversial figures and events in the history of the nation.

Basic human values, political values, and the values of the far-right

Broadly defined, values are guiding beliefs about the desirable related to people's perceptions of how they should conduct their lives (see Hofstede, 2003; Inglehart, 1971). While the study of values encompasses several key theorists, in this paper we primarily draw upon Shalom Schwartz's (1992) foundational model of basic human values. Validated through a series of empirical studies (for an overview, see Schwartz, 2012), the model features ten core values common to many societies: universalism, benevolence, tradition, conformity, security, power, achievement, hedonism, stimulation, and self-direction. The model also features distinct relationships between values, where some conflict (e.g., seeking personal power is negatively associated with benevolence) and others are compatible (e.g., individuals who value conformity also value security).

Schwartz and his collaborators have also investigated the relevance of basic values for interpreting political behavior (Schwartz et al., 2010). Drawing on the hypothesis that political values are the expression of basic personal values in the political domain, they developed a list of eight core political values: traditional morality, blind patriotism, law and order, free enterprise, equality, civil liberties, foreign military intervention, and accepting immigrants. In a series of empirical studies, researchers have found that basic values inform political behaviors, with voting patterns being the most prominent example (Vecchione et al., 2013).

In parallel to the Schwartzian tradition of value research, researchers have drawn on a broad theoretical repertoire to identify a distinctive set of values associated with the far-right. Caiani et al. (2012) identify hierarchy and order, a state-centered economy, and authority as defining commitments. In their view, the far-right is also characterized by ideologies of inequality that justify political violence such as racism, sexism, homophobia, and totalitarianism. Using the lens of populism, Mudde and Rovira Kaltwasser (2018) argue that the far-right combines a nativist discourse that takes pride in one's own national culture and tradition with aggressively xenophobic narratives that reject all non-conforming groups. This might entail, for example, celebrating the extraordinary life achievements of in-group members as proof of national superiority. Finally, far-right movements reject many of the values associated with modernity (e.g., individualism, rationalism, pluralism, and egalitarianism), especially as embedded in the procedures and institutions of liberal democracy (Caiani et al., 2012).

Examining this characterization of the far-right in light of Schwartz's value theory, we argue that the core political values of far-right movements are law and order, blind patriotism, and traditional morality, accompanied by a rejection of the values of equality, civil liberties, and accepting immigrants. In turn, these political values are an expression of the basic human values of tradition/conformity, security, and power, paired with a rejection of universalism and self-direction.

While Schwartz and his colleagues make an important contribution to the study of political values, they do not engage with the ways in which values are constructed in everyday communication. Focusing on alternative calendar commemoration memes, we seek to test the applicability of Schwartz's model to the analysis of values in digital content. In particular, we wish to examine whether the theory of contrasting values holds when the method of inquiry is not a survey but an analysis of real-life content posted by individuals. As noted above, we assume that values in such spheres are multi-layered due to the various contexts in which they are produced; in our case, both the context of the far-right and that of memetic expression.

The communicative values of Internet memes

While memes have been widely studied as forms of political expression, the ways in which they contribute to the social construction of values has not yet been systematically considered. Following Shifman (2019), we argue that memes articulate values through a dual process that takes place at the level of content and communicative stance. Simply put, values do not only reside in what is said, but also in how it is said, by whom, and to whom. As such, memes convey values about the external world and the process of communication itself.

The content of memes may communicate sharply divergent values. For example, the emancipatory values of the aforementioned feminist photos posted with the hashtag #distractinglysexy (Brantner et al., 2020) could not be further from the anti-Semitic connotations that Pepe the frog acquired over time (Hagen, 2018). Somewhat surprisingly, however, these differences tend to diminish when we look at memes in terms of their communicative values, or stance (Shifman, 2019). Drawing on several key works in the field

(Douglas, 2014; Milner, 2016; Miltner, 2014), Shifman articulated a list of five core communicative values characteristic to memes: authenticity, creativity, communal loyalty (i.e., demonstration of affiliation to online communities), freedom of information, and expressive egalitarianism (i.e., the notion that self-expression by memes is a basic imperative). Of these five, authenticity and creativity seem to be most at odds with existing literature on far-right values. In contrast, communal loyalty, freedom of information, and freedom of expression have previously been associated with the far-right (Titley, 2020).

Authenticity is perhaps the most pivotal memetic value as it pertains not only to expression via memes but also to broader patterns of communication in digital spheres (Senft & Baym, 2015). This value relates to the correspondence between utterances and an external truth that can be scientifically observed (also referred to as 'external authenticity') and also to the connection between a statement and the internal essence of the individual speaking it – their emotions, experiences, and core values (also referred to as 'internal authenticity' in Shifman, 2018). As such, authenticity is closely related to the individualistic value of self-direction defined by Schwartz, yet emphasizes its mode of expression.

In what follows, we build on these notions to look into the construction of values in the memes of the Italian far-right, addressing the following research question: what values are explicitly and implicitly conveyed in alternative calendar commemoration memes? While we anticipate that such memes will convey the collectivistic values of the far-right, we also expect they will introduce some elements of individualism, thus troubling the dichotomy between the two as charted in Schwartz's work.

Sites and modes of analysis

The context

In the Italian setting, the far-right enjoys broad institutional recognition. Far-right parties have long enjoyed mainstream visibility and served as a reliable government ally to most center-right coalitions since 1994 (Caldiron, 2001, p. 15). Following the General elections in 2018, Matteo Salvini's *Lega* ('The League') became the second-largest force in parliament (Albertazzi et al, 2018), and joined two of the three coalitions governing the country since then. More recently, Giorgia Meloni's *Fratelli d'Italia* ('Brothers of Italy') has experienced unprecedented success. Both parties have overtaken their moderate allies in terms of popularity (Bruno & Downes, 2020).

Direct access to the public via social media platforms is often listed as one of the factors supporting Salvini's and Meloni's rise to popularity and the mainstreaming of far-right populism in parliamentary politics (Cepernich & Bracciale, 2018). Furthermore, social media have facilitated the creation of transnational alliances between the Italian far-right and far-right movements from abroad, resulting in a shared set of tropes and a partial internationalization of its audience (Caiani & Kröll, 2015; Froio & Ganesh, 2019). Before the advent of commercial social media, however, the Italian far-right already used the affordances of Web 1.0 such as websites and forums to circulate tropes, expand its ranks, and create a closely-knit network of grassroots organizations (Padovani, 2008; Caiani & Parenti, 2013). To this day, the most prominent actors in the Italian far-right make parallel use of social media to expand their reach and cement collective

Figure 2. Examples from each of the ten "memetic commemorations."

uncreative form that features a narrow set of cue-words such as honor (e.g., honoring those who died for the fatherland), duty (e.g., remembering them as one of the duties of a far-right constituent) and nativist pride (e.g., taking pride in having ancestors imagined as honorable). A particularly poignant example comes from an Instagram post commemorating the National Memorial Day of the Exiles and Foibe (*Giornata del Ricordo*), instituted as a national day to keep the memory of the Italians persecuted in the borderlands contested with Yugoslavia in 1943-47:

> The tri-color [flag] decorated for mourning, to remember the dramatic events of the foibe, and the Istrian-Dalmatian exodus. We let our history guide us.

In this example, the author-protagonist makes multiple references to the imagined 'us' of the Italian nation. We interpret these as expressions of belonging that embed an orientation towards the Schwartzian value of 'security.' The post also voices an orientation towards conformity insofar as it refers to a duty to remember those who died for the fatherland.

For the inspirational figures subgenre, the textual component was more mixed. These posts overwhelmingly feature a strong commitment to security via nationalism and conformity through tribute to the forebearers of the movement. However, these values appear alongside a general fascination with the commemorated individuals' willingness to live an exceptional life. For example, one of the posts published on the anniversary of the death of Primo Carnera, the first Italian to become world heavyweight boxing champion, states:

> Life slips away, but you changed your fate, from Italy to New York City, females courting you as you redeemed yourself from the shadows, for the whole nation, because you were able to hit harder than anyone and become the champion!!!

Like other posts in our sample, this example clearly invokes the nation and, therefore, the value of security. In addition, it celebrates Carnera's heterosexual appeal with a sexist choice of words, thus expressing one of the ideologies of inequality that characterizes the far-right. However, the post also voices a fascination with Primo Carnera's willingness to change his fate by acting upon internal wishes. This is evident through reference to his exceptional boxing skills and history of personal redemption through emigration. This tweet serves as an example of how the inspirational figures subgenre combines an orientation towards traditionally far-right values of conformity and security with the celebration of individualistic values such as achievement and self-expression. The general tone of the subgenre is undoubtedly one of commemoration. However, it also celebrates the lives of mentor figures who are imagined as overcoming hardship in order to live and express their truth. In our view, this part of the narrative reads as a celebration of internal authenticity that Shifman (2018) identifies as central to memes. By celebrating heroes who stood out because they dared to express their true 'authentic' self, the constituent of the far-right indirectly endorses authenticity as one of their values.

The values in the captions are both confirmed and problematized when examining the interplay between the text and the visual material. As pointed out above, the commemorating constituents subgenre features a member of the far-right holding, looking at, or standing next to an object connected to the commemorated event. The presence of the user in the space of the representation is crucial. While these users could have just posted a photo of the monument itself, they chose to locate themselves within the frame. Furthermore, the protagonist and the object usually occupy the same amount of space in the representation, suggesting a balance between self-expression and the collectivist values represented by the object.

With their embodied presence, users mark the photo as authentic in two ways. In terms of external authenticity, the image serves as evidence of the physical appearance of the protagonist at a commemorative site. Perhaps more importantly, however, the pictures convey internal authenticity: the users present themselves as individuals 'speaking their truth' and making their deeply held values materially visible by standing next to objects that recall them. Thus, while the captions of this subgenre overwhelmingly lean towards far-right values such as conformity and security, the visual component stresses the value the authentic self-expression typical of memes.

The visual component of the inspirational figures subgenre encapsulates the same duality between individualistic and collectivistic values found in the captions, as well as a general orientation towards the memetic value of authenticity. Foregrounded as the solo protagonists of a close-shot, the mentors and martyrs of the far-right are singled out as role models worthy of commemoration (conformity, tradition) because of their willingness to live their truth and realize their full potential (achievement, self-direction). Arguably, however, the most interesting feature of such pictures is the ubiquitous use of monochromatic toning (black and white or sepia palettes). While some of the figures lived after the invention of color photography, almost all the pictures in our sample were black and white or sepia. Even the pictures that were taken before the invention of color photography are often filtered to exaggerate the original monochromatic tones. In our view, the use of these filters constructs the heroes of the far-right as 'historical' figures worthy of consideration as 'authentic' role models. As such, monochromatic toning imbues these figures with an aura of external authenticity that supports the celebration of internal authenticity expressed in the captions.

Overall, alternative calendar commemoration memes combine a focus on collectivistic values with an individualistic orientation. This combination is also evident in the framework of the memetic commemoration itself: far-right constituents perform their reactionary values mostly individually, yet the shared ritual brings them together. The general tone of the commemorations is rather solemn, with sober and standardized visual and verbal patterns followed by every user participating in the meme without significant expressions of creativity. Finally, although we detected undertones pointing to vaguely defined 'enemies' that echo Tuters and Hagen's (2020) notion of 'nebulous othering,' we found that the genre primarily focuses on in-group construction and nativist pride rather than out-group antagonism.

Concluding remarks

This paper offers a foray into the values of far-right social media content through an inspection of a photo-based meme genre prominent in Italy. Our analysis of the values voiced in the *captions* of the sampled posts points to an overall orientation towards conformity and security, which is unsurprising in light of the literature on the far-right. We also found somewhat expected references to stimulation. Far-right adherents chose 'defiant' individuals who embraced the reactionary values of the movement as heroes and mentor figures, looking up to them and vicariously taking pride in their achievements as members of the same ingroup. These findings suggest that alternative calendar commemoration memes convey some of the core political values of the far-right.

Yet the *visual display* of the memes tells a much more interesting story in terms of values. Here, we can see how the logics of communication governing memes more generally are infused into far-right commemoration memes. The mandate for authenticity intrinsic to memetic communication is strongly associated with notions of self-expression, as meme creators are expected to expose their 'true' inner self. In the case of the commemorating constituents subgenre, this idea materializes when the user posting the meme literally enters the space of representation as the protagonist, regardless of their position in the ranks of the far-right. The authentic self is also pivotal in the construction of the inspirational figures subgenre, in which far-right constituents endorse the value of internal authenticity by expressing admiration for mentor figures who 'dared' to live according to their personal truths, sometimes at great cost.

While we acknowledge that the specificity of our case and sample size does not allow for broad generalizations, we wish to highlight three contributions derived from our findings. First, we discuss how commemoration may act as a shield to protect far-right discourse from criticism and contribute to its mainstreaming. Second, taking a broader theoretical angle, we demonstrate how our study challenges the applicability of established value theories to the analysis of digital spheres, charting a path for new ways of investigating value expression. Thirdly, we emphasize that a full account of the work performed by political memes should take into consideration the key values of specific social media platforms.

Our first observation is that alternative calendar commemorations are a form of memory activism (Hoskins, 2011; Kubal & Becerra, 2014) that exploits the respectable façade of commemorations as a cover for hyper-nationalist re-readings of historical events, symbolic places, and key figures. This façade provides a shield from condemnation comparable to that offered by humor. The inherent polysemy of online humor (Phillips & Milner, 2018) has proven effective in shielding far-right content from criticism (Topinka,

2018), facilitating its circulation on mainstream platforms. We suggest that the aura of respectability inherent to commemorations might do similar work through different means. While the object of commemoration might be controversial, the visual tropes featured in these memes – the national flags, monuments and black and white photography – resemble those used in mainstream national ceremonies. Thus, the social norms demanding respect in the context of commemorations (e.g., respect the flag, don't speak ill of the dead) shield users participating in the alternative calendar commemorations of the far-right, so much so that the meme easily fits within the 'face culture' of commercial social media and individual constituents can proudly participate with their own embodied presence.

Second, and more broadly, our findings suggest that memes can, and at times do, convey allegedly conflicting values. Schwartz's (1992) model posits that so-called individualistic and collectivistic values tend to be incompatible. However, our findings show that supposedly contrasting values such as 'tradition' and 'stimulation' actually coexist in the memetic commemorations of the Italian far-right. This complexity may stem from our conceptualization of values. While veteran studies adopted a deductive approach and examined *perceptions* of values (Inglehart, 1971; Schwartz, 1992; Hofstede, 2003), we focused on verbal and visual *expressions* of values. Questionnaire-based studies are designed to capture people's internal value systems but cannot do justice to the complex entanglements that emerge when individuals communicate their values in everyday mediated interactions. In addition, while these veteran theories tend to decontextualize values, our analysis demonstrates the importance of context in shaping them. Thus, our study both problematizes the distinctions promoted by existing value theories and exposes the need for a more nuanced theory capable of mapping values in action.

Finally, our findings show that the pivotal social media value of authenticity interacts with and even shapes how social movements communicate their deeply rooted ideologies. This amounts to saying that general values promoted in social media settings influence the ways in which constituents appropriate, re-work, and express their political values. Memes are not empty vessels through which far-right tropes propagate beyond the boundaries of the movement. Rather, they are sites where the values of the far-right as a movement and values intrinsic to communication in digital spheres meet and influence each other. Our work thus highlights the potential of investigating political memes not only in the context of social movements' ideologies, but also in relation to the values associated with communicative genres (Kumar, 2021; Shifman, 2016) and the values embedded in the design and culture associated with social media platforms (Hallinan et al., 2021).

We hope that follow-up research on photo-based meme genres of the far-right, as well as other social movements, will address some of the limitations of this case study-based paper. One possible research trajectory is to systematically map far-right photo-based meme genres in mainstream social media platforms across countries, in order to expand on our findings regarding the manifestation of 'face culture' in far-right memes. A second proposal is to expand the focus beyond the far-right to explore photo-based memes of other social movements. Researchers could fruitfully explore the interplay of the intrinsic values of memes as a communicative genre with different sets of political values, such as the universalism of the environmentalist movement. Finally, studies that focus on reception (through interviews, for example) would lead to a deeper understanding of how photo-based memes such as alternative calendar commemorations are perceived by potential audiences.

Such follow-up studies will hopefully build on the conceptual and methodological paths charted in this paper to further explore the values articulated in popular meme genres in general, and far-right meme genres in particular. A tentative conclusion of this study is that the blurred line between the two may increase the appeal of the far-right (and its values) for mainstream audiences. While inside jokes may be a powerful tool to consolidate a community, they also exclude those who are not in the know. The simple act of commemorating an individual alongside national symbols is much more accessible to the general public. The familiarity of the formats (a person featured in a place they care about) and the broad appeal of the 'authentic self' on mainstream social media may provide a form of far-right messaging that is more palatable to outsiders. In this sense, photo-based far-right memes circulating on commercial social media may contribute to rebranding and popularizing the far-right in the twenty-first century.

Acknowledgement

We are indebted to the two anonymous reviewers, special issue editors Mette Mortensen and Christina Neumayer, as well as to Blake Hallinan and Ofra Klein for their useful and insightful comments. We also thank Anna Balestrieri for her meticulous coding of the content surveyed in this study.

Disclosure statement

No potential conflict of interest was reported by the author(s).

Funding

This project has received funding from the European Research Council (ERC) under the European Union's Horizon 2020 research and innovation programme [grant agreement No 819004].

ORCID

Tommaso Trillò http://orcid.org/0000-0003-2830-528X
Limor Shifman http://orcid.org/0000-0002-2616-9491

References

Albertazzi, D., Giovannini, A., & Seddone, A. (2018). 'No regionalism please, we are Leghisti!' The transformation of the Italian Lega Nord under the leadership of Matteo Salvini. *Regional and Federal Studies*, *28*(5), 645–671. https://doi.org/10.1080/13597566.2018.1512977

Benford, R. D., & Snow, D. A. (2000). Framing processes and social movements: An overview and assessment. *Annual Review of Sociology*, *26*(1), 611–639. https://www.jstor.org/stable/223459 https://doi.org/10.1146/annurev.soc.26.1.611

Bhat, P., & Klein, O. (2020). Covert hate speech: White nationalists and dog whistle communication on twitter. In J. E. Rosenbaum, & G. Bouvier (Eds.), *Twitter, the public sphere, and the chaos of online deliberation* (pp. 151–172). Springer.

Bogerts, L., & Fielitz, M. (2019). 'Do you want meme war?': Understanding the visual memes of the German far-right. In M. Fielitz, & N. Thurston (Eds.), *Post-digital cultures of the far-right* (pp. 137–154). Transcript.

Brantner, C., Lobinger, K., & Stehling, M. (2020). Memes against sexism? A multi-method analysis of the feminist protest hashtag #distractinglysexy and its resonance in the mainstream news media. *Convergence: The International Journal of Research Into New Media Technologies*, *26*(3), 674–696. https://doi.org/10.1177/1354856519827804

Bruno, V. A., & Downes, J. F. (2020, February 27). The case of Fratelli d'Italia: How radical-right populists in Italy and beyond are building global networks. *Democratic Audit*. https://www.democraticaudit.com/2020/02/27/the-case-of-fratelli-ditalia-how-radical-right-populists-in-italy-and-beyond-are-building-global-networks/

Caiani, M., & Della Porta, D. (2018). The radical right as social movement organizations. In J. Rydgren (Ed.), *The Oxford handbook of the radical right* (pp. 52–80). Oxford University Press.

Caiani, M., Della Porta, D., & Wagemann, C. (2012). *Mobilizing on the extreme right: Germany, Italy, and the United States*. Oxford University Press.

Caiani, M., & Kröll, P. (2015). The transnationalization of the extreme right and the use of the internet. *International Journal of Comparative and Applied Criminal Justice*, *39*(4), 331–351. https://doi.org/10.1080/01924036.2014.973050

Caiani, M., & Parenti, L. (2013). *European and American extreme right groups and the internet*. Routledge.

Caldiron, G. (2001). *La destra plurale: Dalla preferenza nazionale alla tolleranza zero [The plural right: From national preference to zero tolerance]*. Manifestolibri.

Caren, N., Jowers, K., & Gaby, S. (2012). A social movement online community: Stormfront and the white nationalist movement. In J. Earl, & D. A. Rohlinger (Eds.), *Media, movements, and political change* (pp. 163–194). Emerald Bingley.

Castelli Gattinara, P. (2017). The 'refugee crisis' in Italy as a crisis of legitimacy. *Contemporary Italian Politics*, *9*(3), 318–331. https://doi.org/10.1080/23248823.2017.1388639

Castelli Gattinara, P., & Bouron, S. (2020). Extreme-right communication in Italy and France: Political culture and media practices in CasaPound Italia and Les identitaires. *Information, Communication & Society*, *23*(12), 1805–1819. https://doi.org/10.1080/1369118X.2019.1631370

Castelli Gattinara, P., & Pirro, A. L. P. (2019). The far right as social movement. *European Societies*, *21*(4), 447–462. https://doi.org/10.1080/14616696.2018.1494301

Cepernich, C., & Bracciale, R. (2018). Hybrid 2018 campaigning: The social media habits of Italian political leaders and parties. *Italian Political Science*, *13*(1), 36–50. http://hdl.handle.net/11568/924550

Couperus, S., & Tortola, P. D. (2019). El (ab)uso del populismo de derechas del pasado en Italia y en los países bajos [The (ab)use of the past by right-wing populism in Italy and the nethelands]. *Debats. Revista de Cultura, Poder i Societat*, *133*(2), 11–25. https://doi.org/10.28939/iam.debats.133-2.2

DeCook, J. R. (2018). Memes and symbolic violence: #proudboys and the use of memes for propaganda and the construction of collective identity. *Learning, Media and Technology*, *43*(4), 485–504. https://doi.org/10.1080/17439884.2018.1544149

de Zeeuw, D., & Tuters, M. (2020). Teh internet is serious business. *Cultural Politics*, *16*(2), 214–232. https://doi.org/10.1215/17432197-8233406

Douglas, N. (2014). It's supposed to look like shit: The internet ugly aesthetic. *Journal of Visual Culture*, *13*(3), 314–339. https://doi.org/10.1177/1470412914544516

Falasca-Zamponi, S. (1997). *Fascist spectacle: The aesthetics of power in mussolini's Italy*. University of California Press.

Finkelstein, J., Zannettou, S., Bradlyn, B., & Blackburn, J. (2019). A quantitative approach to understanding online antisemitism. *Proceedings of the International AAAI Conference on Web and Social Media*, *14*(1), 786–797. http://arxiv.org/abs/1809.01644

Fridman, O. (2015). Alternative calendars and memory work in Serbia: Anti-war activism after milošević. *Memory Studies*, *8*(2), 212–226. https://doi.org/10.1177/1750698014558661

Froio, C., & Ganesh, B. (2019). The transnationalisation of far right discourse on twitter: Issues and actors that cross borders in western European democracies. *European Societies*, *21*(4), 513–539. https://doi.org/10.1080/14616696.2018.1494295

Greene, V. S. (2019). 'Deplorable' satire: Alt-right memes, white genocide tweets, and redpilling normies. *Studies in American Humor*, *5*(1), 31–69. https://doi.org/10.5325/studamerhumor.5.1.0031

Guenther, L., Ruhrmann, G., Bischoff, J., Penzel, T., & Weber, A. (2020). Strategic framing and social media engagement: Analyzing memes posted by the German identitarian movement on facebook. *Social Media + Society*, *6*(1), https://doi.org/10.1177/2056305119898777

Hagen, S. (2018, March 1). 4chan/pol/ image walls: Memes. *OILab.Eu*. https://oilab.eu/4chanpol-image-walls-memes/

Hall, K. (2016). Selfies and self-writing: Cue card confessions as social media technologies of the self. *Television & New Media*, *17*(3), 228–242. https://doi.org/10.1177/1527476415591221

Hallinan, B., Scharlach, R., & Shifman, L. (2021). Beyond neutrality: Conceptualizing platform values. *Communication Theory*, https://doi.org/10.1093/ct/qtab008

Heikkilä, N. (2017). Online antagonism of the alt-right in the 2016 election. *European Journal of American Studies*, *12*(2), 1–22. https://doi.org/10.4000/ejas.12140

Hill, C. E., Thompson, B. J., & Williams, E. N. (1997). A guide to conducting consensual qualitative research. *The Counseling Psychologist*, *25*(4), 517–572. https://doi.org/10.1177/0011000097254001

Hofstede, G.. (2003). *Culture's consequences: Comparing values, behaviors, institutions, and organizations across nations* (2nd ed.). Sage.

Hokka, J., & Nelimarkka, M. (2020). Affective economy of national-populist images: Investigating national and transnational online networks through visual big data. *New Media & Society*, *22*(5), 770–792. https://doi.org/10.1177/1461444819868686

Hoskins, A. (2011). 7/7 and connective memory: Interactional trajectories of remembering in post-scarcity culture. *Memory Studies*, *4*(3), 269–280. https://doi.org/10.1177/1750698011402570

Inglehart, R. (1971). The silent revolution in Europe: Intergenerational change in post-industrial societies. *American Political Science Review*, *65*(4), 991–1017. https://doi.org/10.2307/1953494

Klandermans, B., & Mayer, N. (Eds.). (2005). *Extreme right activists in Europe: Through the magnifying glass*. Routledge. https://doi.org/10.4324/9780203004395

Klein, O. (2020). Misleading memes. The effects of deceptive visuals of the British national party. *PArtecipazione e COnflitto*, *13*(1), 154–179. https://doi.org/10.1285/I20356609V13I1P154

Kozinets, R. V. (2010). *Netnography: Doing ethnographic research online*. Sage.

Kress, G. R., & Van Leeuwen, T. (1996). *Reading images: The grammar of visual design*. Psychology Press.

Kubal, T., & Becerra, R. (2014). Social movements and collective memory. *Sociology Compass*, *8*(6), 865–875. https://doi.org/10.1111/soc4.12166

Kumar, S. (2021). *The digital frontier: Infrastructures of control on the global web*. Indiana University Press.

Marino, G. (2015). Semiotics of spreadability: A systematic approach to Internet memes and virality. *Punctum. International Journal of Semiotics*, *1*(1), 43–66. 10.18680/hss.2015.0004

Massanari, A. L., & Chess, S. (2018). Attack of the 50-foot social justice warrior: The discursive construction of SJW memes as the monstrous feminine. *Feminist Media Studies, 18*(4), 525–542. https://doi.org/10.1080/14680777.2018.1447333

McSwiney, J., Vaughan, M., Heft, A., & Hoffmann, M. (2021). Sharing the hate? Memes and transnationality in the far right's digital visual culture. *Information, Communication & Society*, 1–20. https://doi.org/10.1080/1369118X.2021.1961006

Milesi, P., & Chirumbolo, A. (2005). Italy: The offspring of fascism. In B. Klandermans, & N. Mayer (Eds.), *Extreme right activists in Europe* (pp. 85–110). Routledge.

Miller-Idriss, C. (2018). *The extreme gone mainstream: Commercialization and far-right youth culture in Germany*. Princeton University Press.

Milner, R. M. (2016). *The world made meme: Public conversations and participatory media*. MIT Press.

Miltner, K. M. (2014). 'There's no place for lulz on LOLCats': The role of genre, gender, and group identity in the interpretation and enjoyment of an Internet meme. *First Monday, 19*(8), https://doi.org/10.5210/fm.v19i8.5391

Mouffe, C. (2013). *Agonistics: Thinking the world politically*. Verso.

Mudde, C. (2016). *The study of populist radical right parties: Towards a fourth wave* [working paper]. C-REX Center for Research on Extremism. https://www.sv.uio.no/c-rex/english/publications/c-rex-working-paper-series

Mudde, C., & Rovira Kaltwasser, C. (2018). Studying populism in comparative perspective: Reflections on the contemporary and future research agenda. *Comparative Political Studies, 51*(13), 1667–1693. https://doi.org/10.1177/0010414018789490

Nagle, A. (2017). *Kill all normies: The online culture wars from tumblr and 4chan to the alt-right and trump*. Zero Books.

Nissenbaum, A., & Shifman, L. (2017). Internet memes as contested cultural capital: The case of 4chan's /b/ board. *New Media & Society, 19*(4), 483–501. https://doi.org/10.1177/1461444815609313

Öner, S. (2020). 'Europe' of populist radical right and the case of *lega* of salvini: Pioneer of a 'parochial Europe'? *European Politics and Society*, 1–16. https://doi.org/10.1080/23745118.2020.1842700

Padovani, C. (2008). The extreme right and its media in Italy. *International Journal of Communication, 2*, 753–770. https://ijoc.org/index.php/ijoc/article/viewFile/314/191

Pavan, E. (2020). We are family. The conflict between conservative movements and feminists. *Contemporary Italian Politics, 12*(2), 243–257. https://doi.org/10.1080/23248823.2020.1744892

Phillips, W., & Milner, R. M. (2018). *The ambivalent internet: Mischief, oddity, and antagonism online*. John Wiley & Sons.

Rentschler, C. A., & Thrift, S. C. (2015). Doing feminism in the network: Networked laughter and the 'binders full of women' meme. *Feminist Theory, 16*(3), 329–359. https://doi.org/10.1177/1464700115604136

Schwartz, S. H. (1992). Universals in the content and structure of values: Theoretical advances and empirical tests in 20 countries. *Advances in Experimental Social Psychology, 25*, 1–65. https://doi.org/10.1016/S0065-2601(08)60281-6

Schwartz, S. H. (2012). An overview of the Schwartz theory of basic values. *Online Readings in Psychology and Culture, 2*(1), 1–20. https://doi.org/10.9707/2307-0919.1116

Schwartz, S. H., Caprara, G. V., & Vecchione, M. (2010). Basic personal values, core political values, and voting: A longitudinal analysis. *Political Psychology, 31*(3), 421–452. https://doi.org/10.1111/j.1467-9221.2010.00764.x

Segev, E., Nissenbaum, A., Stolero, N., & Shifman, L. (2015). Families and networks of internet memes: The relationship between cohesiveness, uniqueness, and quiddity concreteness. *Journal of Computer-Mediated Communication, 20*(4), 417–433. https://doi.org/10.1111/jcc4.12120

Senft, T. and Baym, N. (2015) What does the selfie say? Investigating a global phenomenon. *International Journal of Communication, 9*, 1588–1606. https://ijoc.org/index.php/ijoc/article/viewFile/4067/1387

Serafini, F., & Reid, S. F. (2019). Multimodal content analysis: Expanding analytical approaches to content analysis. *Visual Communication*, 1–27. https://doi.org/10.1177/1470357219864133

Shifman, L. (2013). *Memes in digital culture*. MIT press.

Shifman, L. (2014). The cultural logic of photo-based meme genres. *Journal of Visual Culture, 13* (3), 340–358. https://doi.org/10.1177/1470412914546577

Shifman, L. (2016). Cross-cultural comparisons of user-generated content: An analytical framework. *International Journal of Communication, 10*, 5644–5663. https://ijoc.org/index.php/ijoc/article/view/5730/1847

Shifman, L. (2018). Testimonial rallies and the construction of memetic authenticity. *European Journal of Communication, 33*(2), 172–184. https://doi.org/10.1177/0267323118760320

Shifman, L. (2019). Internet memes and the twofold articulation of values. In M. Graham & W. H. Dutton (Eds.), *Society and the internet: How networks of information and* communication are changing our lives (2nd ed., pp. 43–57). Oxford University Press.

Siapera, E., & Veikou, M. (2016). The digital golden Dawn: Emergence of a nationalist-racist digital mainstream. In A. Karatzogianni, D. Nguyen, & E. Serafinelli (Eds.), *The digital transformation of the public sphere* (pp. 35–59). Palgrave Macmillan UK. https://doi.org/10.1057/978-1-137-50456-2_3

Spangler, P. T., Liu, J., & Hill, C. E. (2012). Consensual qualitative research for simple qualitative data: An introduction to CQR-M. In C. E. Hill (Ed.), *Consensual qualitative research: A practical resource for investigating social science phenomena* (pp. 269–283). American Psychological Association.

Titley, G. (2020). *Is free speech racist?*. Polity.

Topinka, R. J. (2018). Politically incorrect participatory media: Racist nationalism on r/ImGoingToHellForThis. *New Media & Society, 20*(5), 2050–2069. https://doi.org/10.1177/1461444817712516

Tuters, M. (2017). LARPing & liberal tears: Irony, belief and idiocy in the deep vernacular Web. In M. Fielitz, & N. Thurston (Eds.), *Post-digital cultures of the far-right* (pp. 37–48). Transcript Verlag.

Tuters, M., & Hagen, S. (2020). (((they))) rule: Memetic antagonism and nebulous othering on 4chan. *New Media & Society, 22*(12), 2218–2237. https://doi.org/10.1177/1461444819888746

Vecchione, M., Caprara, G., Dentale, F., & Schwartz, S. H. (2013). Voting and values: Reciprocal effects over time. *Political Psychology, 34*(4), 465–485. https://doi.org/10.1111/pops.12011

Zannettou, S., Caulfield, T., Blackburn, J., De Cristofaro, E., Sirivianos, M., Stringhini, G., & Suarez-Tangil, G. (2018). On the origins of memes by means of fringe web communities. *Proceedings of the ACM SIGCOMM Internet Measurement Conference, IMC* (pp. 188–202). http://arxiv.org/abs/1805.12512

Zhukova, E. (2020). How cultural traumas occur on social media: The case of the Ukrainian famine, 1932–1933. *International Journal of Politics, Culture, and Society*, https://doi.org/10.1007/s10767-019-09348-1

Sharing the hate? Memes and transnationality in the far right's digital visual culture

Jordan McSwiney ⓘ, Michael Vaughan ⓘ, Annett Heft ⓘ and Matthias Hoffmann ⓘ

ABSTRACT
Current research on visual media and the far right creates two expectations: that memes play an increasingly salient role in the far right's digital visual culture, and that the visual and participatory dimensions of internet culture facilitate greater transnationality. We explore these expectations with a comparative research design, situating memes in relation to other genres of visual content and across different country contexts. Taking a mixed methods approach, this article examines the digital visual culture of 25 far-right alternative media and other non-party organisations in Australia, Italy, Germany, and the United States. We assess the salience of memes and other visual genres, as well as three forms of transnationality: the circulation of images, direct communicative references, and transnational similarities. Unexpectedly, we find that memes play only a limited role in the digital visual culture of far-right non-party organisations, with their uneven concentration in Anglophone alt-media suggesting the potential pitfalls of assumptions about 'global' internet culture. We also find little evidence of transnationality through the circulation of the same visuals across countries, whether memes or other genres. Instead, transnationality works through transnational references within the images themselves and through more parallel practices of reproducing visuals in similar ways with similar themes, but with elements specific to an organisation's national and political context. Within this, we identify three distinct visual discourses – fascist continuity, western civilisational identity, and pop cultural appropriation – which highlight different practices of transnationality and collective identity construction within the far right online.

Introduction

Memes are seen as a key element of digital visual media for the far right.[1] Memes are described as 'key strategic digital items of communication' (Moreno-Almeida &

Gerbaudo, 2021, p. 21), a vital form of 'digital propaganda' (DeCook, 2018, p. 501) that is central to the far right's digital visual culture (Marwick & Lewis, 2017). In repackaging old ideas like fascism, racism and white supremacy, memes enable the far right to appeal to broader audiences (Askanius, 2021; Bogerts & Fielitz, 2019; Hakoköngäs et al., 2020). As internet memes draw on a shared internet tradition, with roots in platforms like 4chan or Reddit, there is an expectation of a common memetic culture across borders (Nissenbaum & Shifman, 2018). For the far right, this transnational meme culture was popularised by the rise of the so-called 'alt-right' (Askanius, 2021; Hermanson et al., 2020; Moreno-Almedia & Gerbaudo, 2021). This reflects broader assertions in the literature on far-right visual cultures, which suggest an enhanced capacity for transnational exchange due to the relative translatability of images compared to text (e.g., Doerr, 2017; Hokka & Nelimarkka, 2020; Miller-Idriss, 2018). The development of a more transnational far right communication ecology presents a challenge for democratic politics, since extremist actors who are marginalised at a national level may nevertheless be able to draw on informational resources and mutual recognition from counterparts in other countries.

However, the interest in memes as a specific form of online visual media often omits the broader 'cultural soup' (Lovink, 2019, p. 125), with research designs focusing on memes at the exclusion of other elements of the digital visual cultures (e.g., Askanius, 2021; Bogertz & Fieltis, 2019; Guenther et al., 2020; Lamerichs et al., 2018; Merrill, 2020; Moreno-Almedia & Gerbaudo, 2021). Moreover, these welcome interventions into the far right's use of memes are largely single country or single organisation studies, and do not account for the potential transnationality of memes. Our study aims to put the far right's use of memes in context, firstly in terms of their position within a broader visual culture, and secondly in terms of variation between countries. Through the analysis of the digital visual cultures of 25 far-right alternative media and other non-party organisations across Australia, Italy, Germany and the United States, we ask two research questions. First, how salient are memes in the far right's visual culture compared with other genres of visual content? Second, how does visual content facilitate transnationality in the far right's visual culture, either through the circulation of the same content across borders, direct communicative references, or cross-national similarities?

To address these questions, we adopt a mixed-methods approach combining a quantitative manual content analysis and a qualitative critical visual analysis of far-right digital visual culture across the social media platforms *Facebook* and *Twitter*, and the encrypted messaging service *Telegram*. We focus on aspects of image production and genre to compare memes with other kinds of visual content, before analysing image composition, scope, and symbolic repertoire in order to assess transnationality through direct communicative references and cross-national similarities.

Despite our initial expectations, we find that memes play only a limited role in the digital visual culture of the non-party sector of the far right. Instead, meme usage is closely related to national context and organisational logics, and concentrated in Anglophone alternative media. In comparison to other visual genres, memes substitute an ideological literacy of far-right iconography for a more generic internet meme literacy, while still incorporating far-right content. We also find against our expectations limited evidence of the digital circulation of the same images across borders. However, evidence of transnationality can still be found in direct transnational references within images

(Koopmans & Erbe, 2004), and in similarities in the usage of symbols, such as those associated with Christianity or (neo-)Nazism. That is, a tendency to produce and distribute visual media in similar ways and with similar themes but using nationally specific elements (Eder, 2000), what Risse et al. (2001) call transnationality 'with national colours'. Further, we identify three distinct visual discourses, each illustrating transnationally shared practices of meaning creation and collective identity construction. The first two, which we call fascist continuity and western civilisational identity, deploy a transnationally shared symbolic repertoire to construct exclusionary collective identities centring white racial supremacy, uniformity and action readiness. In contrast, the third, pop cultural appropriation, works to deactivate far-right group boundaries through the use of memes and the remixing of visual media drawn from popular culture to appeal to wider audiences.

Memes, visual culture, and transnationality

Internet memes are groups of digital items that share common characteristics constituting a template, created and circulated with awareness of each other (Nissenbaum & Shifman, 2018; Shifman, 2014). Like political symbols more generally, memes often require a specific (sub)cultural knowledge for interpretation (Shifman, 2014). The creation and dissemination of memes is typically an individual practice (Shifman, 2014). Nevertheless, memes provide a means for far-right organisations to engage with a wider audience, 'adopting humour, irony and ambiguity' to inscribe 'popular culture iconography' with hateful messaging (Askanius, 2021, p. 148, 154). As such, memes help the far right to repackage their ideology to make it more palatable for a broader audience (Askanius, 2021; Bogerts & Fielitz, 2019; Greene, 2019; Hakoköngäs et al., 2020). This has made memes an important part of the global far right's communication strategies (Askanius, 2021; DeCook, 2018; Lamerichs et al., 2018; Marwick & Lewis, 2017; Moreno-Almeida & Gerbaudo, 2021). However, memes are not the only form of visual media utilised by the far right, but rather one aspect of their broader digital visual culture.

Visual culture refers to the extensive place of the visual in social life, emphasising the way visual media are embedded into a wider culture (Rose, 2016). Visual culture provides insight into how the far right view themselves and the world (Sturken & Cartwright, 2001), and how they wish to be perceived by their audiences. It also highlights the potential use of aesthetic and visual dimensions to build bonds of exclusionary solidarity and political activism across borders (Doerr, 2017), and construct a shared sense of identity (Bhat & Klein, 2020; Nikunen et al., 2021; Richardson & Wodak, 2009). Whether deployed as inward or outward orientated communication, visual media function as arenas of 'political and identity construction' (Castelli Gattinara & Bouron, 2020, p. 1807), activating or deactivating particular social boundaries which then form the basis for future contentious collective action (Tilly, 2004).

In the transnational context of the internet, memes and other visual media have a greater propensity to bridge language barriers by communicating messages visually, such as through the direct appropriation and reproduction of images and symbols (Doerr, 2017; Hokka & Nelimarkka, 2020). The rise of a more transnationally networked far right points to the affordances of digital networks to foster a sense of global community and build overarching group identities (Caiani & Parenti, 2016; Knüpfer et al., 2020).

Transnational circulation and direct references can strengthen cross-country alliances, with visual media used to 'create and sustain connections with each other' across borders (Hokka & Nelimarkka, 2020, p. 787). In addition, 'transnationally and globally produced and circulated material' is used to strengthen the ideology of supporters (Hokka & Nelimarkka, 2020, p. 787). Those processes of image production, cross-referencing and circulation are fostered by networks of partisan online news sites and social media channels providing an infrastructure through which far-right content can be easily diffused (Heft et al., 2020).

Integrating research on visual communication and the transnationalisation of political communication more broadly, we conceptualise transnationality in three ways. The first type of transnationality captures the process of explicit circulation and reproduction of specific images across country borders, such as the circulation of memes between different countries (Hokka & Nelimarkka, 2020). The second type of transnationality is established through direct communicative references across borders within the visual material itself (Koopmans & Erbe, 2004), such as an Australian far-right group sharing an image of Donald Trump. Conceptually, we differentiate between vertical and horizontal references. Vertical references consist of communicative links between national and supranational entities, for example, if national organisations refer in their visual communication to supranational political institutions. Horizontal communication consists of the links between actors or organisations from different nation states (Koopmans & Erbe, 2004). The third type of transnationality is the similarity of visuals across countries, participating in the same discourse at the same time, irrespective of direct interactions (Eder, 2000). In this respect, we understand similarity in visual features used by far-right actors across borders, such as shared use of fascist iconography, as a sign that they adhere to a transnationally shared visual repertoire.

Case selection, data collection, and methodology

To analyse the salience of memes in far-right digital visual culture, and the transnationality of far-right digital visual culture more generally, we employ a cross-country and cross-organisational design that reflects variation in cultural, organisational and ideological features. We take a mixed methods approach, combining quantitative content analysis (Krippendorff, 2013) and qualitative visual analysis drawing on semiotics and discourse analysis (Doerr, 2017; Richardson & Wodak, 2009; Rose, 2016).

Case selection took place at two distinct levels. First, at the country level, we selected two Anglophone countries (Australia and the United States) and two European countries (Germany and Italy). These countries reflect varied historical legacies of fascism and the far right, as well as linguistic and other cultural differences. The US was selected due to the recent emergence of the so-called 'alt-right' and the memetic-turn in far-right visual cultures online (Hermansson et al., 2020). Germany and Italy were selected due to their enduring importance to far-right iconography post-WWII as the birthplaces of Fascism and National Socialism. Australia was included due to its growing importance within the transnational far right, particularly in the wake of the 2019 Christchurch Massacre in New Zealand, which was committed by an Australian white supremacist.

Second, at the organisational level, we selected a sample of alternative media, defined as hyper-partisan online news sites that self-describe as correctives to a perceived media mainstream (Holt et al., 2019), and other organisations comprising the 'non-party sector' of the far right (Veugelers & Menard, 2018). Our sampling is driven by three criteria: organisational form (as described), ideological variance, and platform availability. That is, we desired a sample that reflects a varied distribution of different organisational types, varying degrees of ideological extremity, but still with a publicly accessible online presence. This sample includes, for example, the German and Italian branches of the Identitarian Movement – new-right ethnonationalist groups with a strong focus on 'stylised' digital visual culture – as well as revisionist white supremacist groups like the American League of the South, or far-right alternative media organisations. Details on all 25 organisations of our sample can be found in Appendix A (Table A1).

Our data collection comprises all images from each organisation's public Facebook, Twitter, and Telegram in the period between 01.01.2019–30.06.2020. This includes still images posted in an organisation's main feed or timeline of the respective platform but excludes profile images or cover images and video content. Given the varied accessibility of each platform, we followed platform-specific processes for collecting our data (Pearce et al., 2020). For Facebook images, we used the DownAlbum (2020) plugin for Chrome to download all images stored on each page's timeline. Additionally, we purchased access to the full-archive endpoint of Twitter's Search API and used the Python programming language to collect all Tweets by our sample organisations that contained images. Regarding Telegram, images for each organisation's public channel were collected through the export function in the Telegram desktop application. We collected a total of 71,528 images. To make our data feasible for human coding, we drew a random sample of 100 images for each organisation, preserving the distribution of images across time and across platforms. In the five cases where an organisation had posted less than 100 images during our observation period, we used all images posted by the respective organisation. This led to a total of 2208 images. From this, we excluded all images that were screenshots of social media posts or lacked an explicitly right-wing content or message (see Appendix B, Foreword). The final number of coded images is 1175.

Drawing on the literature on contemporary far-right visuals (e.g. Bogerts & Fielitz, 2019; Hermansson et al., 2020; Miller-Idriss, 2018) we developed a standardised codebook for quantitative analysis (Appendix B). To assess the salience of memes in comparison with other types of content, we code for variables related to the site of production (Rose, 2016) allocating each image to a genre such as meme, photograph or 'sharepost', which we define as an image sharing the template characteristics of internet memes, but predominantly text-based and lacking the participatory impetus. In differentiating shareposts from memes, we adopt a stricter operationalisation of the meme genre (c.f. Guenther et al., 2020; Hakoköngäs et al., 2020; Merril, 2020). Though shareposts do have memetic qualities, namely common characteristics of content and form constituting a template, in differentiating between the two we enhance the conceptual clarity and gain a more precise understanding of the prominence and function of memes in far-right visual cultures online.

In order to look for evidence for the first form of transnationality, the direct circulation of content, we code for duplicated images within our dataset and additionally review images grouped by genre (e.g. memes) to highlight any recurring images appearing in different countries. To investigate the second form of transnationality we coded a series of variables relating to image composition. In particular, in order to assess direct transnational communicative references within the visual media we code for the image's geographical scope, differentiating between domestic/national images as well as vertical and horizontal transnationality (Koopmans, 2002; Koopmans & Erbe, 2004). Finally, in order to assess our third type of transnationality, cross-national similarity in discourses, we further coded for symbolic elements, based on an extensive pre-defined list of far-right codes, symbols and iconography. A complete list of symbols, with description and examples, can be found in Appendix B, Section 5.

Quantitative coding was conducted by three trained coders. We used Krippendorff's Alpha to test inter-coder reliability on a sample of 50 images against generally accepted thresholds (Krippendorff, 2013, p. 325). Excluding the symbol variables, strong reliability was achieved with 4 variables (> 0.8) and sufficient reliability for a further 5 variables (> 0.67, see Table A2 in Appendix A for details). Only the 'Object – Weapon' variable fell below the 0.67 threshold and so was excluded from analysis. Assessing the reliability of symbol variables presented a challenge, since the large number of sparsely populated binary variables involved high chance agreement. Even still, only 6 out of 31 symbol variables fell below the 0.67 threshold for Krippendorff's Alpha, and all achieved > 0.9 when using Holsti's CR which does not account for chance agreement.

Our quantitative content analysis is complemented by a qualitative analysis of a sub-sample of our original material. Here we draw on semiotics and discourse analysis to understand how visual media can be used to construct and represent the social world (Doerr, 2017; Rose, 2016). In doing so, we focus on the overall composition, including symbolic usage, clothing style, colour choices or font (Castelli Gattinara & Bouron, 2020; Doerr, 2017). Situating the images in their broader political and historical context, we deconstruct the layers of meaning and ambiguity to contextualise the images in order to best understand their preferred readings in the context of the digital visual cultures of the far right (Richardson & Wodak, 2009). Our analysis centres on the possibility of transnational exchange or similarity in image composition and self-representation, as well as choices of symbolic repertoire and broader processes of meaning making to which the visual media contribute.

Finally, this research brings with it a risk of inadvertently promoting the far right and their materials, by continuing their circulation (Askanius, 2021). To minimise the potential to 'boost' far-right content by reproducing it in publication, we include only select images from our data, deliberately not reproducing the most racist images and those which target individuals for harassment (Askanius, 2021; Muis et al., 2021). Further, we blur the faces of far-right activists 'so as not to provide them with the publicity or "fame" to which they aspire' (Askanius, 2021, p. 151). Though such research comes with significant challenges, we believe the critical analysis of such visuals to be vital in order to better understand the dissemination of the far-right's hateful and extremist content online (Askanius, 2021; Doerr, 2021).

The salience and circulation of memes

In assessing our first research question regarding the salience of memes in far-right digital visual culture, we found against our expectations that there was a relatively low frequency of internet memes (6%, $n = 66$) vis-a-vis other genres of visual media. Out of the 66 memes in our sample, Anglophone countries were overrepresented, with little use in our European cases (AUS = 41, USA = 21, DEU = 2, ITA = 2). In addition, memes were mostly shared by alternative media (*n* = 60). We make two observations from this. First, though memes form part of the digital visual culture of the far right, it is a relatively small part within the non-party, organisational layer. Second, meme usage relates to national contexts, as well as organisational logics, resulting in a particular concentration in Anglophone alternative media. The memes identified in our sample range from vehemently racist versions of popular templates like the 'Wojak' and 'Daily Struggle' memes, to the comparatively banal, like those in Figure 1. All nevertheless share a remixing approach to digital media, often only adding new text to widely circulating templates. These memes broadly share an irreverent or ironic tone, partly produced by the remixing process, as in Figure 1 which juxtaposes high-stakes partisan politics with cartoons or film.

In contrast to memes, we found the most common image genres to be photography (48%), followed by promotional materials such as posters (22%) and shareposts (16%). We argue that the visual culture of these far-right groups, though still predicated on a digital logic of sharing, largely operates within genres other than internet memes. Shareposts make up a larger proportion of images in the European (DEU = 27%, ITA = 18%) compared to the Anglophone cases (AUS = 8%, USA = 7%). Like memes, shareposts are built on templates designed specifically to be circulated online. Figure 2 illustrates the key differences between shareposts and memes. First, in terms of content and tone, shareposts drop the playful humour and ironic distance of internet memes in favour of a more serious and earnest argument. Second, while shareposts rely on templates, these templates are developed at the organisational level with the goal partly to raise organisational visibility, and lack the participatory culture of internet memes. Third, in terms of transnational diffusion, shareposts are typically anchored to specific national contexts through language.

Our sample of memes and shareposts also enabled us to examine the first type of transnationality outlined in our conceptual framework, namely the direct circulation of images. Within our sample, we did not find examples of the same meme or sharepost being reproduced in different national contexts. Moreover, even though memes often remixed elements drawn from a more transnational internet culture, it was a specific and narrow transnationality: the templates were built using cultural references from the Anglosphere, and were primarily used by groups in Australia and the US. Though

Figure 1. Anglophone meme templates. Left: Tuxedo Winnie the Pooh meme. The Daily Wire (2019). Right: One Does Not Simply Walk into Mordor meme. Ein Prozent (2020).

Figure 2. Examples of shareposts used by the far right. Left: Blocco Studentesco (2020). Right: Ein Prozent (2019).

we found only a small number of memes in the European cases, they still relied on Anglophone cultural references, consistent with the cross-linguistic practices of mainstream meme culture (Nissenbaum & Shifman, 2018).

Transnational references and similarity in far-right digital visual culture

As with memes, we found little evidence of other images being directly shared across borders. We then consider our second conceptualisation of direct transnational references contained within the image. From such a scope-oriented perspective, we find while most images are confined to the domestic scope of the country in which the posting organisation is based (61%), nearly a quarter contain reference to another country or entities with supra- or transnational meaning (23%). Digitally native images, namely memes (26%) stand out in terms of their geographical 'neutrality' in that they often lacked a clear geographical referent. Shareposts by contrast, being primarily text-driven, face the same language boundaries as other textual content and are therefore generally domestic in scope (59%), though do on occasion incorporate transnational references (26%). Alternative media organisations in our sample show higher usage of images that include direct transnational references than the other organisations (33% versus 15%). Lastly, the visual cultures of the Australian (34%) and Italian (29%) organisations are more transnational in this respect and more outward-oriented compared to the German (19%) and especially American ones (15%) (Table 1). For the Australian organisations, this appears to be driven by a focus on US politics and culture.

Table 1. Images' geographical scope by country, in percent (n).

Country Scope	AUS	DEU	ITA	USA	Total
Domestic (own country)	42.1	66.8	61.9	65.2	60.9
	(82)	(231)	(195)	(208)	(716)
Horizontal (other country)	21.0	4.3	5.1	8.5	8.4
	(41)	(15)	(16)	(27)	(99)
Multi-/supranational	12.8	14.2	24.1	6.6	14.6
	(25)	(49)	(76)	(21)	(171)
No scope/not identifiable	24.1	14.7	8.9	19.7	16.1
	(47)	(51)	(28)	(63)	(189)
Total	100.0	100.0	100.0	100.0	100.0
	(195)	(346)	(315)	(319)	(1175)

We therefore find some evidence of transnationality in terms of our second indicator, direct communicative references. However, it is important to restate that this transnationality is not driven by memes as a visual genre. In fact, the exact features that might enable the direct transnational circulation of memes – i.e., their generic and flexible visual templates – also appear to limit their transnationality along this second indicator, by avoiding recognisable geographic markers in favour of visual cues drawn from a more deterritorialised internet culture. Instead, transnationality through direct communicative references appears to be enabled through other visual genres, and driven by country and organisational factors as described above.

Finally, we analysed our data for evidence of the third form of transnationality in our framework, namely cross-national similarity in visual media. Our quantitative coding revealed a set of symbols which recurred consistently across different national contexts. For example, shared usage of symbols pertaining to Christianity, Islam, history, and popular culture can be found across all country cases, although their distribution among organisations within each country varies. There were particularly striking commonalities within the cases of fascist and neo-Nazi organisations in our sample, like the Australian National Socialist Network, German Der Dritte Weg, and Italian Blocco Studentesco and CasaPound Italia, which all draw extensively on the symbols of German National Socialism and post-war neo-Nazi movements. Likewise, there is expected overlap in the symbolic choices of German and Italian Identitarian organisations, unsurprising given the transnational, or at least trans-European, nature of the Identitarian movement.

After qualitative analysis of the subset of images containing transnationally recurring symbols, we identify three distinct discourses in our data. These discourses point to differences in how transnationality functions in the far right's digital visual culture, often converging along organisational and ideological lines, rather than national or linguistic proximity. The discourses also highlight particular approaches to boundary activation or deactivation in pursuit of transnational collective identities, forming the basis for future potential solidarities and collective action.

Fascist continuity

The first discourse centres on a continuity with the fascist past, often deploying a militaristic aesthetic and conflict or violence-oriented anti-left-wing symbols. As a revolutionary form of nationalism (Griffin, 2018) the fascist discourse visually constructs the organisations as 'men of action,' ready to 'smash' communism and reconquer their idealised vision of a racially-pure past. It is explicit in its ideological content and racism, and unashamed of the fascist legacy. While memes have been identified as a key means of rebranding fascism to make it palpable to broader audiences (Askanius, 2021; Hermansson et al., 2020) memes do not play a significant role in the visuals of this explicitly fascist discourse.

Instead, this discourse relies primarily on photographic materials and symbols drawn from the iconography of Nazi Germany and post-war neo-Nazi movements, such as Nordic runes, the swastika, Nazi salute, and *Schwarze Sonne* (Black Sun). These symbolic elements are found across all countries, with the greatest concentration in Australia. The explicit use of these Nazi symbols aligns with the ideological extremism of organisations like the Blocco Studentesco or Patriot Front, while the lack of 'playful' content like memes underscores the serious tone. Figure 3 highlights the different ways these symbols are employed cross-nationally, with their least codified references found in countries with more relaxed laws around the use of Nazi symbolism. Compare below the aggressive use of a Nazi salute by the Australian National Socialist Network against the more subtle inclusion of a *Schwarze Sonne* in the background of an image by Der Dritte Weg.

Similarly, the use of historical imagery points to parallel forms of transnationality, or transnationality 'with national colours' (Risse et al., 2001). While reference to historical figures is used to lend legitimacy to their organisation, constructing themselves as inheritors of a historical fascist mission, each organisation refers primarily to their own 'heroes,' albeit in similar ways. For example, CasaPound Italia and Blocco Studentesco emphasise the Italian veterans of the First and Second World War, while the Patriot Front emphasises the colonisers of the American frontier. Unlike the reliance on Viking imagery in the Scandinavian far right (Kølvraa, 2019; Nikunen et al., 2021), here military leaders and soldiers are used to emphasise a 'warrior-spirit.' The military imagery also allows contemporary activists to establish a continuity between the 'men of action' of the past and the present, with the photographic depiction of activists visually narrating a readiness for action and a sense of collective belonging. Despite significant national and organisational differences in clothing style, there is nevertheless a similar underlying visual logic centring on consistency and uniformity in the composition of these images (Figure 4). Both the National Socialist Network's black-bloc clothing and Patriot Front or Der Dritte Weg's paramilitary-style uniforms represent the subordination of the individual to the whole and highlights their readiness to partake in potentially violent action. Even the casual style of Blocco Studentesco and the Identitarian groups has an underlying uniformity: clean and well-fitting clothing, often athletic in style, and co-opting popular brands (Miller-Idriss, 2018). All emphasise a sense of 'joint masculine power and discipline' (Nikunen et al., 2021, p. 175). This can be further seen in the activities depicted, much of it outdoors, claiming the streets and public spaces, either through posters and stickers, holding vigils, or protest rallies – activities present across all countries. Sharing

Figure 3. Different approaches to the use of Nazi symbolism. Left: Brazen Nazi salutes in Australia. National Socialist Network (2020). Right: A more discrete Schwarze Sonne in the background of promotional materials in Germany. Der Dritte Weg (2020).

Figure 4. Collage of parallel styles of uniformity among far-right activists. Left, top: National Socialist Network (2020). Left, bottom: Der Dritte Weg (2019). Right, top: Generazione Identitaria (2019). Right, bottom: The League of the South (2019).

images of activists posing in varied settings further highlights an awareness of presence (Nikunen et al., 2021, p. 175), with these events deliberately structured to connote values of order and unity (Castelli Gattinara & Bouron, 2020).

Western civilisational identity

The second discourse we identify is one of shared western civilisational identity. Like the visuals of fascist continuity discussed above, there is little connection between memes and this discourse. Instead, photographs, promotional materials and artworks are the central genres. There is a strong emphasis on the symbols of Christianity, classical Greco-Roman architecture and art, broader historical visuals such as those relating to colonisation or medieval Europe, and Islam. Through the use of shared Christian and historical symbols this discourse attempts to appeal to a broader audience than the discourse of fascist continuity, while including both coded and explicit signals to the far right regarding the need to defend (white) European civilisation.

Christian symbolism plays a particularly important role (Figure 5). On the one hand, European organisations, especially the German and Italian Identitarian branches, use Christian symbols as an almost incidental backdrop, portraying their activity on a canvas of European cityscapes defined by churches and bell towers rather than mosques and minarets. Cultural practices of mourning, evoked with grave-crosses and candles are central and point toward a 'secularized Christianity-as-culture,' based on belonging and tradition rather than spiritual belief (Mouritsen, 2006, p. 77). Christian symbols serve not as markers of values or faith, but as the perceived roots of a shared civilisational heritage. On the other hand, there are conflict-orientated uses of Christian imagery, which portrays Christianity as in danger. For example, images of the Notre-Dame Cathedral fire,

Figure 5. Use of Christian symbolism in far-right visual media. Left: Vapourwave-style image of a Christian angel. XYZ (2020). Right: Promotional material for anti-Islam event, with German cityscape including church steeples. Journalisten Watch (2019).

shared mostly by Australian and US cases, function as a synecdochal sign of Christianity (and hence white western civilisation) under threat. At its most extreme, the conflictual component of the civilisational narrative is made explicit in a stylised image of a Christian angel with the text: 'do not make peace with evil … destroy it' (Figure 5).

Like Christian symbolism, classical Greco-Roman motifs are present across all countries (Figure 6). These symbols evoke an idea of a common western civilisational

Figure 6. Collage of classical Greco-Roman symbolism in far-right visuals. Left, top: CasaPound Italia (2020). Left, bottom: Identitäre Bewegung Deutschland (2019). Right, top: Blocco Studentesco (2020). Right, bottom: The Unshackled (2019).

identity rooted in an ancient culture (Bhat & Klein, 2020). The concentration of such symbols in the Italian cases reflects the historical process of legitimation, comparable to the prevalence of Viking imagery among Scandinavian far-right groups (Kølvraa, 2019; Nikunen et al., 2021). At the same time, their presence in the Australian and US cases underscores efforts to reinforce a shared transnational white European identity, despite their geographical distance. Statues of ancient warriors and marble busts invoke exclusionary ideas of white racial heritage and make claim to a legacy of imperialism and empire (Dozier, 2020). Similarly, the Identitarian's use of the ancient Spartan symbol the lambda shield represents 'heritage, ancestry, roots, land, blood, and identity' visually narrating what the Identitarians see as their duty to 'defend' Europe (Miller-Idris, 2020, p. 126).

Pop cultural appropriation

The fascist and civilisational discourses discussed already share two related characteristics. First, they reinforce group identities based on entrenched ideologies like white supremacy using fixed symbolic elements like swastikas and church steeples. Second, they form part of a far-right visual culture which is not specifically digital, in that they rely on the reproduction and recirculation of visual materials produced 'offline' like photographs. In contrast to these two discourses, we identify a third that differs in both of these respects, which we label pop cultural appropriation. This discourse relies on the co-option of pop culture iconography and the extensive use of internet memes. Pop cultural appropriation remixes an undefined and shifting stock of symbols drawn from broader internet culture in order to deactivate far-right group boundaries. In this respect, pop cultural appropriation is distinctively associated with digital culture compared to the other two discourses. The use of re-assembly and collage (van Dijk, 2020, p. 192–3) and adoption of the bricolage aesthetic of globalised digital culture (Deuze, 2006) highlights a strategic shift in far-right online communications present across all four countries in our data.

While leveraging the ambiguity of digital visual media to bridge to potential new audiences, the far right is still able to incorporate coded references to the more extreme ideology of their core constituencies. Figures 7 and 8 provide some examples of the specific

Figure 7. Appropriations of popular culture by the far right. Left: Compact (2019). Right: Blocco Studentseco (2020).

Figure 8. Use of memes to target broader audiences. Left: Drake Hotline Bling meme. The Daily Wire (2020). Right: Pepe the Frog. XYZ (2020).

bridging strategies. Figure 7 includes references to popular culture which do not have a fixed symbolic relationship to right-wing ideology, whether *Marvel's* Thor, or George Orwell's novel *1984*. Yet in both cases, audiences who are already primed by far-right framing can 'get it': the need for white European women to defend themselves from a presumably non-white threat, or the perceived authoritarian overreach of government responses to the Covid-19 pandemic. In both cases, the visual and cultural references resonate more broadly than an exclusively far-right audience, and yet the ambiguity of the visual references can support familiar far-right frames.

Figure 8 shows how the out-group constructed by this discourse is broader and more ambiguous than those for the fascist and civilisational narratives, employing the ironic distance and humour of memes to make their messages more accessible, while at the same time fostering a sense of group identity by 'sharing a laugh at the expense of an out-group (Askanius, 2021, p. 152. See also Gal, 2019). Instead of being constructed in opposition to communism or Islam like the visuals of the preceding discourses, pop cultural appropriation employs a memetic remixing of a deliberately broad and imprecise out-group ('leftists,' 'urbanites') to appeal to a wider potential audience. Nevertheless, there are coded signals for those who already 'belong' to the far right, such as the use of the Pepe meme. It also highlights the way in which this visual discourse can be simultaneously deployed across far-right alternative media, from the more mainstream-facing The Daily Wire, to the explicitly white supremacist XYZ.

Conclusion

Resituating memes in the broader digital visual cultures of the far right, we find that memes have only a limited salience in our dataset. This has important implications for the politics of memes in an organisational context, given their centrality to far-right communication at the subcultural or individual level (e.g., Bogerts & Fielitz, 2019; Marwick & Lewis, 2017). By and large, memes have not flowed through from the subcultural to the organisational layer of the far right, even in the case of organisations which grew from or alongside the characteristically memetic 'alt-right' (Greene, 2019). Where memes are present in our data, they are related to specific organisational and geographical configurations, namely alternative-media organisations in Australia and the US.

Nevertheless, memes still fulfil particular communicative needs for far-right organisations. By virtue of their wide circulation and appropriation, as well as their often humorous tone and pop culture content, memes can help the far right deactivate social boundaries, broadening their appeal and softening their ideological content (Askanius, 2021; Bogerts & Fielitz, 2019; Hakoköngäs et al., 2020). Embedding memes in the digital visual cultures of these organisations, we can see how the boundary mechanisms associated with memes differ from other visual media. Though the ideological content may be 'softened' through the use of pop culture and humour compared to other images like photographs or shareposts, memes still require specific forms of literacy to interpret (Miltner, 2014; Shifman, 2014). Using Tilly's (2004) terminology, we can summarise that the far-right adoption of memes activates social boundaries already constituted through the novel literacy demands characteristic of digital culture (i.e., between the meme-literate and illiterate) while deactivating boundaries aligned with extremist ideological cleavages, which become more covert but nevertheless remain central to these groups' communicative strategy.

Further, despite the shared internet culture underpinning memes (Nissenbaum & Shifman, 2018) and emergence of a transnational 'alt-right' meme culture (Askanius, 2021; Hermanson et al., 2020; Moreno-Almeida & Gerbaudo, 2021) we find limited evidence of transnationality in meme usage among the 25 far-right organisations. We found no evidence of the same memes or templates being circulated or reproduced across the four countries. Evidence of direct transnational references within the memes related only to a stock of Anglo-centric popular culture references, such as the 'One Does Not Simply Walk into Mordor' meme adapted by a German group in Figure 2. A greater degree of transnationality in memes is realised with regard to our third conceptualisation of transnationality, the presence of similar visual features across borders. However, this is restricted to the discourses of pop cultural appropriation, and therefore remains tied to specific practices of group border deactivation. In the context of far-right organisations, the politics of memes are by-and-large dependent on their particular national contexts, or at best, Anglophone cultural referents.

With respect to the digital visual cultures of the far right more broadly, although we expected to find the reproduction and circulation of the same images across borders (Doerr, 2017; Hokka & Nelimarkka, 2020), there is only limited evidence of explicit border-crossing distribution of visual media. Visual transnationality was found in direct transnational references contained within the image, such as references to another country or to entities with supra- or transnational meaning (Koopmans & Erbe, 2004) and in the parallel usage of specific sets of symbols. In particular, we observed symbols pertaining to Christianity, Islam, history and popular culture across organisations and countries, as well as the shared use of (neo-)Nazi symbols across borders among the explicitly fascist organisations in the sample. Overall, rather than the smooth circulation and reproduction of the same or similar images such as memes or posters as we had expected, the non-party sector of the far right instead produces and distributes visual media around similar themes but with the use of nationally specific symbols (Eder, 2000), pointing to a transnationality 'with national colours' (Risse et al., 2001)

In analysing this third form of transnationality we differentiated between three distinct visual discourses: fascist continuity, western civilisational identity, and pop cultural appropriation. Each of these discourses illustrates different practices of collective identity construction and transnationality along the lines of our third conceptualisation, and corresponds to particular image genres. In both the discourses of fascist continuity and western civilisational identity, there are no memes used. Instead, we observe the activation of explicitly transnational social boundaries through shared symbols such as those drawn from Christianity and the classical Greco-Roman period or Nazi Germany. More subtly, transnationality functions through parallel exchange in the form of similar themes and self-representations, but with particular national or organisational flavours (Eder, 2000; Risse et al., 2001). For example, the shared emphasis on uniformity, masculinity, and action readiness in the discourse of fascist continuity, and the parallel use of context-specific historical signs, such as the Notre-Dame Cathedral and Greco-Roman motifs in the civilisational visuals. Both serve to activate social boundaries to construct a shared sense of collective identity structured around white racial superiority in either an explicit (fascist discourse) or implicit (western civilisational identity) manner. By contrast, the pop cultural appropriation discourse relies on the remixing of visuals drawn from popular culture, and includes all instances of memes from our data. In keeping with an understanding of memes as a way to broaden the far right's appeal (Askanius, 2021; Bogerts & Fielitz, 2019; Hakoköngäs et al., 2020), these visuals serve to deactivate the far-right group boundaries present in the preceding discourses in favour of a more ideologically neutral (but still globally circulating) stock of cultural references recognisable by a wider potential audience.

It is important to note that our analysis is targeted specifically at the non-party organisational layer of the far right, active on particular platforms, as opposed to individuals active on image boards or forums. This may partly explain the limited presence of participatory visual media like memes, as well as their limited transnationality, and we therefore want to emphasise the limits to the generalisability of our findings to other sectors of the far right. Our study reveals a far-right digital visual culture which is communicatively heterogenous; within this heterogeneity we maintain that the close study of organisational actors is still vitally important. Their role in coordinating and mobilising contentious collective action (ranging from civil protest to acts of political violence) urges researchers to critically engage with and debunk the visual discourses of the far right. Additionally, the methodological choices in our study which enable comparison among four countries leave several complementary lines of inquiry unexplored, two of which we highlight here as fruitful for future study. In centring our analysis on the transnational dimension (or lack thereof) of memes and far-right digital visual culture, we do not necessarily account for the historical and sociocultural context which underlies the production of these visual cultures. Future research should look to the country-specific practices of legitimation in visual production and symbolic repertoire. Finally, transnationality in our study is explored through the analysis of visual objects themselves; this is far from an exhaustive conceptualisation of transnationality, and other research designs could usefully highlight the role of relational networks and organisational dynamics which cross national borders, further contextualising the shared discourses we identify in our study.

Note

1. The far right is here operationalised as a heterogeneous political family which share an ideological core of nativism and authoritarianism (Mudde, 2007).

Acknowledgements

The authors would like to thank David Rouhani for his excellent work in assisting with quantitative coding and codebook development.

Disclosure statement

No potential conflict of interest was reported by the author(s).

Funding

This work was supported by the German Federal Ministry of Education and Research [grant number 16DII114].

ORCID

Jordan McSwiney http://orcid.org/0000-0003-4317-8012
Michael Vaughan http://orcid.org/0000-0003-3582-3296
Annett Heft http://orcid.org/0000-0001-6637-795X
Matthias Hoffmann http://orcid.org/0000-0001-6480-3679

References

Askanius, T. (2021). On frogs, monkeys, and execution memes: Exploring the humor-hate nexus at the intersection of neo-Nazi and Alt-Right movements in Sweden. *Television & New Media*, 22 (2), 147–165. https://doi.org/10.1177/1527476420982234

Bhat, P., & Klein, O. (2020). Covert hate speech: White nationalists and dog whistle communication on twitter. In G. Bouvier & J. E. Rosenbaum (Eds.), *Twitter, the public sphere, and the chaos of online deliberation* (pp. 151–172). Springer International Publishing.

Bogerts, L., & Fielitz, M. (2019). "Do you want meme war?": Understanding the visual memes of the German far right. In M. Fielitz & N. Thurston (Eds.), *Post-digital cultures of the far right: Online actions and offline consequences in Europe and the US* (pp. 137–153). Transcript.

Caiani, M., & Parenti, L. (2016). *European and American extreme right groups and the Internet*. Routledge.

Castelli Gattinara, P., & Bouron, S. (2020). Extreme-right communication in Italy and France: Political culture and media practices in CasaPound Italia and Les Identitaires. *Information, Communication & Society*, 23(12), 1805–1819. https://doi.org/10.1080/1369118X.2019.1631370

DeCook, J. R. (2018). Memes and symbolic violence: #proudboys and the use of memes for propaganda and the construction of collective identity. *Learning, Media and Technology*, 43(4), 485–504. https://doi.org/10.1080/17439884.2018.1544149

Deuze, M. (2006). Participation, remediation, bricolage: Considering principal components of a digital culture. *The Information Society*, 22(2), 63–75. https://doi.org/10.1080/01972240600567170

Doerr, N. (2017). Bridging language barriers, bonding against immigrants: A visual case study of transnational network publics created by far-right activists in Europe. *Discourse & Society*, 28(1), 3–23. https://doi.org/10.1177/0957926516676689

Doerr, N. (2021). The visual politics of the alternative for Germany (AfD): Anti-Islam, ethno nationalism, and gendered images. *Social Sciences*, 10(1), 20. https://doi.org/10.3390/socsci10010020

DownAlbum. (2020, July 28). DownAlbum (v. 0.20.7.1). Google Chrome Store. https://chrome.google.com/webstore/detail/downalbum/cgjnhhjpfcdhbhlcmmjppicjmgfkppok/RK%3D2/RS%3DmDgC9poZ4RqQR0q69sBxG9BiJaA-

Dozier, C. (2020). Hate groups and Greco-Roman antiquity online: To rehabilitate or reconsider? In L. D. Valencia-García (Ed.), *Far-right revisionism and the end of history* (pp. 251–269). Routledge.

Eder, K. (2000). Zur Transformation nationalstaatlicher Öffentlichkeit in Europa: Von der Sprachgemeinschaft zur issuespezifischen Kommunikationsgemeinschaft. *Berliner Journal für Soziologie*, 10(2), 167–184. https://doi.org/10.1007/BF03204349

Gal, N. (2019). Ironic humor on social media as participatory boundary work. *New Media & Society*, 21(3), 729–749. https://doi.org/10.1177/1461444818805719

Greene, V. S. (2019). "Deplorable" satire: Alt-Right memes, white genocide tweets, and redpilling normies. *Studies in American Humor*, 5(1), 31–69. https://doi.org/10.5325/studamerhumor.5.1.0031

Griffin, R. (2018). *Fascism*. Polity Press.

Guenther, L., Ruhrmann, G., Bischoff, J., Penzel, T., & Weber, A. (2020). Strategic framing and social media engagement: Analyzing memes posted by the German Identitarian movement on Facebook. *Social Media + Society*, 1–13. https://doi.org/10.1177/2056305119898777

Hakoköngäs, E., Halmesvaara, O., & Sakki, I. (2020). Persuasion through bitter humor: Multimodal discourse analysis of rhetoric in internet memes of two far-right groups in Finland. *Social Media + Society*, 6(2), 2. https://doi.org/10.1177/2056305120921575

Heft, A., Mayerhöffer, E., Reinhardt, S., & Knüpfer, C. (2020). Beyond Breitbart: Comparing right-wing digital news infrastructures in six western democracies. *Policy & Internet*, 12(1), 20–45. https://doi.org/10.1002/poi3.219

Hermansson, P., Lawrence, D., Mulhall, J., & Murdoch, S. (2020). *The international alt-right: Fascism for the 21st century?* Routledge.

Hokka, J., & Nelimarkka, M. (2020). Affective economy of national-populist images: Investigating national and transnational online networks through visual big data. *New Media & Society*, 22(5), 770–792. https://doi.org/10.1177/1461444819868686

Holt, K., Figenschou, T. U., & Frischlich, L. (2019). Key dimensions of alternative news media. *Digital Journalism*, 7(7), 860–869. https://doi.org/10.1080/21670811.2019.1625715

Knüpfer, C., Hoffmann, M., & Voskresenskii, V. (2020). Hijacking MeToo: Transnational dynamics and networked frame contestation on the far right in the case of the '120 decibels' campaign. *Information, Communication & Society*, https://doi.org/10.1080/1369118X.2020.1822904

Kølvraa, C. (2019). Embodying 'the Nordic race': Imaginaries of Viking heritage in the online communications of the Nordic resistance movement. *Patterns of Prejudice, 53*(3), 270–284. https://doi.org/10.1080/0031322X.2019.1592304

Koopmans, R. (2002, April 15). Codebook for the analysis of political mobilisation and communication in European public spheres. (ultimate version). http://europub.wzb.eu/Data/Codebooksquestionnaires/D2-1-claims-codebook.pdf

Koopmans, R., & Erbe, J. (2004). Towards a European public sphere? Vertical and horizontal dimensions of Europeanized political communication. *Innovation: The European Journal of Social Sciences, 17*(2), 92–118. https://doi.org/10.1080/1351161042000238643

Krippendorff, K. (2013). *Content analysis: An introduction to its methodology*. SAGE.

Lamerichs, N., Nguyen, D., Melguizo, M. C. P., Radojevic, R., & Lange-Böhmer, A. (2018). Elite male bodies: The circulation of alt-right memes and the framing of politicians on social media. *Participations: Journal of Audience and Reception Studies, 15*(1), 180–206. https://www.participations.org/Volume%2015/Issue%201/11.pdf

Lovink, G. (2019). *Sad by design: On platform nihilism*. Pluto Press.

Marwick, A., & Lewis, R. (2017). *Media manipulation and disinformation online*. Data & Society Research Institute. http://www.chinhnghia.com/DataAndSociety_MediaManipulationAndDisinformationOnline.pdf

Merrill, S. (2020). Sweden then vs. Sweden now: The memetic normalisation of far-right nostalgia. *First Monday, 25*(6), https://doi.org/10.5210/fm.v25i6.10552

Miller-Idriss, C. (2018). *The extreme gone mainstream: Commercialization and far right youth culture in Germany*. Princeton University Press.

Miller-Idriss, C. (2020). *Hate in the homeland: The new global far right*. Princeton University Press.

Miltner, K. M. (2014). "There's no place for lulz on LOLCats": The role of genre, gender, and group identity in the interpretation and enjoyment of an Internet meme. *First Monday*, https://doi.org/10.5210/fm.v19i8.5391

Moreno-Almeida, C., & Gerbaudo, P. (2021). Memes and the Moroccan far-right. *The International Journal of Press/Politics*, https://doi.org/10.1177/1940161221995083

Mouritsen, P. (2006). The particular universalism of a Nordic civic nation: Common values, state religion and Islam in Danish political culture. In T. Modood, A. Triandafyllidou, & R. Zapata-Barrero (Eds.), *Multiculturalism, Muslims and citizenship: A European approach* (pp. 70–91). Routledge.

Mudde, C. (2007). *Populist radical right parties in Europe*. Cambridge University Press.

Muis, J., Klein, O., & Dijkstra, G. (2021). Challenges and opportunities of social media research: Using Twitter and Facebook to investigate far right discourses. In S. D. Ashe, J. Busher, G. Macklin, & A. Winter (Eds.), *Researching the far right: Theory, method and practice* (pp. 147–163). Routledge.

Nikunen, K., Hokka, J., & Nelimarkka, M. (2021). Affective practice of soldiering: How sharing images is used to spread extremist and racist ethos on soldiers of Odin Facebook site. *Television & New Media, 22*(2), 166–185. https://doi.org/10.1177/1527476420982235

Nissenbaum, A., & Shifman, L. (2018). Meme templates as expressive repertoires in a globalizing world: A cross-linguistic study. *Journal of Computer-Mediated Communication, 23*(5), 294–310. https://doi.org/10.1093/jcmc/zmy016

Pearce, W., Özkula, S. M., Greene, A. K., Teeling, L., Bansard, J. S., Omena, J. J., & Rabello, E. T. (2020). Visual cross-platform analysis: Digital methods to research social media images. *Information, Communication & Society, 23*(2), 161–180. https://doi.org/10.1080/1369118X.2018.1486871

Richardson, J. E., & Wodak, R. (2009). The impact of visual racism: Visual arguments in political leaflets of Austrian and British far-right parties. *Controversia, 6*(2), 45–77.

Risse, T., Cowles, M. G., & Caporaso, J. (2001). Europeanization and domestic change: Introduction. In M. G. Cowles, T. Risse, & J. Caporaso (Eds.), *Transforming Europe: Europeanization and domestic change* (pp. 1–20). Cornell University Press.

Rose, G. (2016). *Visual methodologies: An introduction to researching with visual materials*. SAGE.
Shifman, L. (2014). *Memes in digital culture*. MIT Press.
Sturken, M., & Cartwright, L. (2001). *Practices of looking: An introduction to visual culture*. Oxford University Press.
Tilly, C. (2004). Social boundary mechanisms. *Philosophy of the Social Sciences, 34*(2), 211–236. https://doi.org/10.1177/0048393103262551
van Dijk, J. (2020). *The network society: Social aspects of new media* (4th ed.). Sage.
Veugelers, J., & Menard, G. (2018). The non-party sector of the radical right. In J. Rydgren (Ed.), *The Oxford handbook of the radical right* (pp. 285–304). Oxford University Press.

ð OPEN ACCESS

Murder fantasies in memes: fascist aesthetics of death threats and the banalization of white supremacist violence

Tina Askanius and Nadine Keller

ABSTRACT
This paper traces the recent turn to humour, irony and ambiguity embodied in the adaptation of memes into the repertoire of online propaganda of the militant neo-Nazi group the *Nordic Resistance Movement*; in a process, we dub the 'memefication' of white supremacism. Drawing on a combination of quantitative visual content analysis (VCA) and in-depth visual analysis focused on iconography and symbolism, we explore all memes (N = 634) created and circulated by the group around the 2018 general elections in the country. The analysis proceeds in two steps: First, we present the results of the VCA in which we identified five thematic categories of memes crafting white supremacy, xenophobia, homophobia, misogyny and anti-Semitic ideas onto esoteric and popular culture iconography then to map these across a matrix of content and form. We then proceed to the analysis of the cluster of memes coded as violent to explore the iconography and symbolism used to promote violence and death threats and render them banal. We draw on a range of recent scholarship on the entanglement of memes in the rise of the far-right and engage critical perspectives on the necropower of fascism to explore the interplay between ambiguous, playful and jokey imagery on the one hand and the murder fantasies and serious threat of white supremacist violence at the heart of neo-Nazi ideology, on the other.

Introduction

For some time now, memes have been associated with vernacular and participatory digital cultures online (Philips, 2019), the communication repertoire of democratic social movements, vibrant political debate and campaigns for solidarity or justice (Bayerl & Stoynov, 2016; Jensen et al., 2020; Milner, 2013) and even counter-terrorism efforts from below (McCrow-Young & Mortensen, 2021). However, these ephemeral and bite-sized images have recently had 'a reactionary turn' and have become deeply entangled with mischievous and far-right subcultures online (Tuters & Hagen, 2020,

p. 2218) and the propaganda apparatus of violent extremist actors. Memes thus not only abound in fringe and early internet cultural spaces like 4chan and Reddit but also increasingly form an essential part of the toolbox of violent actors within extreme-right movements, including male supremacist and white supremacist groups (Askanius, 2021a; DeCook, 2018). The adaptation of memes by white supremacist groups is an important potential driver in online radicalisation into far-right extremism. Previous research indicates that memes serve as an effective means to convey key ideological narratives, attract new supporters and contribute to rendering extremist thought mainstream (Bogerts & Fielitz, 2019). Because online memes are ephemeral and often shared anonymously, they enable new, experimental and playful engagements with far-right ideas in ways that could act as a gateway to later, stronger commitments (Miller-Idriss, 2019; Moreno-Almeida & Gerbaudo, 2021). Yet, the exact role of memes in processes of online radicalisation and their implications for the visual construction of white supremacism and violent extremism more generally remains relatively unexplored. So too do the workings of the specific symbols and iconography involved in this process, which we might dub a 'memefication' of white supremacism. To understand the political potency of memes and the increasing role they play in contemporary far-right propaganda, we need to understand their main tenets and the litany of coded visual language from which they draw and generate new meaning.

During the insurgency against the Capitol on 6 January 2021, we saw a motley array of symbols and iconography well-known from contemporary white supremacist and extremist groups on full public display in Washington DC. Besides the multitude of different MAGA regalia, confederate flags and Trump merch, the signature Hawaiian shirts of the Boogaloo movement, Crusader crosses and Germanic pagan imagery of right-wing militias and different versions of QAnon iconography, for example, on clothes with the letter 'Q' or banners with slogans like 'Trust the Plan' were on display. Equally omnipresent was the widely recognised insignia of the alt-right, Pepe the Frog and the appurtenant green-and-white flag of Kekistan (mimicking the German Empire's Reichskriegsflagge) – a fictional country where Pepe's avatar Kek rules, all conjured up in the meme-driven culture of 4chan, Reddit and other Alt-Tech platforms. These symbols, many of which were not so long ago relegated to the fringes of online subcultures, today seem to travel seamlessly back and forth between online and offline spaces and transit into real-life political mobilisations. The deadly outcome, the vitriol and violence of the insurgency stand in stark contrast to the colourful and somewhat comic imagery and symbolism on display in DC, which is informed by the very same 'humorous ambiguity' (Bogerts & Fielitz, 2019) or 'mischievous ambivalence' (Philips & Milner, 2017) that saturates memes. However, the events leave little ambiguity around what a 'white nationalist' take-over would look like, and it remains to be seen whether the events will put an end once and for all to the 'just joking' veil in which far-right memes are so often cloaked.

This article takes an interest in the symbols and iconography of white supremacist memes and their role in pushing the boundaries of public discourse by trivialising and normalising messages of hate, violence and death threats. We anchor these concerns in a specific national context, that of Sweden, and through the prism of a particular empirical case, that of the militant neo-Nazi group the *Nordic Resistance Movement*; currently the biggest and most active extreme-right actor with an explicitly violent and 'revolutionary' agenda in Scandinavia, which, in 2017, introduced memes as part of its propaganda repertoire. We ask: *How do neo-Nazi memes promote and banalise violence and death threats and what are the key symbols and iconography involved in this process?* We use the case of NRM to demonstrate how memes allow white supremacism with its cultures of violence, including fantasies of ethno-national 'purity' through violence, public executions and the toppling of democracy, to intersect with the more mainstream political currents and ideas they feed off.

Weaponising the visual: the far-right's turn to memes

As 'bite-sized nuggets of political ideology and culture that are easily digestible' (DeCook, 2018, p. 485), memes employ humour and rich intertextuality and are meant to be shared in social media where they '[pass] along from person to person, yet gradually [scale] into a shared social phenomenon' (Shifman, 2013, p. 364). Far-right actors have co-opted this online phenomenon to dress up hate speech with dark humour, pop-culture references, quirky GIFs and catchy phrases. Tapping into contemporary digital subcultures allows such actors to cloak anti-democratic messages in the attires of depoliticised cultural consumption. Memes feed off a pool of content that appeals to 'multiple audiences far beyond those who unambiguously identify with neo-Nazi and other far-right symbolism' (Bogerts & Fielitz, 2019, p. 150). The co-optation of memes and the digital subcultures from which they stem involve a wide range of iconography and symbols that entail carefully coded references that rely on and market to the observer's knowledge of far-right ideology (Miller-Idriss, 2018, p. 6). The humanoid cartoon frog, Pepe the Frog, is but one such by now well-known example. While memes commonly emerge on so-called Alt-Tech platforms (such as 4chan, 8kun, Reddit, Gab and Imgur, see Donovan et al., 2019), they increasingly tend to leave the fringe communities of the global far-right and travel through what Ebner (2019) describes as a circular online influence ecosystem across mainstream social media platforms in a variety of bigoted guises.

But the weaponisation of visuals in far-right propaganda is not new. Well aware of the power of visuals to appeal to the masses, build affective bonds, package and sell political agendas and transform ideology into a marketable object of consumption, fascist regimes have been prolific in aestheticising politics in the past (Benjamin, (1979 [1930]); Koepnick, 1999; Ravetto, 2001). The concept of the aestheticisation of politics was first coined by Walter Benjamin (1930) in his analysis of German fascism. Although Nazi Germany railed against the poisons of modernity, they knew how to deploy the latest technology to relay their message effectively. Through technologically innovative movies, orchestrated mass rallies, the excessive use of brand symbols and Führerkult imagery, German fascism 'endorsed seemingly unpolitical spaces of private commodity consumption so as to reinforce political conformity' (Koepnick, 1999, p. 52). Culture and entertainment allowed historic Nazism to gain mass support by 'offering something to everyone' (Koepnick, 1999). Placing the role of visuals in fascist propaganda in a historical context helps us understand today's memefication of white supremacism as an evolution of the aesthetisation of fascism. Similar to fascist propaganda of the Third Reich, memes wrap ideology in easily digestible narratives and appealing visuals that are designed and marketed to appeal to 'modern consumers' (Koepnick, 1999).

While the actual political potency of memes remains contested (Wiggins, 2016), research indicates that they are potentially powerful drivers in processes of online radicalisation and work as gateways into more extreme and violent content and communities. Yet, knowledge of how memes and online participatory cultures are deployed and co-opted by the far-right is still scarce, just as we know little of how the various visual codes and symbols at the heart of the meaning-making processes of memes move across and translate in different national contexts. While we have previously examined the meme production and practices of this particular group and how their memes display a convergence of traditional neo-Nazi imagery with the visual aesthetics of the alt-right (see Askanius, 2021a), in this piece, we take a particular interest in the iconography and symbolism at play in the memefication of white supremacist violence. We do so to disentangle the multivalent (and at first sight confusing/nonsensical) array of different symbols dense with intertextual references to historical and contemporary figures, events, places and debates, in their memes. We hope that by bringing clarity to the layers of relationships between dichotomous categories such as mainstream and esoteric/fringe, violent and non-violent, harmful and harmless in this particular mode of online propaganda, we can shed light on the strategic blurring of these boundaries in violent extremists' current attempts to reshape and re-invent political action and discourse associated with white supremacism.

Methods and material

The study focuses on the body of memes produced and circulated by the group around the 2018 general elections in Sweden. The sample includes all publicly accessible memes ($N = 634$) that were published in weekly bundles on NRM's online hub Nordfront.se in the period from May 2017 – when 'Memes of the week' was launched – to December 2018 when the fieldwork ended. To analyse this material, we combine two visual methods, and the analysis proceeds in two steps accordingly. First, we conduct a quantitative visual content analysis (VCA) (Bock et al., 2011; Rose, 2016) that allows us to code our larger sample of memes and classify it into distinct categories. Through the systematic coding of images, we identified five broad thematic categories. These are (i) anti-establishment (214), (ii) 'racial strangers' (145), (iii) anti-Semitism (129), (iv) NRM self-promotion (61) and (v) anti-feminist/LGBTQ (42) memes. The categories were derived inductively and revised multiple times until they were exhaustive and exclusive. We then coded the memes within each category for persons, characters, objects, symbols and text appearing in the images, their intertextual references, and (remixed) stylistic and aesthetic features. This allowed us to further characterise and understand the memes on the spectrum of (a) far-right ideological positions and (b) cultural form.

In a second analytical step, we take an interest in a particular cluster of memes spanning across the five categories that contain markers of violent extremism ($N = 67$) to explore the visual iconography and symbolism used to promote and banalise violent intent and death threats. Within the broader VCA, this coding process allowed us to systematically map the notoriously slippery notion of *våldsbejakande*[1] [adjective signalling someone or something inciting violence], mining the data for explicit and implicit references to violence, genocide, ethnic cleansing and probe for the ways in which coded signs and symbols are weaponised across the thematic clusters of memes. Markers of violence and violent extremism include dead bodies, bodies being beaten/violated, as well as indirect markers of violence such as references to the Third Reich (concentration camps, swastikas, the portrayal of Hitler), explosives, knives, hangman's ropes and weapons in general.

To operationalise the qualitative visual analysis of memes coded as violent, we draw on Miller-Idriss's (2018, 2019) extensive work on the role of symbolism and iconography in contemporary extreme-right youth cultures and social movements. While her research focuses specifically on the commercialisation of far-right ideology in the context of clothing brands and consumer goods, we follow her approach to study the visual codes involved in the memefication of neo-Nazi ideology, which follows a similar pattern of 'encoding historical and contemporary far-right, nationalistic, racist, xenophobic, Islamophobic, and white supremacist references into iconography, textual phrases, colors, scripts [and] motifs' (Miller-Idriss, 2018, p. 4). The concept of iconography is key to understanding the constitutive power of visual culture: 'images convey meaning beyond their mere aesthetic representation; rather, images and pictures are "encoded texts" that need to be carefully deciphered' (p. 33). The imagery of the far-right heavily relies on such codes that are interwoven in (modified) symbols of Nordic mythology and nationalist history, as well as references to the Third Reich, the Holocaust, the colonial era, etc. Symbols are multivalent and 'often do not convey a decisive or direct meaning, but rather an evocative one' (p. 12). This obviously complicates the unambiguous decoding of images. For legal reasons, far-right imagery may also avoid depicting historical scenes from the Third Reich or explicit links to the Holocaust, making it all the more important to look for and carefully examine (strategically) coded references. The ability to detect, decode and correctly interpret the images is dependent on the viewer's background knowledge. We draw on previous international research on far-right iconography and symbolism (Bogerts & Fielitz, 2019; Doerr, 2017; Greene, 2019; Miller-Idriss, 2018, 2019) and on the specificities of Sweden's extreme-right imagery (Askanius, 2021a; 2021b; Ekman, 2014; Kølvraa, 2019; Lööw, 2015; Merill, 2020) to establish the contextual knowledge needed to decipher the visual codes and subcultural ephemera that NRM uses to promote and banalise violence and death threats.

Understanding neo-Nazi memes across (ideological) content and (cultural) form

On 27 May 2017, NRM launched the campaign Memes of the week [*Veckans meme*] as part of a larger effort to boost the humour and entertainment end of their online propaganda. The editors of Nordfront present memes as offering 'a gateway into heavier topics' and 'catching the attention of people outside the movement'. Supporters 'old and young, skilled and unskilled' are called upon to join the 'meme war' on mainstream social media. From its launch to the end of 2020, the weekly meme dump on Nordfront counts 49 editions. The memes antagonise NRM's political enemies and reiterate the logic of discrimination, exclusion and stereotyping. With NRM's white supremacist and explicitly violent agenda, their memes go far beyond remixing LOLCats and funny looking frogs to mock opponents and target minorities and the promise/threat of deadly violence in their proclaimed rise to power and revolutionary 'take-over' is woven into the imagery in both implicit and explicit ways.

Jumping off the initial categorisation of the memes into five categories, we propose a matrix with which to further examine the images across these thematic strands on a spectrum of first, different ideological positions within the broader extreme-right movement in Sweden and second a continuum of visual symbols and pop-cultural references ranging from the esoteric symbols (impalpable to anyone outside the knowing in-group) to the more mainstream cultural references, including well-known cartoon characters, protagonists in children's books, logos and graphic design of public institutions, etc. This analytical distinction largely follows Eatwell's (1996) original categorisation of fascist appeal between the 'esoteric' nods and winks to hardcore members and the more populist and palatable 'exoteric' modes intended for the general public.

The memes draw from a pool of figures and symbols known from mainstream entertainment and popular culture. These include children's television characters, toy brands, cartoons characters and video games aesthetics. Together, these elements and their mixing are so consistently deployed that they qualify as a strategy, one that continues the long history of fascist movements' aestheticising politics. The memes are densely self-referential but also highly intertextual. They display different degrees of explicitness about violent intent and variations over ideological positions on a spectrum between cultural and biological racism and between ethno-nationalism and white supremacy. To make sense of these variations and the juxtaposition of (textual/cultural) forms and (ideological) content, the first steps of the VCA involved positioning the memes in a matrix built around these axes.

(i) **(Ideological) content**: All of the memes are obviously produced from within or circulated by an explicitly neo-Nazi and white supremacist organisation. Yet, some memes draw more explicitly on references to historical national socialism as an ideology using documentary or cartoon images of Hitler's Third Reich, Holocaust imagery (denial and ridicule), the swastika or NRM's own symbol, the Nordic Tyr rune, whereas other memes are discernibly informed by Alt-right ideology and meta-political messages and symbolism. This is the case when, for example, NRM's messages or logo are projected onto memes of Pepe the Frog or other lesser-known symbols and icons of the Alt-Right such as the OK hand sign, the thumbs-up sign or the 1980s style vaporwave filter. At this upper end of the axis, the ideological core ideas are rooted in ethno-nationalism rather than white supremacy and in expressions of cultural rather than biological racism. The vertical line thus represents two ends of the far-right continuum in terms of the ideological positions, from the 'softer' ideas of ethno-nationalism, white identity/nationalism embraced by the Alt-right and identitarian movements to the violent and anti-democratic positions with explicit references to militancy, violence and violent revolution (indicated with weapons, ethnic cleansing, mass executions, race wars, etc.).

(ii) **(Cultural) form**: The second axis positions the memes in accordance with how they draw on pop-cultural references and deploy styles and aesthetics on a scale between the mainstream and the esoteric. With *esoteric*, we refer to memes remixing symbols, icons and images not immediately known to people outside extreme-right circles. They require a high level of shared (sub)cultural knowledge. Several of the memes make references to Alt-Right iconography and discourse, for example, by featuring seemingly harmless characters such as the Moon Man (originating from a 1980s McDonald's ad campaign) and the black and white 'normies' or 'feelsman' image (meant to represent the docile mainstream 'sheeple'). With *mainstream*, we refer to memes re-appropriating familiar, to a Swedish audience at least, popular culture references and icons. These include well-known characters from children's shows such as Alfons Åberg, Skurt and Björne, cartoon characters like Tintin or Bamse; references to Hollywood films or political satire shows (e.g., The Simpsons), commercial brands and merchandise (e.g., Lego and Star Wars). These are symbols with mainstream subcultural currency. Memes at this upper-right end thus possess a certain 'pop-polyvocality' (Milner, 2013) in that they reflect elements of a 'pop-cultural common tongue that facilitate a diverse engagement of many voices' (Milner, 2013, p. 65) and therefore have, at least potentially, a broader public appeal.

The co-optation and 'swedification' of symbols

Miller-Idriss (2019) distinguishes between three types of far-right symbols: those created by or for far-right consumers, in artefacts intentionally laced with far-right symbols and codes; those that at their origins have no relationship to the far-right but have become *co-opted* as far-right symbols; and those which deliberately or accidentally deploy far-right symbols and codes, either through attempts to draw media attention, or through ignorance and coincidence. The first two categories in the Miller-Idriss distinction are represented in the memes. The first category obviously includes NRMs own visual logo, an adaptation of the Tyr rune in Norse mythology, and Third Reich Nazi symbols, such as the swastika and the 'Imperial Eagle'. Co-opted symbols include, for example, the frog puppet Skurt and the teddy bear Björne from 1980s children's television shows, the literary characters Åsa Nisse and Alfons Åberg, symbols and characters from the film such as *Star Wars, Attack on Titan* and *Dracula Untold*. Out of all of these fictional characters co-opted from entertainment and popular culture, the Swedish version of Pepe the Frog, Skurt, occurs most frequently. Originally, Skurt was a small frog-like hand puppet on a Swedish TV show running from 1988 to 2006 – a children's favourite that is widely known among young and old in Sweden today. Today, the frog with the grinning face and colourful hat is remixed into endless variations of racist, misogynist and anti-Semitic memes to the extent that he has become the face of the Swedish far-right within and beyond Sweden. The malleability of the symbol and the relative ease with which a character such as Skurt is repurposed and transposed into new contexts in a fashion that is easily replicable (Shifman, 2013) suggests that these symbols work as empty signifiers; discursive voids into which meaning can be assigned and recruited for different ideological purposes. Today, there are several sites and channels dedicated to producing and posting Skurt memes, and the character has been used frequently and indiscriminately with reference to parties across the far-right spectrum from the Sweden Democrats (SD) and Alternative for Sweden (AfS) to the Nordic Resistance Movement (NRM). Around the 2018 general elections, calls were made on Reddit and 4chan for the international community to help Swedish users make 'the lad go global' and to try to influence the outcome of the elections in support of the far-right. While these efforts did not pan out in any significant way (Colliver et al., 2018), the collective efforts of users in these communities, well-versed in the vernacular arts of remixing open-ended and nebulous symbols, have arguably turned Skurt into a far-right mascot with some degree of success.

But perhaps the most 'creative' example of an elaborately co-opted sign is that involved in the series of execution memes set in the small industrial town Finspång in the northern part of the country, which started to circulate in 2017. The memes recount a fictional/future tribunal to take place after fascist take-over in 2022 in which 'traitors of the people' (politicians, journalists, researchers, feminists and women in relationships with non-white men) will be held accountable for their betrayal against the nation and hanged from lamp posts and cranes across the country. Once 'justice has been served', Finspång will be turned into a 'white reserve' to protect the population's 'biological exceptionalism' from the dangers of the Muslim invasion and/or the collapse of society under the burdens of multiculturalism more generally. The memes are built from stock photographs or caricatures of those considered to fall into the category 'traitor of the people' accompanied by the text 'Finspång 2022' or the more direct 'We are going to Finspång' or 'See you in Finspång', the latter being an allegory to the expression of German extremists who use the phrase 'See you in Walhalla' referencing the halls of death in Norse mythology (Miller-Idriss, 2019). The slogan was also recently referenced at the end of the manifesto of the right-wing terrorist behind the Christchurch massacre in New Zealand. In this manner, 'a real place, rooted in the offline world, became a fantastical place in online spaces and was infused with far-right meanings' (p. 128). To be sure, the Finspång memes represent the most explicit articulation of death threats in the batch of memes examined, an aspect we unpack in the final sections of the analysis focusing on the iconography of death and violence.

Much like other far-right symbols before them, both Skurt and the town of Finspång are arbitrary signs in the sense that there is no clear reason why this exact puppet or town should become symbols of neo-Nazi ideology over others. Such co-optations of symbols and their coincidental evolutions as such defies explanation through traditional theories about how symbols work, according to Miller-Idriss (2018, 2019). At the heart of this disruption between logical and linear association between symbols and their intended meanings are the online subcultural communities and the global nature of the internet, which have profoundly changed the ways in which ideological messages are produced, circulated and consumed.

In this sense, the NRM memes draw on and add meaning to symbols, icons and narrative conventions well-known to far-right supporters globally. But they are also distinctly Swedish and draw on a range of symbols and cultural references one would have to be knowledgeable of the political context of Sweden to fully understand. Both Skurt and Finspång provide ample evidence of how symbols are not merely adopted wholesale but rather translated to make sense in and add meaning to specific national contexts, conflicts and public conversations. The case of NRM and how this particular actor has adopted a cultural phenomenon with the global purchase by tapping into a subcultural lingo of the far-right internationally, thus also shed light on the transnationalisation processes through which memes, and their visual codes, travel and find new meaning in local/national contexts. Further, we might argue that both 'Skurt' and 'Finspång' have become so commonplace in memes and other imagery across the Swedish far-right that they qualify as subcultural icons in this ideological context, although their 'status' as such might turn out to be short-lived. Indeed, as argued by Mortensen (2016), 'online construction of icons is more transient' and 'less controllable and predictable because it involves more actors, more media platforms, and a greater geographical spread' (p. 410). But we may understand these as icons in the sense that they have become embedded into 'standard frames of reference' among the groups, networks, alternative 'news' media and online spaces that make up the far-right in the country to such an extent that they in the end 'seem to require no particular explanation, and are often proclaimed to "speak for themselves"' (Mortensen (2016)) in these circles.

The iconography of death threats and violence

In these final analytical steps, we explore the interplay between the ambiguous, playful and jokey imagery of the memes and the visual constructions of murder fantasies and serious threat of white supremacist violence at the heart of neo-Nazi ideology. The majority of all memes coded as violent ($N = 67$) target those individuals and groups deemed not to belong to or to pose a threat to the nation.[2] The iconography of violence in these memes is intricately tied to symbols of death and dying. This is important, Miller-Idriss (2018) argues, as '[d]eath is the penultimate celebration and valorisation of violence that is so central to far-right identity and ideology' (p. 109). Symbols of death act as straightforward threats of violence and physical harm, evoking both a general and unspecified fear as well as a more specific threat against certain ethnic, religious or racial minorities (Miller-Idriss (2018)). The aesthetic moment in fascist propaganda has a history of reconfiguring perceptions so that they prefigure and culminate in violence and warfare, which constitutes the climax of alternative fascist modernity (Koepnick, 1999, p. 53). Although symbols of violence, often combined with historical or mythological references, are ubiquitous in far-right subcultures, themes of violent threat, dying and death have so far received little to no attention within the scholarship on far-right extremism (p. 108). This second part of the analysis responds to Miller-Idriss's call for the social sciences to further deepen our knowledge on the iconographic representations of death and dying and their relation to militant violence. While the valorisation of violence that characterises these memes clearly places them on the lower, 'race revolutionary', end of the matrix presented in Figure 1, the wide range of symbols and codes

Figure 1. Example of analytical coding in a matrix across content/form 349 × 222 mm (72 × 72 DPI).

deployed to visualise violent intent distributes these memes across the mainstream and esoteric scale of our matrix. This is significant for the potential appeal of the memes to both in-groups and out-groups, as detailed in the sections below in which we follow Miller-Idriss's (2018) typology of three key iconographic representations of death in far-right products and symbols to structure the analysis of *abstract/implicit violence, specific/explicit violence* and *threats of (deadly) violence* at play in the memes.

Abstract/implicit violence

Memes with abstract depictions of violence convey the thought or idea of causing physical harm rather than directly depicting violent action, death or dying. In this category of violent memes, ideological motivation and violent intent are carefully disguised through a range of esoteric far-right codes on the one hand and seemingly harmless 'humorous' mainstream references on the other hand. In the example below, we see this dynamic at work in one of the many Skurt memes (Figure 2).

This meme shows the smiling frog head on the body of a German WW2 Wehrmacht soldier who extends a hand towards the observer, inviting him/her to fight 'together'. The Nazi/WW2 references and their (implicit) violent intent are cleverly nested in esoteric codes and symbols. In the background, we see a blazing Black Sun (or Sun Wheel), an

Figure 2. Skurt German Wehrmacht soldier remix. Text: 'Together'.

ancient European symbol that was appropriated by the Nazis and was inscribed in the SS headquarters of Wewelsburg. With its three superimposed swastikas, the occult symbol is often used as a (less recognisable and not prohibited) substitute for the swastika (Bogerts & Fielitz, 2019, p. 147). The textual references 'REW' for 'rewind' and 'May 7, 1945' place the meme in a specific historical context, namely the day of Germany's official military surrender at the end of WW2. From what the (deliberately) pixelated meme allows us to see, the soldier's uniform has the typical collar patch of the Wehrmacht, and his gun resembles a Mauser Karabiner 98k, the most common infantry rifle within the German Army during the war. The timecode 14:88 is a combination of two popular white supremacist numeric symbols. 14 is shorthand for the 14 words 'We must secure the existence of our people and a future for white children' penned by white supremacist David Lane (1938–2007) as a unifying slogan for an international militant Aryan uprising. The number 88 is a coded symbol for 'Heil Hitler' (H being the 8th letter of the alphabet).

The sympathy with National Socialism and its violent history is thus woven into a bricolage of 'complex layers of intertextual references, which require literacy to decode' (Tuters & Hagen, 2020, p. 8). Impalpable to anyone outside the group, the iconography of this type of meme fosters an in-group belonging among those fluent in neo-Nazi vernacular. The symbols and codes can be understood as a form of 'performative communication' in the sense that they do not only express and market 'ideological beliefs, but also to strengthen a sense of belonging among group members' (Miller-Idriss, 2018, p. 52). This makes this cultural expression a key driver in stimulating in-/out-group distinctions, 'not through political opposition, but rather through the implicit formation of an "us"' and "them" comprised, respectively, of those aware and of those unaware of a meme's subcultural currency' (Tuters & Hagen, 2020, p. 8) . By remixing esoteric far-right symbols with a seemingly innocuous pop-culture character, the iconography of such memes makes it possible to promote and celebrate violent intent in subtle, not overtly violent ways that would otherwise, if spelled out, be abhorred by the general public.

Specific/explicit violence

The second category of violent memes goes beyond abstract depictions and, instead, is characterised by a specific, straightforward display of violence that threatens factual people (politicians, journalists, etc.) with serious/deathly violence and/or those targeted groups considered to pose a threat to 'the nation as a place with particular kinds of ethnic, racial, religious, linguistic, or cultural boundaries' (Miller-Idriss, 2018, p. 116). What makes the violent intent so explicit in these memes is not only the depictions of weapons (guns, (laser)swords, artillery, etc.), dead bodies and blood but also the image-text combinations (titles, descriptions and direct speech) that make it easy to re-contextualise well-known imagery from mainstream popular culture and give them completely new meanings (Bogerts & Fielitz, 2019, p. 150).

The example below (Figure 3) shows a scene from the movie *Dracula Untold* (2014) that retells the story of the historical figure Vlad the Impaler (who later turns into the undead vampire Dracula) in fifteenth-century Transylvania. The movie presents the warlord sociopath Vlad, in this version known for allegedly slaughtering thousands of his

Figure 3. Movie scene from Dracula Untold with the caption '#Refugees welcome'.

Ottoman foes by impaling them on stakes, as a misunderstood hero. The recurring themes of the vilification of Islam and the fear of a Muslim Europe make the narrative well-suited for far-right Islamophobic propaganda.

By adding #refugees welcome – the well-known slogan of the migrant solidarity movement which formed in Europe during the border crisis of 2015–2016 to the gory scene depicting a forest of impaled bodies (Vlad's allegedly Muslim enemies), the meme uses a historic anti-Islam reference to re-direct meaning to what was originally a pro-refugee solidarity slogan to show support for newly arrived refugees a new, diametrically opposite, meaning. The explicitly violent iconography in these memes effectively creates existential antagonisms that juxtapose an organic and classless 'us' with a nebulous 'them' (Tuters & Hagen, 2020). While the white supremacist agenda remains subtle or cleverly disguised in the first category of implicitly violent memes, these latter examples make little or no effort to conceal their message that certain groups are not only unwelcome; – they must be eradicated. Memes in this category clearly assert a willingness to go far beyond what is deemed socially acceptable and, at the same time, demonstrate how the lines of legality regulating hate speech are carefully toed.

Threats of (deadly) violence

While in the previous category, 'violence is celebrated as a strategy to achieve a particular outcome', in this last cluster of violent iconographies, 'the end goal is the restoration of a dying civilization' (Miller-Idriss, 2018, p. 117). The threat of (deadly) violence is framed around the need for the rebirth of a national socialist society. Far-right threats of violence are often embedded in specific future-oriented, hypothetical scenarios that sketch the idea of an 'aspirational nationhood' (Miller-Idriss, 2018). Such 'fantasy expressions of a nation that never existed but that is, nonetheless, aspired to' (Miller-Idriss, 2018, p. 109) are most clearly reflected in the Finspång memes that proclaim the preservation of white purity and the superiority of the Aryan race in remarkably overt and unabashed ways, even for this specific actor in the Swedish context. As a particularly unsettling 'revenge fantasy' built around more mainstream far-right imaginaries of the collapse of Sweden (Titley, 2019, p. 1013), Finspång not only celebrates and valorises violence but normalises linkages between anti-establishment sentiments and racial fantasies of national degeneration with ideas of justifiable violence and ultimately mass murder (Figure 4).

While executions and hangings are not always directly depicted, the noose serves as a recurring symbol of the death threat and a proxy to the broader Finspång narrative. Such death (threat) symbolism against the establishment serves as a 'source of resistance, protest, and cultural subversion against perceived hegemonic authorities' in the extreme-right (Miller-Idriss, 2018, p. 111). The iconography of the Finspång memes feeds off a range of different imagery and symbols that contain intertextual, political and historical references to visualise and bring substance to this ultimate revenge fantasy. A key illustration of the rich intertextuality of the execution memes includes the nod to the fictive event 'Day of the rope' (carved out in detail in the racist novel The Turner Diaries) in which '"race traitors" are summarily lynched, including "the politicians, the lawyers, the businessmen, the TV newscasters, the newspaper reporters and editors, the judges, the teachers, the school officials, the 'civic leaders', the bureaucrats, the preachers", actors and musicians and anyone else who cooperated with the system, as well as anyone who took part in an interracial sexual relationship' (Berger, 2016, p. 12). The execution memes mainly depict 'impending death' rather than dead bodies. This death trope evokes the subjunctive 'as if' – the voice of the contingent, imaginative 'of what might be' stored in the images (Zelizer 2010). As such, they provide an externalisation and visualisation of the 'what if' of this longstanding revenge fantasy in the extreme-right movement.

Figure 4. Series of Finspång memes. Top: Election campaign meme juxtaposing the fast-right party Alternative for Sweden with NRM. Bottom left: Digitally manipulated photo of Holocaust survivors. Bottom right: Picture of executed Soviet Union partisans 349 × 222 mm (72 × 72 DPI).

Such death tropes propelled by the current rise of far-right movements might usefully be understood 'to belong to a new moment' in the long history of the necropolitics that continues to haunt post-colonial liberal democracies (Mbembé 2003, p. 30). The third category of explicitly violent iconography provides an excellent window into what Mbembe (2003) calls the twin issues of death and terror at the heart of necropolitical regimes. In the examples of execution memes above, the (imagined) construction of a Pan-Nordic national socialist state is presented as the consolidation of the politically legitimate 'right to kill' in the name of the greater good of saving the nation culminating in 'the final solution' (i.e., Finspång). In an 'extrapolation of the theme of the political enemy' (Mbembé 2003, p. 17), the memes put concrete faces and names to the list of the 'Sweden-enemies' whose death is both required and just. Such systematic killings are rendered possible/plausible, and necessary even, by the always impending 'state of exception' imagined in the peculiar terror formation that is organised racism. Facing societal collapse, chaos and the disintegration of the white nation 'judicial order can be suspended' and proponents of national socialism granted the 'right to wage war (the taking of life)', Finspång then becomes 'the zone where the violence of the state of exception is deemed to operate in the service of "civilization"' (Mbembé 2003, p. 24). They convey a nostalgic longing for national socialism to once again have the 'sovereignty, power and the capacity to dictate who may live and who must die' (p. 11).

Importantly, the Finspång memes were circulated in a time around the general elections during which the group simultaneously engaged in extensive offline 'base activism' around the country in which the fictive/future trials are interwoven into analogue propaganda distributed across cities in the southern part of the country. For example, in November 2018, 'clear messages to local traitor politicians' were put up on doors and notice boards at the entry of 21 town halls stating: 'To politicians in this building: you will pay for your crimes against the Nordic people when put to justice in the future folk tribunal'. In this manner, the death threats travelled back and forth between online and offline space and reached different audiences, many of whom were themselves directly targeted and named as prospective accused for the tribunal.

Concluding reflections

Beyond the context of Sweden, and certainly, beyond this specific white supremacist group, the likes of which tend to come and go, memes are increasingly part of a broader strategy of the far-right to push the boundaries of what is acceptable in mainstream discourse. In important ways, memes are helping move ideas, previously considered beyond the pale in public discourse, to travel and have bearing online. They are key to ongoing efforts among far-right actors to get rid of or re-invent the symbols and visual codes that once defined far-right ideology and white supremacism, more specifically in the pursuit of making it attractive to a new generation of younger audiences. Bogerts and Fielitz (2019) argue that 'since the far right, too, has undergone a process of (post) modernization, it must be regarded as closely intertwined with post-modern (youth) cultures which express themselves creatively and often ironically on social media' (p. 150). The neo-Nazi movement in the country has not yet succeeded in recruiting youth in large numbers, but they are certainly tapping into the cultural expressions of contemporary youth culture in their efforts to do so. Indeed, NRM's memes find inspiration in early internet culture spaces that are rife with symbols 'easily hijacked by those looking to do harm, whose actions often fly under the radar – because those actions look like the things that used to be fun' (Philips, 2019, p. 3).

The carefully coded and remixed symbols and references that were subject to close examination in this study highlight the multivocality of memes and the strategic attempt by an openly Nazi group with a relatively straightforward agenda of violence to tap into the sentiments of ambiguity and nebulosity around earnestness and intent that saturate the subcultural fringes of the internet. It is this malleability and the fusing (and confusing) of the silly and the banal with murder fantasies and threats of white supremacist violence that allow the group to cater to not only to those already identifying with far-right ideology but also to the broader public and those 'who are keen to avoid the social stigma of the far right while still communicating with insiders' (Miller-Idriss, 2018, p. 62). In this sense, memes work as one of the key techniques in contemporary efforts by far-right movements internationally to counter the stigma of the totalitarianism, genocide and human tragedy still associated with national socialism and help launder white supremacist violence into the mainstream.

To be sure, most of NRM's memes are rife with violence and death. However, what makes those in the final category described above stand out in comparison to all other violent iconographies in the sample is the mimicry and remix of documentary photography, factual places and concrete people in combination with messages directly articulating death threats and/or evoking death symbolism through past atrocities and fantasies of future genocides. They play around with imagined, phantasmic ideas, yet they mirror and tap into real historical events. Public lynching, trials and executions of traitors and the public display of dismembered bodies of dehumanised Others, parades of heads mounted on sticks – these images may in Western audiences all resonate with atrocities elsewhere or atrocities of the past. They are scenarios and ideas easily written off as inconceivable and confined to the perversions of the uncivil fringes of society among groups classified as marginal, extremist and unwanted by the state. Yet as Mbembé (2003) reminds us, anti-democratic groups such as NMR and the broader movements in which they operate are not exterior to or the antithesis of liberal democracy. Rather they represent its dark side, or what he calls its 'nocturnal body', which is based on the very same desires, fears, affects, relations and violence that once drove colonialism. They are the unwelcome reminders of the persistence of necropolitical techniques and ideas *within* liberal democracies in a Europe consumed by the continued desire for apartheid.

Yet, in order to understand the ways in which fascist iconography lingers in the fibres of contemporary culture and how it works as an entry point for far-right recruitment and radicalisation, it is not enough to have an exclusively visual lexicon of fascist aesthetics (Ravetto, 2001). More ethnographically oriented work and audience studies are needed to examine the extent to which out-groups, the mainstream user, and especially youth native to digital subcultural aesthetics, are exposed to memes with violent far-right messaging, how remixed pop cultural references and coded symbols are understood and perceived and what appeal and political potency they may carry. For example, where and how do young people come into contact with such memes in their day-to-day life? What are their ordinary and everyday encounters with radicalisation messages online? Asking these questions will further our knowledge of the extreme right as a site of cultural engagement and help us understand *where* messages of violent extremism circulate and *how* they resonate when travelling back and forth between fringe and mainstream spaces today.

Notes

1. The term 'våldsbejakande' is used consistently by intelligence services, state authorities and researchers in the field of extremism and radicalisation in Sweden. It aims to describe violence beyond physical attacks such as murder or abuse to include threats of physical violence as well as limitations of mobility such as detention and forcible resettlement/ethnic expulsions. Further, the term is meant to go beyond direct invitations to such acts to include anti-democratic ideas which legitimate hierarchies of inferiority and superiority between different groups which in turn work to pave the way for explicit incitement to violence (SOU 2013).
2. This cluster of memes fall under three thematic categories: anti-Semitic (25), 'racial strangers' (20) and finally 'traitors of the people' (16).

Disclosure statement

No potential conflict of interest was reported by the author(s).

Funding

This work was supported by Marianne and Marcus Wallenberg Foundation [MMW.2016.0018] and Myndigheten för Samhällsskydd och Beredskap fÃ¶r SamhÃ¤llsskydd och Beredskap [1-MS-002].

References

Askanius, T. (2021a). On frogs, monkeys, and execution memes: Exploring the humor-hate nexus at the intersection of neo-Nazi and alt-right movements in Sweden. *Television & New Media, 22* (2), 147–165. https://doi.org/10.1177/1527476420982234

Askanius, T. (2021b). I just want to be the friendly face of national socialism. *Nordicom Review, 42* (1), 17–35. https://doi.org/10.2478/nor-2021-0004

Bayerl, P. S., & Stoynov, L. (2016). Revenge by photoshop: Memefying police acts in the public dialogue about injustice. *New Media & Society*, *18*(6), 1006–1026. https://doi.org/10.1177/1461444814554747

Benjamin, W. (1979 [1930]). Theories of German fascism: On the collection of essays war and warrior. *New German Critique*, *17*, 120–128. https://doi.org/10.2307/488013

Berger, J. M. (2016). The Turner legacy: The storied origins and enduring impact of white nationalism's deadly Bible. *ICCT Research Papers*, *7*(8), 1–50. http://doi.org/10.19165/2016.1.11

Bock, A., Isermann, H., & Knieper, T. (2011). Quantitative content analysis of the visual. In E. Margolis & L. Pauwels (Eds.), *The SAGE handbook visual research methods* (pp. 265–283). SAGE Publications, Inc.

Bogerts, L., & Fielitz, M. (2019). 'Do you want meme war?' Understanding the visual memes of the German far right. In M. Fielitz & N. Thurston (Eds.), *Post-digital cultures of the far-right online actions and offline consequences in Europe and the US* (pp. 137–154). Transcript Verlag.

Colliver, C., Pomerantsev, P., Applebaum, A., & Birdwell, J. (2018). *Smearing Sweden: International influence campaigns in the 2018 Swedish election*. LSE Institute of Global Affairs.

DeCook, J. R. (2018). Memes and symbolic violence: #Proudboys and the use of memes for propaganda and the construction of collective identity. *Learning, Media and Technology*, *43*(4), 485–504. https://doi.org/10.1080/17439884.2018.1544149

Doerr, N. (2017). Bridging language barriers, bonding against immigrants: A visual case study of transnational network publics created by far-right activists in Europe. *Discourse and Society*, *28*(1), 3–23. https://doi.org/10.1177%2F0957926516676689

Donovan, J., Lewis, B., & Friedberg, B. (2019). Parallel ports, sociotechnical change from the alt-right to alt-tech. In M. Fielitz & N. Thurston (Eds.), *Post-digital cultures of the far-right online actions and offline consequences in Europe and the US*, (pp. 49–65). Transcript Verlag.

Eatwell, R. (1996). *Fascism: A history*. Allen Lane.

Ebner, J. (2019). Counter-creativity: Innovative ways to counter far-right communication tactics. In M. Fielitz & N. Thurston (Eds.), *Post-digital cultures of the far right online actions and offline consequences in Europe and the US* (pp. 169–181). Transcript Verlag.

Ekman, M. (2014). The dark side of online activism: Swedish right-wing extremist video activism on YouTube. *MedieKultur: Journal of Media and Communication Research*, *30*(56), 21–99. https://doi.org/10.7146/mediekultur.v30i56.8967

Greene, V. S. (2019). 'Deplorable' satire: Alt-right memes, white genocide tweets, and redpilling normies. *Studies in American Humor*, *5*(1), 31–69. https://doi.org/10.5325/studamerhumor.5.1.0031

Jensen, M., Neumeyer, C., & Rossi, L. (2020). 'Brussels will land on its feet like a cat': Motivations for memefying #brusselslockdown. *Information, Communication & Society*, *23*(1), 59–75. https://doi.org/10.1080/1369118X.2018.1486866

Koepnick, L. P. (1999). Fascist aesthetics revisited. *Modernism/Modernity*, *6*(1), 51–73. https://doi.org/10.1353/mod.1999.0009

Kølvraa, C. (2019). Embodying 'the Nordic race': Imaginaries of viking heritage in the online communications of the nordic resistance movement. *Patterns of Prejudice*, *53*(3), 270–284. https://doi.org/10.1080/0031322X.2019.1592304

Lööw, H. (2015). *Nazismen i sverige 2000-2014*. Ordfront.

Mbembé, J.-A. (2003). Necropolitics. *Public Culture*, *15*(1), 11–40. https://doi.org/10.1215/08992363-15-1-11

McCrow-Young, A., & Mortensen, M. (2021). Countering spectacles of fear: Anonymous' meme 'war' against ISIS. *European Journal of Cultural Studies*, *1*, 1–18. https://doi.org/10.1177%2F13675494211005060

Merill, S. (2020). Sweden then vs. Sweden now: The memetic normalization of far-right nostalgia. *First Monday*, *35*, 6. https://doi.org/10.1177%2F1940161221995083

Miller-Idriss, C. (2018). *The extreme gone mainstream: Commercialization and far right youth culture in Germany*. Princeton University Press.

Miller-Idriss, C. (2019). What makes a symbol far right? Co-opted and missed meanings in far-right iconography. In M. Fielitz & N. Thurston (Eds.), *Post-digital cultures of the far-right online actions and offline consequences in Europe and the US* (pp. 123–136). Transcript Verlag.

Milner, R. M. (2013). Pop polyvocality: Internet memes, public participation, and the occupy wall street movement. *International Journal of Communication, 7*, 2357–2390.

Moreno-Almeida, C., & Gerbaudo, P. (2021). Memes and the Moroccan far-right. *International Journal of Press/Politics, 1*, 1–25. https://doi.org/10.1177%2F1940161221995083

Mortensen, M. (2016). 'The image speaks for itself' – or does it? Instant news icons, impromptu publics, and the 2015 European 'refugee crisis'. *Communication and the Public, 1*(4), 409–422. https://doi.org/10.1177/2057047316679667

Philips, W. (2019). It wasn't just the trolls: Early internet culture, 'fun,' and the fires of exclusionary laughter. *Social Media and Society, 5*(3), 1–4. https://doi.org/10.1177/2056305119849493

Philips, W., & Milner, R. M. (2017). *The ambivalent internet: Mischief, oddity, and antagonism online*. Polity Press.

Ravetto, K. (2001). *Unmaking of fascist aesthetics*. University of Minnesota Press.

Rose, G. (2016). *Visual methodologies: An introduction to researching with visual materials*. Sage (atlanta, Ga).

Shifman, L. (2013). Memes in a digital world: Reconciling with a conceptual troublemaker. *Journal of Computer-Mediated Communication, 18*(3), 362. https://doi.org/10.1111/jcc4.12013

Titley, G. (2019). Taboo news about Sweden: The transnational assemblage of a racialized spatial imaginary. *International Journal of Sociology and Social Policy, 39*(11/12), 1010–1023. https://doi.org/10.1108/IJSSP-02-2019-0029

Tuters, M., & Hagen, S. (2020). (((they))) rule: Memetic antagonism and nebulous othering on 4chan. *New Media and Society, 22*(12), 2218–2237. https://doi.org/10.1177/1461444819888746

Wiggins, B. E. (2016). Crimea river: Directionality in memes from the Russia-Ukraine conflict. *International Journal of Communication, 10*, 451–485.

Zelizer, B. (2010). *About to die. How News Images Moves the Public* . New York, NY: Oxford University Press.

Index

Note: **Bold** page numbers refer to tables; *Italic* page numbers refer to figures and page numbers followed by "n" denote endnotes.

Abbas, M. 25, *28*
Abidin, C. 6, 27, 103, 104
abstract/implicit violence 165–166
aestheticisation of politics 158
aesthetic moment in fascist propaganda 164
affective meaning 58
AfS *see* Alternative for Sweden (AfS)
Aladdin, Disney movie *28*
'alternative calendar commemorations' memes 117, 120–122, 124, 128, 131
alternative fascist modernity 164
Alternative for Sweden (AfS) 162
Alt-Right iconography 161
Alt-Tech platforms 158
analytical coding in matrix 164, *164*
ancient European symbol 166
Anglo-centric popular culture references 150
Anglophone alternative media 137
Anglophone cultural referents 150
Anglophone meme templates 142, *142*
Anglo-Saxon bias 83
'anti-Boomer sentiment' in Western societies 95
anti-democratic groups 170
anti-democratic traits 86
anti-elitist strategies 86
anti-fascist legal framework 117
anti-Semitic connotations 121
antithesis of liberal democracy 170
Antoinette, M. 87
Arabic context 17
Arab Israelis 16
Arab society *27*
Arab World 19
Arab youth 19, 23
archiving digital material 83
Aryan uprising 166
Askanius, T. 7, 8
Ask, K. 27
audio memes 96, 104
Australian colonialism 17

Australian far-right group 139
Australian National Socialist Network 145
authenticity 122
'authentic' role models 128
Ayman Odeh 26, *29*

Balfour Declaration in 1917 14
base activism 169
Bayerl, P. S. 39
Bee in the City art trail 44, 46, 47, 49
bee's memetic use 43, 45
beliefs 116
Benjamin, W. 158
Berlusconi, S. 61
Bernie Sanders Wearing Mittens Sitting in a Chair Meme 21
Biden, J. 21
Blocco Studentesco 145
Bogerts, L. 169
'Boomers' 93–95; grievances 94–95; self-defence and self-deprecation by 107–108; TikTokers *108*
'Boomer Woah' 107
brands 39, 49; merchandising and bandwagoning by 108–109; scheme 47
Brantner, C. 118
British aristocracy 85
British politicians 85
British 'Stay at Home' campaign 86
brokered 'peace deal' 21
#Brusselslockdown 60
'Burioni effect' 69
Burioni, R. 69
Burj Al Arab 12, 21
Burnham, A. 37

Caiani, M. 121
Canary Mission 15
Carnera, P. 127–128
Casa Pound Italia 123

'centrifugal' or 'centripetal' convergence 57
Chagas, V. 81
4chan 1, 137, 157
Christchurch Massacre in New Zealand 139, 163
Christian symbolism 146, *147*
circular online influence ecosystem 158
circulation of memes 141–143
circumscribed creativities 96
classical Greco-Roman motifs 147, *147*
cluster of violent iconographies 167
codebook 125
coding categories 113–114
Codogno 56
cognitive meaning 58
colloquial Palestinian Arabic 23
colonial capitalism 15
Coma, F. M. 79
'commemorating constituents' subgenre 126
commercial social media platforms 118
communicative function 97
communicative strategy 79
communicative values of Internet memes 121–122
consensual qualitative research 125
conservative politics 102
constitutive antagonism 59
contemporary digital environments 57
contemporary internet culture 3
contemporary youth culture 169–170
the context 122–123
context-specific historical signs 151
controversial issues: conservative politics 102; gender and sexuality norms 101–102; young people's lifestyles and well-being 99–100
co-optation: of pop culture iconography 148; of symbols 162–164
corpus mix popular culture 30
'the corrupt elite' 86
cosmopolitanism 47, 49
countering populist ideology 85–88
COVID-19: communication strategies 84; crisis 82; memes 56, 62, 77; memetics of Italian Twitter 70
craft activism 105–106
creative political expressions 3
criterion-based sampling strategy 84
critical visual methodologies 43
'cue card confessions' 117
cultural diversity 27
cultural form 161–162
'CURING CORONAVIRUS IS RACIST' 84

The Daily Wire 149
D'Amelio, C. 109
data gathering 124–125
death threats, iconography of 164–169
Democratic Football Lads Alliance (DFLA) 49, *50*
democratic pluralism 5
Denisova, A. 3, 39, 81
'depression' memes *100*
Der Dritte Weg 145
De Saussure, F. 57
DFLA *see* Democratic Football Lads Alliance (DFLA)
Diehl, P. 79
digital activism 39
digital communicative *genres* 79
digital culture research, Palestine 18–19
digital environments 58
digital logics, non-digital materialisation of 41
digital methods 63
digital propaganda 137
digital spheres, remixing far-right values in 116–118, *127*, 129–131; communicative values of Internet memes 121–122; The context 122–123; descriptive overview of 126; far-right memes 118–120; methods of analysis 125; The sample 123–125; values of 120–121; verbal and visual representations, values in 126–129
digital visual cultures 150
digital visual media for far right 136
direct communicative references 139
discursive practices 62
discursive weapons 81
distinct visual discourses 138
'Dodim' culture 23, 28
'Down with the experts' 68–69, *69*
'Down with the leader' 66, 68, *68*
Dracula Untold (2014) 166, *167*
Drago, I. 86
'dress-coded,' by Boomer *101*
DuckDuckGo search engine 83–84

Eatwell, R. 161
Ebner, J. 158
'The Election of Memes' 2
embedding memes 150
'enjoyment of incongruity' 65
Ernest, N. 80
'esoteric' nods 161
esoteric symbols 161
European integration 123
'everyday social media practices' 62
'exoteric' modes 161
external authenticity 122

Facebook 137, 140
Farquaad, M. 86
far-right actors 158
far-right adherents 129
far-right commemoration memes 129
far-right digital visual culture 137, 143–149

far-right iconography 137
far-right iconography post-WWII 139
far-right ideology 169
far-right memes 7, 118–120
far-right movements 116, 169
far-right organizations 116, 150
far-right parties 122
far-right's communication strategies 138
far-right's digital visual culture 136–138, 149–151; case selection, data collection, and methodology 139–141; memes, visual culture, and transnationality 138–139; salience and circulation of memes 141–143; transnational references and similarity in *see* transnational references and similarity, in far-right digital visual culture
far-right spectrum 162
far-right subcultures online 156
Fascism 139
fascist continuity 144–146
fascist iconography 170
fascist propaganda, aesthetic moment in 164
'fast food' communication of social media 81
Ferrari, E. 61
Fielitz, M. 169
Finspång memes 163, 167–168, *168*, 169
Five Star Movement (Movimento Cinque Stelle) 61
Forza Nuova party 123
Fratelli d'Italia ('Brothers of Italy') (Meloni) 122

Galli, M. 69
Gal, N. 58
game-streaming videos 103, *104*
gender norm 101–102
generational tensions 95
generic criticism 72
Gen Z 109–110; climate activism 102, *102*; generational sentiments 99; politics 93–95; TikTokers 95–96, 100–102, 104, 105, 107; use of #OkBoomer memes 107
German fascism 158
German National Socialism 144
'Get Brexit Done' slogan 83
globalised digital culture 148
'Good citizens and rule breakers' 66, *67*
Google algorithms 83
Grillo, B. 61

Hagen, S. 5, 129
Haifa Memes 19
Haifa tower 12, *13–14*, 23, *24*, *25*, 33
Hartley, J. 60
Hawkins, J. M. 84
Hebrew language 28
Heft, A. 6
'Heil Hitler,' coded symbol 166

'historic' and/or 'peace' agreements 14
'historic peace deal' 12
Hodson, D. 83, 89
Hoffmann, M. 6
Holocaust 160
horizontal communication 139
'humorous ambiguity' 157
humour, in memes 2–3, 149; and nonsense 57–59; playful humour 3–5; pop culture and 150
hybridity of post-terror togetherness 41
hybrid togetherness 40
hyper-partisan online news sites 139
hypocrisy type 24

Iannelli, L. 61
iconographic tracking 42
iconography, of death threats and violence 164–165; abstract/implicit violence 165–166; specific/explicit violence 166–167; threats of (deadly) violence 167–169
Identitarian Movement 140
identity politics 4
ideological content 161
'IF HE DIES, HE DIES,' iconic quote 86
image-based communication 42
IMAGE ('url') function 63
'image macro' 118
img2vec models 43, **43**, *44*
indigenous lingua franca 58
individualistic and collectivistic values 130
Inglehartian political culture 61, 62
in-group lingo 5
in-group Palestinian diversity 21
Instagram 6, 19, 117
instagrammability 45
Instaloader 42
integrating research on visual communication 139
intergenerational politics on TikTok: and Boomer grievances 94–95; controversial issues *see* controversial issues; meme forms *see* meme forms; meme functions *see* meme functions; methods of 97–99; political memes 96
internal authenticity 128
Internet cultural spaces 157
Internet culture 96
Internet memes 12–17, 38–39, 41, 57, 137, 138; communicative values of 121–122; findings of 20–29; as mapping tools 29–33; methods of 19–20; Palestine and digital culture research 18–19; and politics 17–18
intertextual web 58
ironic humour, on social media 58
Israel: Jewish citizens 20; music 28; settler colonialism 31; *vs.* UAE, diplomatic relationship 12, 20
Israeli Knesset 25

Israeli State, navigating dynamics with 24–26
Italian anti-vaccination movement and politicians 69
Italian far-right constituents 124, **125**
'The (Italian) model does not work' 69–70, *70*
Italian pandemic memes 61, 62, 64
Italian social media 56
Italian Twitter 65
IwMCR branding campaign 41, 46

@james.bee 93, 103, *104, 109*
'Je Suis Charlie' 40–41
'the Jewish conspiracy' 119
Jewish Israeli society 30
Johnson, B. 6, 76, 78, 82–89
Johnson, D. 20

Kaltwasser, C. R. 78, 79
Katz, Y. 58
Keller, N. 7, 8
key commemorations 124
'key strategic digital items of communication' 136
Kozinets, R. V. 123
Kress, G. R. 125
Krippendorff, K. 141
Kristensen, N. N. 6, 8

Laclau, E. 3, 5
Laineste, L. 58
Lane, D. 166
Lega ('The League') (Salvini) 122
lens of populism 121
LGBTQIA+ community 101
LGTBQ+ 46
liberal democracy 118, 121; antithesis of 170
Lindgren, S. 6
linguistic silliness 58
lip-sync activism 103–104
literary characters 162
local politics, pandemic memes as 64–70
LOLCats 4, 160
lolcat template 60
#LoveMCRBees campaign 46
Luigi Di Maio 68

MacDonald, S. 58
Machiavellianism 86
machine learning method 38
machine learning mode of image classification 43
#manchesterbee(s) 41–44, *42*, 47, 49, 50
Manchester charities 47
Manchester Charity Appeal Trust 41–42
Manchester City Council 41, 46, 47, 49
Manchester Evening News 45
Manchester's civic symbols 38
Manchester Tattoo Appeal 45
Manchester Together 46, 47, 48
Manchester Unity March 49–50

Manchester worker bee 51
Mancunian community 45
mapping tools, memes as 5–7, 29–33
Marino, G. 118
Marvel's Thor 149
'mask culture' of meme 119
Massey, D. 20
Mbembé, J. -A. 169, 170
McSwiney, J. 6
Meloni, G. 122
@mem3a_fe_alda5el, Instagram profile 19
meme culture 17, 22
memefication 39, 49; of neo-Nazi ideology 160; of political discourse 2, 80; of politics 2; of white supremacism 7, 157
meme forms 97, 103; craft activism 105–106; lip-sync activism 103–104; reacts *vs.* duets 104–105, *105, 106*
meme functions 106, 114–115; merchandising and bandwagoning, by TikTokers and brands 108–109; retorts and criticism by Gen Z 107; self-defence and self-deprecation, by Boomers 107–108
memejacking 39, 47, 49
meme-making ecology of TikTok 103
memes 1, 138–139; with abstract depictions of violence 165; 'alternative calendar commemorations' memes 117, 120–122, 124, 128; audio memes 96, 104; circulation of 141–143; communicative values of Internet memes 121–122; COVID-19 memes 77; 'depression' memes *100*; 'The Election of Memes' 2; embedding memes 150; far-right commemoration memes 129; far-right memes 7, 118–120; Finspång memes 167–168, *168, 169*; Haifa Memes 19; between humour and nonsense 57–59; humour in *see* humour, in memes; Internet memes *see* Internet memes; Italian pandemic memes 61, 62, 64; as mapping tools 6, 29–33; murder fantasies in *see* murder fantasies in memes; Nazareth Memes 19; neo-Nazi memes 160–162; normative memes 66; #OkBoomer memes *see* #OkBoomer memes; online memes 157; Palestinians in Israel 20; pandemic memes, as local politics 64–70; photo-based memes 119, 124, 131; playful politics of *see* playful politics of memes; political memes *see* political memes; politics and humour in 2–3, 5, 39, 59–60; populist political leaders, during COVID-19 crisis *see* populist political leaders, during COVID-19 crisis; resituating memes 149; salience and circulation of 141–143; sampling memes 84; shared Internet culture underpinning memes 150; templatable memes 71; text *13–16, 23, 25–27, 32–34*; TikTok *see* TikTok; white supremacist memes 157; 'Wojak' and 'Daily Struggle' memes 142

INDEX

memetic antagonism 119
memetic authenticity 58
memetic commemorations 116–118, 120, *127*, 129–131; communicative values of Internet memes 121–122; The context 122–123; descriptive overview of 126; far-right memes 118–120; methods of analysis 125; The sample 123–125; subgenres *124*; values of 120–121; verbal and visual representations, values in 126–129
memetic content, identification of 123–124
memetic culture 59
memetic practices 71
memetic protest 2
memetic unit of analysis *64*
meme war 4, 160
Merelman, R. M. 60, 62, 71
Merrill, S. 6
Middle East 'peace deal' 14
'migration crisis' of 2014–15 123
military imagery 145
Miller-Idriss, C. 160, 162–165
mixed-methods approach 137
mode of communication 58
Modern Standard Arabic 23
moral principle of coherence 68
Mortensen, M. 6, 8, 163
Mouffe, C. 3, 5
@mrbeardofficial 104
Mudde, C. 78, 79, 83, 121
multi-modal analysis 117, 126
mundane forms of social media communication 61, 63
mundane memetics 57
mundane political culture 60–62, 72
mundane Twitter practices 62
murder fantasies in memes 156–158, 169–171; co-optation and 'swedification' of symbols 162–164; far-right's turn to memes 158–159; iconography of death threats and violence *see* iconography, of death threats and violence; methods and material 159–160; neo-Nazi memes across (ideological) content and (cultural) form 160–162
Murru, M. F. 6

Nai, A. 79
national autonomy 123
National Memorial Day of the Exiles and Foibe 127
national socialism 139, 166, 169
national sovereignty 123
navigating Palestinian cultural diversity 26–29
Nazareth Memes 19
Nazi Germany 158
Nazi iconography 119
Nazi salute 145
Nazi symbolism 145, *145*

neoliberal norms 58
neo-Nazi ideology 163, 164
neo-Nazi memes 160–162
neo-Nazi movement 169
neo-Nazi organisations 144
Netanyahu, B. 24, 25, *27, 28*
netnographic approach 123
new media technologies 18
new-right ethnonationalist groups 140
Nissenbaum, A. 57, 64
non-digital materialisation of digital logics 41
Nordfront 160
Nordic Resistance Movement (NRM) 157, 160, 162, *168,* 170
normative memes 66
Norse mythology 162, 163
notions of community 40
Nowell, L. S. 84
NRM *see* Nordic Resistance Movement (NRM)

Obama Hope Poster 59
'offline' culture 17
#OkBoomer memes 93–94, 99, 101, 102, 105, 106; controversial issues *see* controversial issues; intergenerational politics and boomer grievances 94–95; meme forms *see* meme forms; meme functions *see* meme functions; methods 97–99; political memes on TikTok 96
'One Does Not Simply Walk into Mordor' meme 150
One Love Manchester 44, 45
online memes 157
online radicalisation process 157, 158–159
online visual media 137
Orwell, G. 149
Our Manchester 47, *48,* 50
overriding themes 85

Palestine: communities 16–17; context 16; culture 30; and digital culture research 18–19; group identity 27; as indigenous people 17; meme makers 12, 15, 24; youth 6, 18–19, 26, 29, 30, 32
'Palestinians in Israel' 16, 17, 19
pandemic memes, as local politics 64–70
Pan-Nordic national socialist state 169
participatory place branding 39
'Pepe the Frog' meme 2, 8, 62, 77, 119, 121, *149,* 157, 158, 161, 162
Pepper Spray Cop 2
performative characteristics 79
'performative communication' form 166
phantasmic ideas 170
phatic communication 58
photo-based memes 117, 119, 124, 130, 131
photo-based 'testimonial rallies' 117
playful humour 3–5

playful politics of memes 1–2; mapping 5–7; moving and demarcating frontiers 7–9; playful humour 3–5; politics and humour 2–3
Plebs 85
'political and identity construction' 138
political culture 62
'politically correct' culture 119
political memes 77, 80–82, 88; on TikTok 96
political participation 61
political populism, academic literature on 78
political protests 2
political resonance 59
political significance: of memes 57; of mundane memes 70
political symbols 138
politicisation of memes 70
politics: aestheticisation of 158; Internet memes and 17–18; in memes 2, 5–7, 39, 59–60; playful humour and 3–5; of post-terror togetherness *see* post-terror politics
pop cultural appropriation 138, 148–149
'popular culture iconography' 138
populism 72, 78, 79, 82; lens of 121
populist: crisis (mis)communication 86–87; leadership 88–89; *vs.* people 85–86; politicians 77; style 84
populist political leaders, during COVID-19 crisis 76–78; context and cases 82–83; ideology, communication and style 78–80; methodology 83–84; political memes 80–82; populist crisis (mis)communication 86–87; populists *vs.* people 85–86; reproducing populist style 87–88
post-modern (youth) cultures 169
post-terror contexts 38
post-terror politics 37–38, 51; analysis of 43–51; material and method of 41–43; memes, brands and politics 38–40; social media and 40–41
post-war neo-Nazi movements 144
preliminary online ethnography 123
pre-WWII fascism 123
primary memetic dimensions 57
prior research 96
'programme and anti-programme approach' 63
pro-refugee solidarity slogan 167
Python programming language 140

QAnon iconography 157
qualitative critical visual analysis 137
quantitative coding 141
quantitative content analysis 141
quantitative manual content analysis 137
quantitative visual content analysis 159
Qubek 45, 47
Queen Elisabeth 76

radical democracy 3–5
reacts *vs.* duets 104–105, *105, 106*
Reddit 137, 157

'#Refugees welcome' 166, *167*
reinforce group identities 148
remixing far-right values, in digital spheres 116–118, *127,* 129–131; communicative values of Internet memes 121–122; The context 122–123; descriptive overview of 126; far-right memes 118–120; methods of analysis 125; The sample 123–125; values of 120–121; verbal and visual representations, values in 126–129
reproducing populist style 87–88
resituating memes 149
revisionist white supremacist groups 140
revolutionary form of nationalism 144
Rintel, S. 59
Riot Hipster 2
Rovira Kaltwasser, C. 121

salience of memes 141–143
Salvini, M. 68, 122
The sample 123–124
sampling 82, 140; core users 123; memes 84; strategy 123
Sanders, B. *22, 31*
Sandri, G. 126
scholars stress 79
Schwartzian tradition of value research 121
Schwartzian value of 'security' 127
Schwartz, S. H. 117, 120, 125, 130
Schwartz's model 117, 120, 130
Schwartz's value theory 121
Schwartz Value Survey 125
Schwarzenegger, C. 89
Schwarze Sonne 145
SD *see* Sweden Democrats (SD)
'secularized Christianity-as-culture' 146
Seiffert-Brockmann, J. 58, 59
self-defence and self-deprecation, by boomers 107–108
semiotic model 118
settler colonialism 18
sexuality norm 101–102
shared internet culture underpinning memes 150
shared transnational white European identity 148
Shifman, L. 3, 6, 17, 39, 57, 58, 63, 64, 97, 117, 118, 121, 122, 128
Sicart, M. 3
silly citizenship 60–61
Skurt German Wehrmacht soldier remix 165, *165*
snowballing additional 'core' users 123
social identity form 95
'social justice warriors' 119
social media: artifacts of 8; channels 139; 'everyday politics' 60; 'fast food' communication of 81; ironic humour on 58; Italian social media 56; mobilization 118, 123; mundane forms of 61, 63; and politics of post-terror togetherness 40–41; techno-commercial infrastructure of 1

social movement 117
'soft visceral side of politics' 38
Sorensen, L. 78
Spangler, P. T. 125
specific/explicit violence 166–167
'starter pack' meme template 15
'Stay Alert. Control the Virus. Save Lives' slogan 86
'Stay home. Protect the NHS. Save lives' slogan 86
Stoynov, L. 39
street art cluster 45
'strong-man' style of political leadership 83
'stylised' digital visual culture 140
'Super Mario & Boomer' meme 103
supremacist ideology 116
Sweden Democrats (SD) 162
'swedification' of symbols 162–164
Swedish context 168, 169

'tactical social action' 17
Tawil-Souri, H. 18
TCAT *see* Twitter Capture and Analysis Tool (TCAT)
techno-commercial infrastructure of social media 1
techno-cultural environment 117
technological-spatial-political relationship 18
tech-savvy far-right movement 117
Telegram 137, 140
templatable memes 71
#The22BeesProject 46
thematic analysis 84–85, 88
'thin-centred' ideology 78
Third Reich 158–160
Third Reich Nazi symbols 162
threats of (deadly) violence 167–169
TikTok 18–19, 93–95, 106; case on 101; everyday politics and identity politics on 110; 'generation anthem' 93; intergenerational politics on *see* intergenerational politics on TikTok; @irishmanalways *106*; meme categorisation 97; meme-making ecology of 103; memes 100; memetic momentum on 94; #OkBoomer campaign on 94; #OkBoomer challenge viral in 97, 105; #OkBoomer memes on 93, 99, 109–110; #OkBoomer merchandise creators on 108; Palestinian youth 18; political memes on 96; vernacular styles of videos on 103; video memes 6, 115
TikTokers 99, 103, 110; Boomer TikTokers 107–108; Gen Z TikTokers 95, 100, 101, 104, 105, 107; merchandising and bandwagoning by 108–109; #OkBoomer trend 101; with performative talents 106; transgender Gen Z TikTokers 102
Tilly, C. 150
'trajectories of publicness' 40
transgender Gen Z TikTokers 102

transnationality 138–139; 'alt-right' meme culture 150; communicative genre 117; context of the internet 138; far right communication ecology 137; meme culture 137; of political communication 139; social boundaries 151
transnational references and similarity, in far-right digital visual culture 143–144; fascist continuity 144–146; pop cultural appropriation 148–149; Western civilisational identity 146–148
Trillò, T. 6
Trump, D. 2, 6, 8, 21, 22, *22*, *23*, 76, 78, 79, 82–89, 102, 139
'Trust the Plan' slogan 157
Tuters, M. 5, 119, 129
Twitter 4, 6, 59, 60, 117, 137, 140
Twitter Capture and Analysis Tool (TCAT) 63

United States (US): brokered agreement 21; elections, 2020 *31*; institutional politics 21; politicians 22; popular culture 22, 23
UN summit 2
US Capitol 8

våldsbejakande 159, 171n1
Van Leeuwen, T. 125
VAT *see* Veterans Against Terrorism (VAT)
Vaughan, M. 6
verbal and visual representations, values in 126–129
Veterans Against Terrorism (VAT) 49, *50*
Vicari, S. 6, 61
violence-gesturing content 119
violence, iconography of 164–169
violent extremism 157
visual culture 138–139
visual transnationality 150
Voolaid, P. 58

Wagner, A. 89
We Are Manchester 46
western civilisational identity 146–148
Western societies, 'anti-Boomer sentiment' in 95
WEwMCR Charity 42
white nationalist 157
white supremacism 157, 169
Wiggins, B. E. 3, 80
Williams, R. 47
Wittgensteinian language games 61
'Wojak' and 'Daily Struggle' memes 142
'worker bee' 41
World Health Organization 82

Zeng, J. 6, 97
Zidani, S. 6, 7
'Zoomers' 93–94
'Zoomer Sweater' 108–109
Zurovac, E. 61